Glacier From the Inside Out

Best stories from *The Inside Trail*

Glacier From the Inside Out

Best stories from *The Inside Trail*

Edited by
Ray Djuff and Chris Morrison

The Glacier Park Foundation

Copyright © 2012 Glacier Park Foundation

All rights reserved. No part of this publication may be reproduced, stored in a retrieval system or transmitted in any form or by any means—electronic, mechanical, audio recording or otherwise—without the prior written consent of the publisher, the Glacier Park Foundation.

Glacier Park Foundation
P.O. Box 15641
Minneapolis, MN 55415
U.S.A.
www.glacierparkfoundation.org

Cataloging information

Editors: Djuff, Raymond J.
        Morrison, Chris D.

Glacier From the Inside Out
Best stories from *The Inside Trail*

Includes biographical references and index.

ISBN 978-0-615-62680-2

1. Glacier National Park - Montana - History
2. Great Northern Railway - Montana - chalets
3. Montana - economy - national parks
4. National parks - Montana - Glacier
5. Transportation - Glacier National Park - Red buses
6. Tourism - Montana - Glacier National Park
7. Going-to-the-Sun Road - Red buses - gearjammers
8. Tourism - employment - recreation

Cover design and page design by Ray Djuff
Title by Chris Morrison
Cover photo: Becky Hill, 1970s housekeeper at Prince of Wales Hotel, viewing Heavens Peak from the west tunnel portal on Going-to-the-Sun Road. Chris Morrison photo.
Back cover photo: Gordon Doggett washing his bus, No. 89.
    Courtesy, Sabra Doggett.

Printed and bound in the United States of America

Dedicated to Ray Kinley, Ian B. Tippet
and the members
of the
Glacier Park Foundation

Table of contents

	Introduction	11
Chapter 1	**Our first days**	14
Chapter 2	**Staff and antics**	26
Chapter 3	**The entrance hotel**	44
Chapter 4	**Gearjamming down life's highway**	56
Chapter 5	**Bear country**	78
Chapter 6	**Chalets, tent camps and motor inns**	88
Chapter 7	**Showplace of the Rockies**	100
Chapter 8	**Glacier's dragons: fires and floods**	126
Chapter 9	**Lake McDee**	142
Chapter 10	**People famous and obscure**	158
Chapter 11	**Afoot in the backcountry**	184
Chapter 12	**Why we keep coming back**	206
	Index	218

Foreword

This project came about out of the realization that after publishing *The Inside Trail* over a period of 30 years, the Glacier Park Foundation had created a priceless collection of personal stories about time spent in a much-loved place, Montana's Glacier National Park. As the "voice of the Glacier Park Foundation," *The Inside Trail* is a forum for former concession employees, and others, to share their love of people, place and time. All the authors graciously gave us permission to republish their stories and each reviewed and approved the edited version of his or her work.

For the authors whose writing appears in this book, a summer working at one of the resort facilities, driving a Red bus or other pursuits in Glacier was worth more than the money earned—it was an experience of a lifetime. One summer was not enough for many, though, and some returned for years, sometimes decades, with friendships formed and a life-long appreciation of the park.

As editors of this collection, we had a difficult job deciding which stories to select and which to leave out—and then having to pare them to fill a finite space. Like these authors, we are not only fellow foundation members but also Glacier aficionados in both the front and backcountry.

Our thanks to John Hagen for his help in making the final selection. Hagen is president and a co-founder of the foundation, and the man behind *The Inside Trail* from its very first issue, in April 1981.

Locating the authors for their permission to republish the articles was a challenge of its own. While many kept contact with the Glacier Park Foundation, others drifted away and some had died. In some cases, we were looking for the grandchildren of the authors as heirs, remembering that the first articles appeared decades ago. Of course, people also moved over the years. In two cases, we found authors had traveled from the Lower 48 states to Alaska, then back, but to a different state. In one of those instances we were looking for a granddaughter who had married, twice. To say we got lucky finding all these authors to get their copyright permissions is an understatement.

The illustrations in this book were supplied by the authors and when we couldn't reuse their images from *The Inside Trail*, supplemented them with pictures from our collections. We've also included a few of the drawings done by John Hagen to illustrate the original articles.

Over the decades places in Glacier have changed, as have their names. Some places no longer exist: Cutbank Chalets, St. Mary Chalets, Going-to-the-Sun Chalets and Many Glacier Chalets. The seasonal tent camps are also no more. Names change. Crossley Lake, site of a tent camp, has been redubbed Cosley Lake, for ranger Joe Cosley. The original spelling was a misunderstanding. Goathaunt, site of another defunct tent camp and chalet, has become an active, though remote, interpretive location. It is now spelled Goat Haunt.

Built accommodations have seen slight name alterations. Glacier Park Hotel and Lake McDonald Hotel are now called lodges. Two Medicine Chalets, Granite Park Chalets and Sperry Chalets are now referred to in the singular. In the case of Two Medicine, only one building left is used commercially. We have used the location title appropriate to the era the author has written about. To assist you, we've included a map on Page 33 showing names and places as they were.

A further challenge is the fact Glacier has its own lexicon, which we've done our best to make evident or explain. The "entrance hotel," or just "entrance," is Glacier Park Lodge, although technically it is outside the park boundary. "Many" or "Many G" refers to Many Glacier Hotel. "The Pass" is usually Logan Pass on Going-to-the-Sun Road, although it can mean Marias Pass crossed by Highway 2—deciding which is a matter of context.

Glacier's historic buses were for the longest time referred to as "Reds," denoting their color, although they were made by the White Motor Company of Cleveland, Ohio. The drivers are called gearjammers or jammers, for the non-synchromesh manual transmissions whose gears they would sometimes grind. It's common now for the buses to be referred to as "jammers" or "jammer buses," even though they are all equipped with automatic transmissions, courtesy of a $6.5-million refurbishing by Ford Motor Company in 2001-02. We've stuck with the earlier terms, used by most of the authors.

For all that has changed, the beauty of Rocky Mountains remains as stunning as ever. Again and again the authors pause from the telling of their activities in the park to remark on the landscape. It's an overarching constant in the stories and as much as the people and familiar buildings, it's what draws us back to Glacier.

The stories that follow provide a glimpse of the past that only those who have lived it can explain. They may not consider themselves special, but in many ways these authors, during their time, are the sparkle that makes Glacier one of the brightest gems among the jewels known as America's national parks.

Editors Ray Djuff and Chris Morrison, 2012

Introduction

By John Hagen
President of the Glacier Park Foundation

When I was a young employee in Glacier Park in the 1970s, I loved to sit at the feet of old Ray Kinley and listen to his tales of the park. Ray worked at Many Glacier Hotel from 1919 to 1977 and had a vast repertoire of stories which he retold with color and verve. He was a character in his own right, with innumerable hats (which he was constantly donning and doffing) and various whimsical turns of phrase (he called hotel manager Ian Tippet "Mr. Tibbets," said "extry" where you or I would say "extra," and rounded out many observations with "don't you see" or "don't you know").

Ray had a strong influence on the Glacier Park Foundation from its inception. In 1980 the hotel concessioner sought to sell its assets to a casino corporation. A group of employees, past and present, formed the Foundation to block the sale. We were inspired, in part, by the sense of tradition and history Ray had instilled in us, and we thought that the pending buyer would be ill-suited to preserve them.

John Hagen, left, and fellow Many Glacier Hotel bellman Tim Vadheim make unusual Red bus fender ornaments in 1973.
Courtesy, John Hagen

A federal lawsuit ensued (with the 93-year-old Ray on the stand as a witness). The casino company blessedly chose not to pursue the sale, and the concession ultimately came into the hands of excellent management. The Foundation endured as a citizens' group devoted to historical preservation and to promoting the public interest in Glacier. We have many hundreds of members, most of whom are former concession employees dating back to the 1930s.

For more than three decades we have published *The Inside Trail* as a membership journal. Besides park news and public affairs, *The Inside Trail* always has featured stories by former Glacier employees and visitors. Ray set the tone from the very first issues, contributing many wonderful tales. The values which he embodied—community spirit, tradition, humor, adventure, a delight in personalities—infuses *The Inside Trail*.

A number of Ray's fine tales enliven this anthology, including his account of the runaway Heavens Peak Fire of 1936. His description of Swiftcurrent

Valley after the fire is a signature line—"It was like Dante-land: the Inferno, don't you know." Ray's tales often had a Dante-esque quality, in which misbehavior was subjected to appropriate punishments (see "Foiling the flirtatious cook" (p. 36) and "The rowboat race" (p. 115)).

Some *Inside Trail* stories charm us as archetypal accounts of things that almost all Glacier employees have known. Other stories arrest us by their uniqueness. Tales of the latter sort abound in this anthology—the Red bus gingerly backing out of the avalanche (p. 60), the ocean of gasoline nearly blowing up the Glacier Park Transport Company garage (p. 58), the employees swimming in the drinking water for Going-to-the-Sun Chalets (p. 96), the hitchhikers clinging for dear life to the luggage rack of a car with a maniac at the wheel (p. 187).

Also memorable are the stories of ingenious pranks—the "millionth visitor" extravaganza (p. 34), the Red bus filled with water and disgorged upon a transport agent to protest its leaky roof (p. 71), the Wild West party descending on a tour group and abducting its escort (p. 73). In bygone decades, when bearskins were draped on the hotel balconies, employees would dress up in them and prowl the grounds, sometimes with surprising results (p. 83).

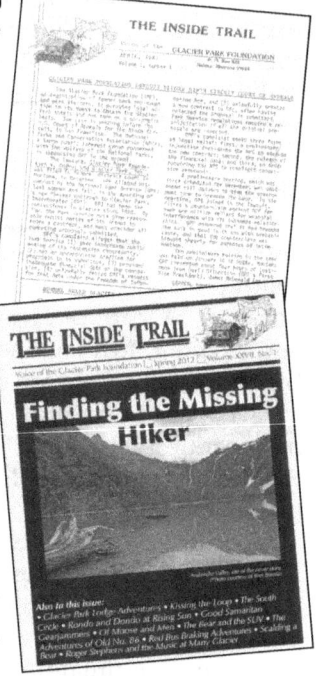

The first edition of *The Inside Trail*, top, and the spring 2012 edition.

The Inside Trail has showcased legendary people who spent many seasons in Glacier and left their mark there. We've run many stories about Cy Stevenson, the irascible engineer who maintained the creaking old lodges for decades. We've published descriptions of Ma Perkins of Granite Park Chalets, Mama Frase of Lake McDonald Hotel, Omar (the Terrible) Ellis of Many Glacier, Hugh and Margaret Black of St. Mary Lodge, Art Burch and Joy Paulsen of the boat crew, and the timeless transport agents Ino Belsaas and Sid Couch, the latter "almost blind, but he always saw what he wasn't supposed to see" (p. 58).

Foremost among those personalities is Ian B. Tippet, whose storied career began in 1955 and continues today. Mr. Tippet was personnel director for all the hotels for many decades. He corresponded with thousands of people—he may have written more letters than anyone in the history of the world. He managed Many Glacier from 1960 to 1983 and created a legendary program of employee music there. Mr. Tippet has been a beloved presence in the park and among alumni of the lodges for generations. He appears in a multitude of stories in *The Inside Trail*.

My earnest gratitude goes to Mr. Tippet, to Ray, to the hundreds of members of the Glacier Park Foundation, and to all who have helped create *The Inside Trail* over the decades. I especially thank our editors, Rolf Larson and Katryn Conlin, our membership director, Carol Dahle, our secretary, Mac Willemssen, and our historian, Tessie Bundick. And I thank the creators of this anthology, Ray Djuff and Chris Morrison, for their devoted work.

I wish every reader delightful hours enjoying these scores of vivid tales.

Glacier Park Station on the Great Northern Railway line was a main arrival and departure center for not only tourists, but hotel staff.
Great Northern Railway collection, Minnesota Historical Society

Chapter 1

Our first days

Glacier National Park: Is that in Oklahoma or New Mexico?
Tessie Bundick
(Many Glacier Hotel 1972-73, 1976-80)

I had never even heard of Glacier National Park when a fellow Texas Tech University actress mentioned that she had thoroughly enjoyed last summer in this glorious place. I was a dyed-in-the-wool Texan who had never traveled farther north than the Panhandle, and Glacier Park might as well have been a recreational area on Mars as far as I was concerned.

After carefully listening to this former Glacier hotel employee prattle on in glowing terms, I decided to apply. I was immediately accepted for a maid's job because Ian Tippet, the hotel company's employee recruiter, was fond of prospects from Texas Tech because, he said, "No one from there has ever broken their contract."

I had my doubts, and would really have been quite content to stay in Lubbock that summer, but off I went on the trail of adventure to far-off Montana.

In those days, the thing to do upon arrival by plane into Great Falls was to get a taxi straight to the Rainbow Hotel in the downtown area. This hostelry had seen its glory days pass by. However, it was a tradition and the bus station was only a block away, so one could drag one's luggage down the sidewalk (before wheels), and purchase a ticket to East Glacier.

Of course, I was impressed by the great lodge at the entrance to the park, but my sense of history appreciation had not been honed to a very sharp edge and I was not as impressed as I should have been.

I was put up in a communal room overnight with other employees bound for Many Glacier and the next morning saw us off in a shiny Red bus to Many Glacier. The intensity of the excitement rose amongst the old-timers as they lovingly named each landmark and mountain on our 55-mile journey. Finally we came to the tiny village of Babb. There was some snickering about this, and then we turned down that long road to dear old Swiftcurrent Valley.

As we neared the hotel, misty-eyed returnees all but stood at attention and saluted, each thrilled at the first sight of the beloved old barn. I could only wonder at such rapture. As we disembarked, people seemed to appear out of nowhere and there was much screaming and hugging as old friends recognized each other.

I took a hard look around. Yep, there were those mountains all right and, "gosh, they were big," I thought with a flatlander's sensibility.

Since I was on opening crew, we ate our meals in the tiny lobby of the Lower Dorm. I was innocent of all employment as I had never held a job, so mucking out a winter's worth of dirt from the hotel's rooms came as something of a shock. It was hard, physical labor and just when we thought we were too exhausted to go on, we had a big party in the communal living room of the Lower Dorm and somehow found energy reserves for whooping it up.

It probably took about two days for me to catch on to exactly where I was. In retrospect, I cannot fathom why it took that long as it was obvious from the get-go that I had somehow landed into a combination of Never-Never Land and Paradise Regained. Or at least it should have been.

The spell of those mountains was so strong, the television-free, radio-free, car-free atmosphere so charged with pure fun, the intense bonding of the employees from all over the nation so instantaneous, the music was so beautiful, the history of the hotel so fascinating that I quickly shed the Texas dust from my shoes and exchanged it happily for the magical sand on Swiftcurrent's lake shore.

I returned for seven more summers, never regretting a moment spent in these magnificent northern Rockies and grateful for the good luck that had sent me there.

The "Chalet City" and Howard Eaton
Ray Kinley
(Many Glacier Hotel 1919, 1922-77)

In the summer of 1913, at the age of 21, I was a brakeman on the Pennsylvania Railroad. One night in Ohio, a switchman forgot to close a switch and the train I was riding ran into a hopper train full of coal. Sixty-five people were killed. I was trapped beneath a baggage car and lost my right hand, which was pinned by the undercarriage.

The following summer, still recovering from the accident, I went to visit my uncle in Vaughan, Montana. He ran a hotel which catered to passengers on the "Galloping Goose," a spur train that ran from Great Falls to the Great Northern's main line.

Uncle Henry decided to take me to Glacier Park, which was just four years old. We rode north on a wagon, known as a democrat, loaded with blankets for us and oats for the horses. We went by way of Conrad,

Part of the Many Glacier Chalets complex circa 1915. Ray Djuff collection

Blackfoot and Browning, and then up the Duck Lake Road (which just had been built). Uncle Henry took this route to avoid the hill climbs closer to the park.

At Babb we passed the original Thronson's Store (which was closer to the turnoff than the present store). I saw Oscar Thronson there for the first time; a small boy back among the shelves. The store was run by Oscar's father.

We passed the newly built Sherburne Dam, with a steam shovel still in place at the dam site. Then we trotted on up the Many Glacier Valley. I just fell in love with it, don't you know; I thought that it was the most magnificent sight I had seen in all my life.

Many Glacier Hotel had not been built yet (it opened the following summer, and Great Northern workers were busy on the site). A whole city of chalets was scattered beside the falls and on the slopes of Mount Altyn. We went farther up the lake and made our camp in a secluded spot.

While we were there, Howard Eaton came through with one of his enormous horse parties. They had bull cooks who fed the people and put up the tents or teepees in which they slept. Mary Roberts Rinehart traveled through Glacier with  **Howard Eaton** Eaton the following two summers and wrote books about the experience [*Through Glacier Park: Seeing America First with Howard Eaton* (1916) and *Tenting Tonight* (1918)] which helped to make the park very popular.

Chapter 1 — Our first days

After my visit with Uncle Henry, I went back east. I sold artificial arms and did railroad work for several years. In the summer of 1919 I came back again and worked in Glacier for more than 50 summers, through 1977.

Mice in the wastebasket
Liz Gehring Coddington
(Many Glacier Hotel 1956-59)

During the summer of 1955, the hottest summer I can remember, I was working in a doctor's office in downtown St. Paul. A college friend kept sending me postcards about her most wonderful first summer working in Glacier. I decided right then that I would spend the summer of 1956 in Glacier. So what if the pay was only 55 cents an hour?

My friend encouraged a group of us from college to work at Many Glacier Hotel. We were all excited climbing aboard the Great Northern milk train, which stopped at every little town. After 28 hours, we arrived at East Glacier in time for lunch, and then we boarded the bus for Many Glacier. We felt like total greenhorns, as those who had previously worked at Many talked endlessly about their experiences and named all the mountains we passed as if they were old friends.

The first week was never to be forgotten. I was employed as a front desk cashier. The new auditor couldn't figure out how to run the posting machine that I would be using to bill the guests for their stay. And, of course, there was a convention that first week.

We literally worked day and night trying to figure out this machine and then cranking out the bills for a full house of guests. By the time the week was over, we newcomers felt that we had paid our dues and were now part of the establishment.

One experience stands out concerning that first week of dorm life. It was a very cold week and the dormitory was not heated. Every night we had to listen as mice got into our wastebasket and would jump and jump trying to get out. It was so cold in our room that no one wanted to get out of a warm bed to do anything about it. In the morning, we would have a wastebasket full of frozen mice. We never thought to tip the wastebasket over before turning in for the night. It was a very effective mousetrap.

Snow and mosquitoes
Cathy Crossland Woods
(Many Glacier Hotel 1971)

On May 31, 1971, I began a journey that would take me from my hometown of Plainview, Texas (a town aptly named to describe the scenery), to

Glacier, the place I quickly determined would be the closest to heaven I would ever find in this life.

At Texas Tech, my friends and I had been sunbathing on our balcony since February. Though I had packed sensibly for the summer, I was psychologically unprepared for the early June weather of the park. When we arrived, there was a pile of snow that had been plowed from the parking lot and ran the length of the hotel and was up to the second story windows.

Cathy Woods

Being part of the skeleton crew that cleaned the hotel in preparation for opening had advantages. Staying warm was not one of them; I don't think I thawed out until July.

I learned several things the first week of that most idyllic summer of my life. I learned that friendships blossom quickly in such an environment. I learned that mountains and lakes and people that you may never see again can take root in your heart and never let go. I also learned that the state bird of Montana is the mosquito. How do those things survive and thrive in those freezing temperatures?

A southerner in the north country
John Cotham
(Many Glacier Hotel 1972)

My first days in Glacier in the summer of 1972 were unforgettable, not in the least because I almost didn't make it there.

Glacier Park employees were offered a discounted train fare from Minneapolis to East Glacier, Montana, so I decided to make the entire trip from Tennessee by train—a trip that was to take at least two full days.

On the day of departure, I arrived at Union Station in Nashville at the appointed time only to find the train station deserted. I wandered around and finally found a workman down by the tracks who said that only two passenger trains departed Nashville daily, one northbound and one southbound, and the northbound train had departed about four hours earlier.

The ticket agent who had sold me my ticket several weeks earlier in Memphis, where I was attending college, had evidently given me departure times from Memphis, not Nashville. So much for catching the train that day.

Luckily, however, I was able to fly from Nashville to Minneapolis the next day, where I caught the same train I would have been on had I been able to start my rail journey in Nashville. I still wonder if manager Ian Tippet would have kept me on if I had arrived in Glacier a day late.

The trip across the northern plains was largely uneventful, except I remember puzzling over unscheduled stops seemingly in the middle of nowhere, and being amazed by the sight of snow lingering in sheltered areas in the high plains as we approached the mountains. Snow? In June? In 75 degree weather? That didn't seem right to my southern eyes, and I was truly amazed after my arrival at Many Glacier to see several feet of snow still on the trails in the park.

The day of my arrival in Glacier was a day of luminescence—warm and bright, with a clarity that only autumn days can bring in the South. When I arrived I learned that I was among a small group of employees to bring Many Glacier Hotel out of its winter hibernation. There were probably no more than eight to 10 of us that first day.

Pat O'Connor, John Harris, Pat Kinsella and I were to be lobby porters (boy, was that a misnomer) and a few housekeepers had come early. I was glad to be among the chosen few, not only because it meant that I had the opportunity to spend a few extra days in such a magical place, but also because I was somewhat shy and felt much more comfortable in a small group of strangers than in a large group. Little did I expect that I was soon to be the center of attention.

While eating breakfast the very first morning, I became aware that the room had become suddenly very quiet and all eyes were trained on me. That was the last thing I wanted, and I had no idea what I might have done or said to draw such attention.

Finally, someone said that they were just listening to me talk. With some relief I came to realize that this group of mostly Midwesterners had the crazy notion I had an accent, a notion they somehow kept all summer and probably still have today.

A snowy night in the Upper Dorm
Ray Kozel
(Many Glacier Hotel 1972)

I was born and raised in the Midwest and never knew anything different from the hot, humid summers on the farm. But my parents, unlike most of our neighbors, took a summer vacation. The summer before I was a senior in high school we made it as far west as the Little Bighorn battlefield.

The next summer we made it to Glacier Park. My dad and I took a short hike around Swiftcurrent Lake. We saw a beaver and heard it slap the water with its tail. The rugged mountains, clear blue lake and magnificent wildlife made quite an impression on this flatlands teenager. Before we left Glacier, I was already asking how to get a job.

The next year I applied and was accepted at Many Glacier Hotel, probably due to my high school music background. I was on the early crew, arriving the first week in June.

I drove my car out to East Glacier only to have to park it for the summer.

The Upper Dorm for staff at Many Glacier Hotel. Ray Djuff photo

[Employees in those days were not permitted to have vehicles.]

I still remember the cloudy sky as we pulled into Many Glacier late in the day. I was shown to the Upper Dorm and my room. I was to be a busboy and share a room with two other busboys.

The first night I will never forget. During the night a storm blew in and I discovered that there was a hole in the window in my room. The howling wind actually blew snow into the room. I found a rag to plug the hole, but the tiny heater couldn't keep me warm. I remember shivering all night.

The next day I truly wondered what I was doing there. Snow in June! How could I survive in such harsh conditions? But I did survive.

Being on the early crew was great for a newcomer. I had no trouble meeting the few employees already there and was mostly able to keep up with the new people coming in every night. The early crew worked hard, scrubbing and cleaning. I still remember all the employees getting together in the lobby of the Lower Dorm to play a game. I always pitied the people who arrived late and had to try to catch up with all the new names and faces at once.

Working at Many Glacier Hotel was one of the highlights of my life. The fun-loving, friendly employees made me feel like I was in a family I had known all my life.

Starting with a loan
Rey Holmen
(Many Glacier Hotel 1935)

My first sight of Glacier Park occurred near the end of the 1935 summer season. I had been the photo-finisher for the Crandall Studios, at Moran in Grand Teton National Park, that summer. Before heading home for Rock Island, Illinois, I took the opportunity to visit the Jardine Ranch near Wisdom, Montana, home of our studio's clerk, cook, and housekeeper, and to drive on to Glacier.

I was very impressed with the beauty of the park, its expansiveness, and its peaks, even though they were not of the same alpine character as the Tetons. I harbored a wish to have a job there the following summer.

In the early months of 1936, my last semester as a senior at Augustana College in Rock Island, I wrote to Tomer J. Hileman at his Kalispell, Montana, studio, asking about a photo-finishing job in his Glacier Park concession.

I mentioned my experience at Crandall's Studios the prior summer, and my work as portrait photographer and photo-finisher for the yearbook during my senior year in high school and during two of my college years. There wasn't much encouragement in his reply.

It wasn't until shortly before graduation that the word came from him that, after all, he would have an opening at the East Glacier hotel location, at Two Medicine Chalets, and at Lake McDonald. I was elated.

Tomer J. Hileman
Ray Djuff collection

The day after commencement my classmate, Keith Hussey and I started westward in my 1928 Dodge sedan. Our elation was short-lived. Just a few miles out of Muscatine, Iowa, a connecting rod bearing failed and the rod went through the cylinder block wall.

I phoned around Muscatine to locate someone who would tow the car into town and junk it without charging me. I finally found one who would do so and pay me $35 for the remains.

Keith decided to hitch hike to his job in Grand Teton Park. I hitched a ride back to Rock Island and bought a round-trip railroad ticket to Spokane, Washington, via Denver, Salt Lake City, and Pendleton. This was cheaper than a round-trip ticket to Glacier Park.

I finally arrived at Kalispell bereft of money in Salt Lake City by a couple of con men and having to ask Hileman for an advance from my future pay. What a start.

A scene from the road over Looking Glass Pass. Chris Morrison photo

Seasick on Looking Glass Pass
John Hagen
(Many Glacier Hotel 1970-80)

I first departed for Glacier Park in the wake of a punishing week of final exams at the end of my junior year in college. I stayed up all night to finish a term paper, flung a few items into a suitcase, and drove 100 miles to Minneapolis, barely catching the train. As I blearily walked through the old Great Northern depot, I was impressed by a mural depicting the Many Glacier Valley, not realizing that this was the very location where I was going to work.

I fell asleep at once after climbing aboard the train, and continued sleeping soundly all that day and night. I woke up the next morning on the high plains of Montana, not far from the park.

I recall the dramatic sight of the front range of the Rockies, surging suddenly up above the prairie horizon as the train came over a rise. The morning sky was bright blue, the spring grass was a vivid green, and the snowy peaks looked like a line of tremendous icebergs rising out of an emerald sea. For an hour I was spellbound, watching the contours that I would come to know as Chief Mountain, Merritt, Going-to-the-Sun and Rising Wolf growing larger and larger as we crossed the miles of windswept grass.

Around mid-morning, we arrived at the Glacier Park Station, a few hundred feet from Glacier Park Lodge. There were quite a few employees bound for Many Glacier, and we all put our luggage aboard a Crown bus.

Before the bus departed, the company fed us lunch—a forbidding goulash—in the East Glacier cafeteria. Shortly afterward, as the lumbering old Crown [bus] went swaying around the many curves on Looking Glass Pass, I found myself feeling distinctly seasick. I gritted my teeth at the sight of Lower Two Medicine Lake, looking eerily green as it rolled in and out of view every time the bus lurched around a corner.

I was vastly relieved when we reached the open road between St. Mary and Babb.

Shortly afterward we rolled into sight of Many Glacier Hotel. The first person out of the hotel to greet the bus was a room clerk, resplendent in a scarlet blazer bearing the white Swiss cross above one pocket. He looked like a sort of medieval herald. Within a few minutes, I met perhaps the three most colorful personalities I ever have known in my life—Ian Tippet, our illustrious manager; Ray Kinley, the aged gardener and storyteller; and my longtime roommate Chris Vick. They gave rise to hundreds of merry tales.

From those first minutes I was captivated by the old hotel, its traditions and its rich community, in which I was blessed to share each summer for the next 10 years.

First memories of the park
John Slater
(Glacier Park Lodge 1965)

As I rode the Great Northern Railway across the plains, I was filled with anticipation at arriving at my summer job. I was bound from Michigan through Chicago that June of 1965 for Glacier—a place I had never been before.

At dawn, after three days on the train, I looked out the window and realized that the clouds I was seeing on the western horizon were actually the snow-capped peaks of Glacier. The air was cold when we stopped momentarily at Browning, and the mountains had drawn much closer now.

I took in the full blast of the mountain-scented air as I stood peering out through the opening between train cars as we headed down the last 13 miles of track to East Glacier. The click-clack of the wheels echoed off the canyon walls of the Two Medicine River gorge as we crossed on a high bridge. Minutes later, around 7 a.m., we pulled into the station at East Glacier.

I had arrived on the train I would be loading and unloading many times over the course of the summer. I walked up the path to the extraordinary old hotel built of massive Douglas firs—Glacier Park Lodge. The lawn was covered with snow. I was here.

A week later or so, wanting to see the park, a friend and I hitched a ride in front of the hotel. This was only the first of many such rides, but this one was especially memorable because I rode in the back of a pickup truck. My senses were overwhelmed by the marvelous, unobstructed view of beauty as we wound up the curving mountain road. The smells of the forest, the cool air and the warm sunshine filled my soul.

John Slater atop Mount Gould in 1965.
Courtesy, John Slater

I was hooked. Something inside me I had not known about came alive. That magical spirit of the park has been with me ever since.

It always will be.

The Glacier Park Hotel dining room "indian" hostess looking for "dudes."
Alice Porter photo, Ray Djuff collection

Chapter 2

Staff and antics

The great green underwear caper
Annette (Haussler) Walker
(Many Glacier Hotel 1967-68)

In 1967, when the rest of the country was heating up around the Vietnam War, civil rights, and a swirl of political activism, there was a place of sustained innocence and peace known as Many Glacier Hotel. It was one of the years when there was an abundance of Texans among the college-age staff. I suspect manager Ian Tippet liked us because we were relatively obedient, pretty darn trustworthy, generally loyal, and quick with a "Yes, sir!" when asked to perform menial chores.

Among the Texans was a particularly beautiful and relentlessly cheerful maid named Mary Ann. Her trademark statement, "Well, gre-a-a-a-t!" (Texas style), cheered any mood, any situation.

Equally memorable, for different reasons, was a Montana fellow named Mark (known affectionately as E!), who daily wore his trademark green sweatshirt. Many of us wondered how, or if, he ever managed to wash it because he always seemed to be wearing it.

Annette Walker

Eventually it came to pass, as the Many Glacier bunch grew to know and, in some cases, harbor affection for one another, that a mob of males stormed the women's dorm one night in what was in those days known as a panty raid. They thundered from room to room rifling through dresser drawers, grabbing bras, undies, stockings, slips (we wore slips in those days), and then ran back to the upper men's dorm with the loot.

The outstanding victim of this crime was Mary Ann, who arrived at the dorm just after the dust had settled and was greeted by her frantic roommates.

"Mary Ann. There was a panty raid."
"Well, great."
"No, Mary Ann. The guys came down and went through your dresser."

"Oh, great."
"No. You don't get it. They took stuff."
"That's great."
"No, no! They took a bunch of your underwear."
"Oh-h-h-h, . . . gre-a-a-a-a-t!"

After the damage had been assessed, we put our heads together and agreed almost instantly that it was time to plot revenge. With remarkable feminine restraint, we planned our attack, divvied up the territory, gathered flashlights, suited up in jeans and tennis shoes, ascended the hill in the dark of night and stormed the men's dorm.

The operation was over in a flash, and the take, which we heaped on the floor in one of our rooms, was astonishing. Shrieking and laughing, we sorted through the pile of decidedly masculine garb—shorts, T-shirts, socks, and what-have-you—wondering what belonged to whom, until we uncovered a pair of green jockey briefs.

Whoa, green? Well, that answered that question. E! had managed to wash that sweatshirt, after all. Got a free lesson in sorting laundry, too.

The triskaidekaphobiac
John Hagen
(Many Glacier Hotel 1970-80)

One June day in 1979, a traveler entered Many Glacier Hotel. He had no reservation and asked if there were any rooms available. Bonnie Brown, the room clerk, scanned the board to find a vacancy.

"Room 409 is free," she said, and turned to the pigeonholes for a key.

"I don't want that room," said the man emphatically.

"Hmm." Bonnie thought. "That's odd. He's young and looks physically fit, but maybe he doesn't want to climb three flights of stairs."

She scanned the board again.

"We can give you Room 58," she said.

"I don't want that room, either," the man replied, more emphatically than before.

"Sir," Bonnie remonstrated, "you haven't even seen those rooms, so how can you be so sure that you won't like them?"

The man drew himself up rather archly. He was thin, intense and humorless.

"Well," he said, "I could give you a long numerological explanation. The gist of it is that the sum of the digits in both those rooms is 13."

Bonnie's eyes grew wide at this. However, she went back to scanning the rooming board. She soon found a vacancy in the inoffensive Room 441.

The man took the key to this room and solemnly departed for the fourth floor.

That evening at dinner in the employee cafeteria, Bonnie recalled the triskaidekaphobiac (one who fears the number 13). All the listeners were fascinated.

In looking back upon the episode, we all were struck by the sheer statistical improbability of Bonnie drawing two sum-of-the-digits-is-13 rooms in a row. There were only 14 among roughly 210 revenue rooms at Many Glacier.

Alligator in the Annex
Douglas Batson
(Many Glacier Hotel 1968-70)

One of my duties as front office manager in the summer of 1970 was to oversee the bellmen, as if that could really occur. Overseeing the bellmen was like herding cats.

I remember that the bellmen were huddled, talking at the front door of the hotel lobby. What I can't remember is which bellman it was that told me, "You probably ought to go up to Room 312 in the Annex."

As I walked away from the front desk toward the Annex, I remember hearing part of the ongoing discussion between the bellmen.

"So how did you get it up there?"

"Well, I just sort of flopped it up on the luggage cart for the trip to the Annex and then took it up the stairs wrapped in a blanket."

I was obviously a late arrival to the party because the maids, housemen and assorted others were four to five bodies deep in the hallway, each attempting to peer through the door of Room 312. Feeling now that I was truly on a mission of some importance and in my official capacity as front office manager, I needed to get to the bottom of whatever had happened in that room.

I worked my way through the layers of people. I steeled myself not knowing what gruesome scene might next present itself. As I worked my way into the room, I could see one of the maids sitting on the end of the twin bed closest to the window. She was petting something and it was a pretty big something at that. I quickly estimated the length at about three and one-half or maybe four feet. Its weight was . . . how the heck did I know? I hadn't exactly read about this being one of the woodland creatures native to Glacier.

How much does an alligator weigh by the foot, anyway?

Now I knew what "just sort of flopped it up on the luggage cart" meant. It sure didn't have any handles that I could see. I hadn't even seen it check in at the front desk. But there it was docilely resting on the bed being petted by one of the maids. It had that sinister alligator smile that I had seen in Disney movies, and it scared me.

"Don't be afraid," said a woman with a German accent. At least I think that it was German ... maybe Austrian, whatever. "You can pet it if you like."

My official status as front office manager was really on the line here in front of all of my on-looking cohorts. I kept thinking, "My status, my hand, my status, my hand."

I opted for my hand and passed on the cordial invitation to pet the reptile.

"Oh, don't be alarmed, Manfred (name changed to protect the innocent) is perfectly tame. He travels everywhere with us," she said, pointing to her husband, who was standing in the corner of the room.

I wasn't sure if she meant that the husband traveled with the alligator and her or that Manfred traveled with the two of them.

"We are from California (that cleared up a lot of things) and we are on our vacation. We have had him for 11 years."

"Food—what about food?" I asked.

"Well," she said, "we feed him every three or four days." (I envisioned a trail of one-handed maids across the Rocky Mountain states.) "We get him several chickens at the grocery store and that fills him up for a while."

I wanted to say, "We don't have a grocery store in the hotel, we don't serve pets in the dining room and, by way, the how long has it been since he has eaten?" but I didn't. I wanted to know if they carried a 100-pound bag of "gator litter" with them when they traveled, but I figured that was a question that the maids would really want to ask.

I had often heard Ray Kinley tell the stories about the fire of 1936, but I bet that fire didn't spread as fast as the story of the alligator that checked into Room 312.

Ship of fools
Jim Lees
(Many Glacier Hotel 1970-73)

As anyone who has ever lived in the Upper Dorm at Many Glacier can verify, one of the most neglected tasks in the dorm (although it was one of the simplest) was answering the telephone.

The phone was located near the front entrance on the first floor, and there were two main reasons why the residents did not like to answer it. Invariably, the call would be for someone in a room that was farthest away, or if the person who answered the phone did take the time to go to the person's room, the person was almost never there.

It was easier just to let the phone ring until Ray Kinley (the octogenarian dormitory supervisor) would shuffle grumbling out of his room and answer with his characteristic two phrases—first, "Upper Dorm," and then (irascibly), "What's he do? What's he do?"

One midsummer afternoon in 1973, a few dining room waiters were gathered in one of the rooms on the first floor, relaxing and talking, as was customary after we were done serving lunch and before dinner.

The phone started to ring and, as usual, was allowed to ring for a couple of minutes without anyone answering it. After the ringing had continued for some time, one of the waiters decided to answer.

He picked up the receiver and jauntily announced, "Ship of fools. Captain speaking."

Two seconds later, the waiter quickly hung up the phone.

Jim Lees

He returned to the room, his face as white as a waiter's jacket, and said, "Guess what, guys. That was Mr. Tippet calling." (Mr. Tippet's response to his greeting had been a decidedly icy "Who is this?")

As he spoke, the phone again began to ring ferociously, and this time was allowed to go on ringing until it was answered by Ray Kinley.

The Tabasco four-top
Hank Overturf
(Many Glacier Hotel 1970-72)

I was preparing my waiter's station when the Many Glacier dining room opened for breakfast. It was one of those beautiful mornings and I was on the lake side of the dining room, so it was necessary to give the guests a few extra minutes to look out the windows before asking for their breakfast orders.

The first table seated was a four-top of two couples. I walked over, introduced myself and endured the normal questions about my major in school and where was the best place to see a glacier, etc. Their deep southern accents were pleasant and cultured.

They all ordered the normal fare of bacon and eggs and potatoes, with lots of coffee.

I brought their coffee with cream and sugar when one of the gentlemen asked for something that was new to me.

"Son, could you bring me the Tabasco sauce?" the gentleman I'll call Joseph asked.

"Certainly, sir," I stated, and retired to my station to fetch the hot sauce. When I brought it back, I watched as they passed the bottle around and each shook 15 to 20 drops of the hot pepper sauce into their coffee.

"Hank, you'd better bring another bottle of this sauce, as this one is only half full and we'll use what's left before the main course gets here," Joseph said.

I left to place their order, pick up their orange juice and fruit, and get another bottle of Tabasco sauce. Once in the kitchen, I remarked to several of my fellow waiters and waitresses and busboys that they should look at my four-top and watch those folks guzzle Tabasco sauce.

Then I recounted their use of Tabasco in their coffee and their request for additional sauce.

I served them their juice and fruit along with a fresh bottle of Tabasco. They drowned everything in the sauce. Grapefruit with Tabasco, prunes with Tabasco, orange juice with Tabasco and, finally, something I had seen before—tomato juice with Tabasco.

I was going to need an additional bottle of Tabasco sauce, a big one.

The morning was fairly slow and I didn't have another table. I had the opportunity to converse with these nice folks and answer a lot of questions. Then I went back to the kitchen to get their breakfasts.

By now I couldn't contain my curiosity.

I blurted out, "You folks must really like Tabasco sauce."

They all chuckled. Joseph said, "Hank, this stuff is amazing. It is a disease preventative and helps keep us young. We go through two bottles per meal, and none of us have had any health problems. We hike and travel all over the world. Notice none of us are wearing glasses, and we all have our own teeth."

As Joseph and the rest of the guests talked about Tabasco sauce, I learned that they were members of the family that produced it. The business was family-owned and operated.

The family would gather for several weeks a year and produce Tabasco sauce. Then they all would go their separate ways and enjoy the income generated by diners who enjoy a hot pepper sauce.

I picked up their orders and placed them in front of the diners and refreshed their coffees. Again everything, including the oatmeal, got a healthy dose of Tabasco.

The brand new bottle soon was empty. I pulled out the reserve bottle that I had brought out with their orders and offered it to them.

"Oh, thank you, Hank. We were running low," Joseph said with a grin.

They were friendly people. At the end of breakfast, we parted with handshakes and they left me a nice tip.

When lunch came around, they asked for me as their waiter, and I made sure that I had three full bottles of Tabasco on hand.

I was off duty for dinner, and I always have wondered who had the good fortune to wait on those folks. I sure hope that they had lots of Tabasco sauce on hand.

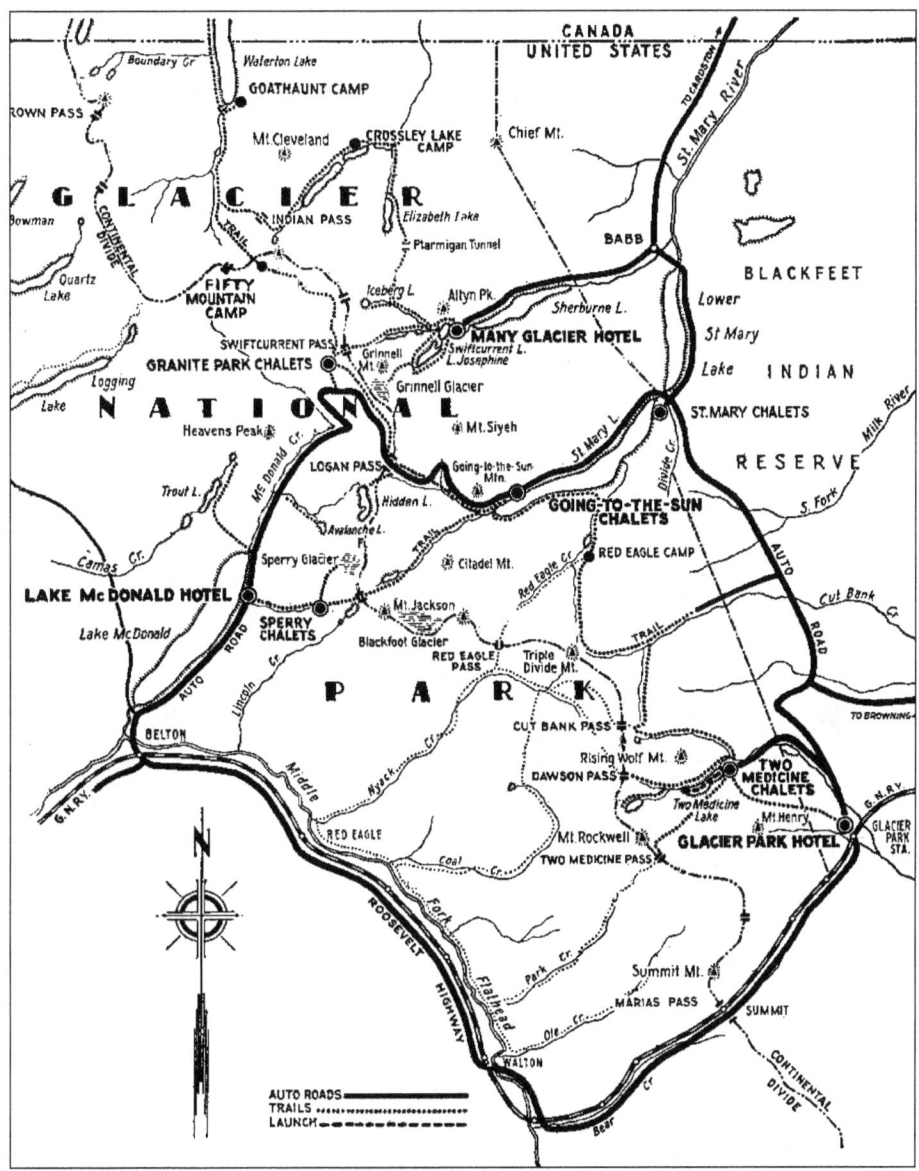

This map of Glacier National Park dates from 1934 and is an adaptation of what appeared in a Great Northern Railway brochure promoting the park. It shows facilities such as Going-to-the-Sun Chalets and St. Mary Chalets, which no longer exist, and place names, such as Crossley Lake, referred to in the text, which have since been changed. It's now Cosley Lake. Chief Mountain International Highway would not be completed until 1936.

Ray Djuff collection

Many Glacier's millionth guest
Mac Willemssen
(Swiftcurrent Motor Inn, 1967; Many Glacier Hotel 1968-70)

In 1969 I was a bellman at Many Glacier Hotel. Our manager was the inimitable Ian B. Tippet, a man who was very conscientious in his duties. In fact, there was only one night per summer that he would be away from the hotel and that was for the annual managers' meeting at Lake McDonald.

Trying to give credence to the adage that "when the cat is away the mice will play," my fellow bellman Eric Norby, front desk clerk Claude Matney and I attempted to come up with a proper way to celebrate Mr. Tippet's absence.

We finally hit upon the idea of honoring Many Glacier Hotel's "one millionth visitor." We had no idea how many people had been guests at the hotel since its opening in 1915. Obviously, as a seasonal operation, it had not been one million. But the number had a nice ring to it.

Our next concern was to pick the worthy recipient of this honor. The thought of selecting one of the many senior guests on tour gave way to the visions of coronaries, strokes and lawsuits. So we decided to find an appropriate young visitor upon which to bestow this honor. Careful and secretive planning took place during the week before Mr. Tippet's anticipated absence. Once he was on his way, it began.

Early in the afternoon, a young couple approached the front desk and Claude Matney, his face flushed with excitement, joyfully announced over the public address system that Many Glacier Hotel had just received its one millionth visitor.

Upon his cue, a trumpet trio gave a resounding fanfare from the first balcony. The somewhat befuddled guests were then presented with a cornucopia of gifts from the hotel staff which included a room (paid for by the housekeeping department and the bellmen), dinners (paid for by the dining room staff), complimentary pie (provided by the kitchen), and beverages (paid for by the bar staff).

The gearjammers and trail hands also participated. A Red bus, bedecked with colorful crepe paper, was driven into the portico, accompanied by several cowboys carrying American flags. The lucky visitors were each given a cardboard crown and taken on a complimentary ride through the parking lot in the bus.

At their honorary dinner in the Ptarmigan Room, the one millionth visitors were serenaded by the dining room staff and presented with a bottle of "vintage" wine by the bar captain. Needless to say, the couple was the envy of every hotel guest.

I think that by early Monday the one millionth visitors had ascertained they were part of a good-natured joke. The couple kept their humor, which was very easy to do because their stay at Many Glacier Hotel had cost them absolutely nothing. As they boarded their bus for another destination in Glacier National Park, they were given a goodbye serenade by a large contingent of the hotel's staff.

We never knew if Mr. Tippet was aware of our guest tribute. If he learned of it, it was never mentioned. But the next year, when I became head bellman at the hotel, Mr. Tippet chose not to attend the annual managers' meeting.

Switchboard tales
John Hagen
(Many Glacier Hotel 1970-80)

In the 1970s, Many Glacier Hotel had an old-fashioned switchboard with plugs on cords and long rows of holes and lights connecting to all the telephones in the hotel. The operators picturesquely spent their days manipulating the complicated spaghetti-work of cords and responding to calls of every description.

Hotel manager Ian Tippet liked to place employees from the Deep South in the front office, and I have fond memories of mellifluous Texas and Georgia voices intoning, "Many Glacier Hotel, may Ah help you?"

The operators fielded all sorts of requests and complaints from room guests. They generally would scrawl these messages on notepaper and pass them to the bellmen—

An operator at the Many Glacier Hotel switchboard. Ray Djuff collection

calls for ice, cribs, rollaways, and blankets, complaints about heat, noise, plumbing malfunctions and, of course, the ubiquitous bats.

Once I was handed a note complaining of a frog in the sink—Room 405. This seemed extraordinary as frogs aren't often seen in Glacier, and if one had somehow crept into the hotel, you wouldn't think to find it on fourth floor.

The "frog" proved to be a bat, sitting in the drain like a soldier in a foxhole with his head just peeping out. The guests let it be known that they would have been happier with a frog.

Another daily chore for the operators was to make wakeup calls. The bellmen's log of 1975 records an episode where Cheri Hinrichs, the early-morning maid, was allowed to make the 6 a.m. calls. Cheri went down the list of room numbers, crisply punching in plugs and announcing sweetly, "Good morning, it's 6 a.m."

Groggy voices repeatedly grunted back, "Thank you."

After a dozen calls or so, Cheri suddenly realized that she had been arousing the wrong guests. She had been sticking switchboard plugs into wrong holes. None of the guests uttered a word of protest.

Foiling the flirtatious cook
Ray Kinley (as told to John Hagen)
(Many Glacier Hotel 1919, 1922-77)

In Ray Kinley's heyday as a fishing guide at Many Glacier Hotel, he took out many celebrities. Among them were Harriet Parsons (the daughter of Louella), a Hollywood columnist, and her friend Edie Adams, who was then a star with the Ziegfield Follies.

Ray took this pair fishing on Lake Josephine on a cold day around 1940. The women produced a pint of Old Thompson to ward off the chill and traded sips while Ray, strategically positioned at the oars between them, enjoyed a healthy pull from the bottle both coming and going.

Back at the hotel, Ray took the ladies down to the "steam room" on Stagger Alley to warm up. They were soon discovered there by Ray's roommate, Butch, who was one of the cooks.

He dragooned the trio down to the rooms which he and Ray shared and served them all hot coffee. Then he began to make plans to join their next day's excursion, proposing that he take Miss Adams out in one boat while Ray took Harriet in the other. He couldn't keep his eyes off the gorgeous Edie.

Ray chafed and cast about him, but couldn't think of a way to gracefully turn down his roommate's proposal. The ladies listened in cool silence, clearly less than captivated by Butch.

"We'll leave it to your good judgment, Ray," said Harriet, as they left.

Early next morning, Ray went to breakfast and sat down with Lydia (Casey) Jones, the hotel chef. He explained the situation and asked if she could lend a hand.

"He'll ruin the whole day for me," lamented Ray. "I'm in this for the money, Lydia. If he horns in and makes it a foursome, then the ladies will look on it as a date, and I'll lose my tip."

"Why, that womanizing so-and-so," exclaimed the sympathetic Casey. "I'll tell you what I'll do, Ray. I have steak listed on the menu tonight, but I'm going to change it to chicken. East Glacier just phoned me and said that they have 300 fryers down there on ice, whenever we want them. I'll order them up this morning and set Butch to cleaning the batch of 'em. That should hold him until you've gotten those girls safely out of here."

Noon rolled around and Ray escorted the ladies down to the boat dock, where they were to catch the launch to Lake Josephine. Ray asked the skipper to hold the boat while he went to run an errand, and also to let off a tremendous blast on the whistle in about five minutes' time.

Ray walked to the hotel kitchen and found a scene there that utterly defied description. Chickens were strewn across every level space: stoves, tables, window ledges. In the midst of them stood Butch, almost beside himself with indignation, hacking off heads and gutting carcasses, and hurling scraps into garbage cans.

"Why, Butch! What are you doing?" Ray said. "We're supposed to be on that boat right now."

"I know, Ray," Butch sobbed plaintively. "You go along without me. That witch. That witch! I'll get even with her if it's the last thing I ever do."

Ray could see Casey Jones behind the coffee urns, smothering uncontrollable laughter. He turned on his heel to hide his own amusement, and ran down to the boat dock, where the ladies expressed satisfaction at being spared the company of Butch.

An afternoon in the Browning jail
Steve Berg
(St. Mary Lodge 1960-67)

Hugh Black, co-owner of St. Mary Lodge, had a great sense of humor, and a temper. It was never dull when he was around. He occasionally, though, acted in strange ways.

While driving the company truck to Browning one sunny day in 1962, I was ticketed by the highway patrol for driving without a chauffeur's license. Thinking it was appropriate that Hugh pay the ticket, and noting the fine represented half my monthly income, I gave it to him for payment.

Until a couple of arrest warrants were sent to me implying non-payment, I thought no more about it. I informed Hugh of the increased tension and understood he would pay the mounting fine.

A few weeks later, I was arrested and taken to the Browning jail with four miscreants from Babb. After five hours behind bars in a facility not approved by the Geneva Convention, and failing to engage my cellmate with my views on Camus, we got the word about 6 p.m. of our imminent transfer to the Cut Bank jail.

Steve Berg with the St. Mary cabin cleaning crew in 1961. Courtesy, Steve Berg

Convinced I was spiraling into the gulag, I asked to use the telephone. I called an old friend of Hugh's, Don MacRae, who was in the lumber business in Browning. He agreed to bail me out for $100, and by 6:30 p.m. I was again 18 years old and free.

I hitchhiked back to St. Mary and en route saw Hugh headed in the opposite direction toward Browning. Arriving at St. Mary, I was heralded as a hero and ordered to report to Margaret Black, Hugh's wife and co-owner of St. Mary Lodge. She was angry with Hugh for not paying the ticket.

Since I hadn't eaten, she treated me to a steak dinner in the dining room. There I held forth to the waitresses embellishing this story to include torture and other perfidy.

Hugh and I never spoke of it, but Don MacRae later told me Hugh reimbursed him. Hugh was one of the great men in my life. He viewed life as black or white with gray appearing perhaps once or twice each year.

Bearing with an obnoxious employee
John E. Daubney
(Many Glacier Hotel 1930s)

It seems that most of my memories of Glacier Park are tied in with the grizzly bear, and not just my own personal encounter with one of those large, unpleasant creatures.

One incident sticks in my memory because it involved one of my fellow students from the University of Minnesota who bragged incessantly about his family's social connections in Minneapolis and their high standing in the financial community—in short, a jerk.

On the evening in question, the loud mouth, who for purposes of this story will be called "George," had invited a female employee for a late evening walk.

About one-half mile from the hotel, George and the girl were seated on a log discussing things that people do under similar circumstances. Suddenly from behind them, and out of the dark, came a fearsome roar, and the apparition of a huge grizzly, walking on his back legs.

George, thrusting out his arms in an endeavor to gain his balance, knocked the young lady off the log and took off alone at a speed that could only be described as jet propelled. When he got back to the hotel, he reported the bear attack and his unsuccessful attempt to ward it off.

Luckily, the people he reported the incident to were in on the gag. What had really happened was that one of my co-employees, in a well-justified attempt to put George in his place, had borrowed a grizzly bear skin from the hotel lobby and had quietly approached where George and the girl were on the log.

The rug was carefully restored to its position of prominence in the hotel lobby, and George became the laughingstock of the other hotel employees (the story was never extended to include management, who would have frowned on such use of hotel property).

No longer were we required to listen to George's accounts of parties at the Minikahda Club and of his father's business prowess. All we had to do was to stand behind George, utter a fearsome growl, and everyone else in the room would collapse in laughter.

Fast times in the Many Glacier kitchen
Jeff Selleck
(Many Glacier Hotel 1980)

The summer after I graduated from college, I worked in the kitchen at Many Glacier Hotel. I was a morning cook for an excellent and well-respected chef.

Around midsummer, the chef decided that our cooking habits were growing lackadaisical. He herded the staff together around the grill for a brush-up session on proper methods for cooking hash browns. Tossing a hefty batch of our frozen, packaged potatoes on the grill, he sternly instructed us, "I want it done just like this. Don't mess with them so much. Cook them exactly as you see me doing here."

An unusual sizzling was arising from the grill. One cook blurted timidly,

"But chef, there's still waxed paper on one side. You don't really want us to cook 'em exactly like that, do you?"

The chef (turning slightly red) chuckled good-naturedly, "I guess you've got me this time."

All through the summer, the kitchen was constantly being visited by sanitation inspectors from the park service. The chef, who ran a very clean and well-organized kitchen, was exasperated over these constant visits.

Since our oven space was so limited, prime ribs had to be finished cooking a number of hours before they were served, but there was no room for them, with their pans and gravy, in the cramped refrigerators. The chef thus had us store them on open kitchen shelves before reheating them for dinner.

One day the park service held a grandiose inspection of the entire hotel, with numerous officials. At noon, the chef rounded up a group of us, and said, "Our friend the inspector's here again. We've got to work fast and hide the prime ribs."

This was an ambitious undertaking, since there were 11 prime ribs weighing 40 to 50 pounds each. We swarmed up on the storage shelves and removed huge pots and cauldrons. In their places, we set the ribs, and hurriedly covered them with foil. Then we replaced the pots and pans, or whatever else was suited for purposes of concealment.

Soon the inspector arrived, with a line of other officers in tow—all carrying clipboards and looking important. They marched expectantly to the shelves where the prime ribs customarily lay. The inspector gaped to find the shelves empty.

"Why, they're not here," he exclaimed. "This is where he always keeps them. Well—I just don't know what he's done with them today."

The inspector led his troupe away, with a crestfallen air. The chef watched him go, with a look of enormous satisfaction.

"We really fixed him, didn't we?" he remarked to the kitchen help, as we brought the ribs out of hiding once again.

A feisty Fourth of July
Einar Hanson
(Many Glacier Hotel 1976-77, 1979)

Many Glacier Hotel is a strange and wonderful place. In the 1970s, its Fourth of July parade was a tradition. Each year, the hotel employees, college kids mostly, assisted by the Park Service, would stage a parade past the front of the massive lodge to celebrate our nation's birthday.

First would come the mounted park rangers, looking impressive in their Smokey Bear hats and gray-green uniforms. Then each hotel department (housekeeping, front desk, dining room, etc.) would follow in one of the vintage Red touring buses with its canvas roof pulled back. Decorated like parade floats, they would roll past, with chosen representatives seated in and on the vehicle, like small-town royalty. Finally, the park fire truck, lights flashing and siren blaring, would finish off the annual event. Given that the parade was so short, sometimes it would loop through the upper parking lot and sweep past the hotel once again, just to make the parade last longer.

Mike Accardo, a fellow bellman, and I had schemed to make this parade more memorable than most. We had an innocently simple plan: ambush the hotel maids. We would sit in wait by the parade route, buckets of water in hand, and when the housekeeping bus came by—kersplosh.

All summer the traditional war between the bellmen (not bellboys, thank you) and housekeeping had raged delightfully. One by one we had thrown practically every maid into the lake, hauling them from their duties in guest rooms, down the stairs, onto the boat dock, and then with a hearty heave-ho, into the icy water of Swiftcurrent Lake. Salvos of pranks of impressive creativity had been hurled back in retaliation by the maids and housemen (not houseboys, thank you).

We knew the maids had planned something for the bellmen for this parade. Pat Wontorski, the head maid, had bragged about the ditties they would sing of the bellmen's defects while going by the hotel. Pat was an amazing adversary. A petite, wiry brunette from Tok, Alaska, with a wisecracking air you would think came from Brooklyn, she was fearless and witty.

That it might make sense to enlist more than Accardo to take on the entire housekeeping department never occurred to me. Mike was a son of Chicago, a short, broad-shouldered guy with a swagger like a young James Cagney. His ringing, early-morning renditions of *Nine Pound Hammer*, as we swung through the hotel's hallways picking up luggage for departing bus tours, was a great favorite of mine, though in later years I've sometimes wondered if his singing was enjoyed as much by the guests trying to catch a little more shut-eye.

The parade was scheduled to start at 4 p.m. I had worked the early shift and had gone to my dorm room after lunch. I'll just lie down and rest a little, I told myself. I listened to the mountain breeze, breathed in the smell of warm pine and drifted off. Suddenly, I heard the siren of the rangers' fire truck. Rats! I was late.

I leaped out of bed, still in my lederhosen, and ran to the front of the hotel. The maids' Red bus was parked in front of the building. Pat, sitting on the back of the bus like an elf princess, was leading the full busload of maids in a song, whose lyrics seemed specially designed to delight the large crowd of guests in front of the hotel with the pathetic qualities of bellmen. I saw Mike, who had come prepared with an arsenal of four cottage cheese containers of water.

"That's it?" I cried. "Well, it's all I could carry," he shot back. "Where were you?"

I shut up and grabbed two; so did he. We strode out, intent on ending this outrage. Suddenly, out of the bushes sprang a crew of housemen, armed with five-gallon buckets of water.

In the ensuing melee our pitiful supply was quickly gone and Mike and I were sloshed with bucket after bucket.

We stood there, dripping, as Pat turned from us, back to her busload of maids, to lead another chorus of her bellman ditty. In unison, the maids waved toilet brushes and crowed (to the tune of *The Stars and Stripes Forever*): "Oh, we are the Samurai maids."

I firmly believe that sometimes, in moments of crisis you can read another person's mind. Mike looked at me; I looked at him. We both looked at the pile of soft, brown balls at our feet, a gift of the wranglers' horses that had passed by only moments before. In a flash Mike and I both reached down and scooped up a handful.

A fire hose is used to spray one of the participants in the Fourth of July parade at Many Glacier Hotel.
Courtesy, Rolf Larson

The choir of maids in the bus, facing Pat, saw us, their eyes widening in disbelief. As we wound up, their heads descended into the bus, like gophers ducking for shelter.

Pat, her back toward us, was completely unaware of the oncoming bombardment. My first volley caught her right between the shoulder blades with a satisfying splat. The driver scrambled to jam the bus into gear and drive off, but could not before a couple more of our volleys had hit home. The crowd of tourists gathered for the parade gasped and roared at our onslaught.

Now, the ranger fire truck came zooming up behind us. At its rear, stationed at the turret water gun, was Ray, the maintenance man. Ray, carried away by the excitement, turned on the water, and though aiming for Mike and me, instead shot a rope of water across the crowd of tourists. I was soaked again, but so was the crowd, which swayed like a wheat field in the wind trying to avoid the spray.

John Hagen, our head bellman, ran up yelling, "Let's return the favor." We ran into one entrance of the hotel and unrolled the standpipe fire hose hanging in the hallway. I ran out the door with the business end, while John waited for my signal to turn on the water. Ray, in the fire truck, having circled through the upper parking lot, approached for another run. I yelled, "Turn on the water." Nothing happened.

"I did," yelled John. "There's no water!"

As so often happened at Many Glacier in those days, the plumbing had failed. The fire truck zoomed past unscathed, and with that the Fourth of July parade fizzled to an end.

Or so I thought. The next morning as I stumbled from the dormitory to the hotel, I heard someone softly swearing by the road. It was the maids' driver. He had a bucket of water, and was stooped over trying to wash away every bit of horse debris from his bus. Suddenly, I felt very guilty. I slipped by him unnoticed in the dark, ducked into the rear hotel entrance and went downstairs.

I stumbled down Stagger Alley, the basement hallway renowned for its lack of right angles, to the porter's lobby closet, where our brooms, mops and other implements of cleanliness were stored. I opened the door, flicked on the light and reached for a floor mop. My hand closed around the handle, but instead of smooth hard wood it felt squishy and sticky. Jolted awake, I jerked back my hand and looked closer. Thick brown goop covered the handle. I sniffed my hand. Peanut butter. The handle was coated in peanut butter. So were the handles of every other broom and mop in the closet.

Oh, well, I thought. It could have been worse.

Glacier Park Lodge was known as the "entrance hotel," where guests arriving by train could relax or start their visit to Glacier Park via a Red bus trip.
Great Northern Railway collection, Minnesota Historical Society

Chapter 3

The entrance hotel

Waitressing at the entrance hotel
Joan Fritz Shipley
(Glacier Park Hotel 1948)

I was a waitress at the entrance hotel, as Glacier Park Hotel was then called by employees, in 1948. I had just graduated from Tracy High School in southern Minnesota. A high school classmate and I went to St. Paul, Minnesota, to the headquarters of the Great Northern Railway to interview for the job.

The Great Northern's interviewer, a gentleman named Ralph Erickson, asked, "How old are you?"

I said, "Eighteen."

He folded my application and said, "Well, you know you have to be 21."

I quickly retorted with, "But Mr. Erickson, I'm far more qualified than some of the girls who are already accepted, and who are not 21. I'm not going to lie to you about my age. The Finley girl and her friend are going because they have pull. Mr. Finley is the vice-president of Great Northern. They have no waitress experience at all. I've worked my way through high school as a waitress. They're going out there for a joy ride. I have to earn money for college—I need this job because I have to work my way through."

Joan Shipley

He answered, "Young lady, can you carry a tray with 12 dinners on it, balanced on your shoulders with one hand, while you pass through a swinging door from the kitchen to the dining room?"

I said, "No, but I can learn."

He said, "You're in. But I do not want you to let any of the other employees out there know that you're only 18. You don't need to lie about it. Just carry on as if you're 21."

The worst part of being a waitress was that Mrs. Chadwick, the woman in charge of us, had us wear hair nets, ugly black shoes, maroon-red waitress dresses with white collars, and funny little white waitress hats. Our uniforms and hats had to be starched and ironed, which was a pain. Mrs. Chadwick trained us in the proper etiquette of serving guests.

The waitresses at the entrance hotel were always jealous of the ones at Many Glacier, because the gearjammers spent a lot more time at Many Glacier. I was a girlfriend of one jammer for half the summer, and then of another for the last half. We always were delighted when the jammers arrived. The MO was to have a powwow, which meant bringing a six-pack of beer, building a bonfire and crawling under blankets to keep warm.

The waitresses would work the breakfast shift, go back to the dorm and sleep until the lunch shift, work that and then go back to the dorm to sleep until the dinner shift. After the evening shift, we danced till the lounge closed, then went to Dusty's Tavern (about five miles west of Glacier Park Hotel), sang and danced and gambled till they closed at 2 a.m., then went to the powwow back at entrance. We were literally up all night, and got back in time to start the breakfast shift. Ahh, the vigor of youth.

One night a group of us rented horses and rode up Mount Henry in the full moonlight, to watch the sun come up.

I particularly enjoyed waiting on Lord and Lady Astor, with their British accents. I remember they ordered a bottle of wine with dinner, drank only one glass each, and told me that the rest of it was part of my tip. They also left me $5, which was, as I remember it, generous. And the wine was very popular with the jammers at the powwow that night.

The Bishop of Helena was another memorable guest. He would come in for breakfast and would say with an Irish brogue, "I'll have a bowl of stirabout."

I didn't know what that was.

He grinned and said, "You just tell the chef that's what I ordered and you'll find out."

Of course, it was oatmeal.

For some reason, the Bishop took a liking to me and liked to tease me in an innocuous sort of way. He ordered soft-boiled eggs one morning. The waitresses cooked the eggs in little timed containers. I thought I knew how long it took for a soft-boiled egg, but when I brought them to him, they were raw. He laughed and gave me a bad time about it, but in the process I learned that I had not accounted for the altitude. I thoroughly enjoyed the challenge and all the repartee with the guests.

I once waited on Winold Reiss and Carl Link. Reiss was the German-born artist who painted the marvelous Indian portraits that were used on the Great Northern Railway calendars. Shortly after waiting on them, I had the day off and decided to hitchhike with friends to Two Medicine Lake. We took off early that morning with our lunch in little brown paper bags so that the visitors would recognize us as Glacier Park employees and give us a ride. Two elderly gentlemen gave us a lift. It was Reiss and Link, who had recognized me from the dining room.

The artists asked us if we would like to go to Browning, the Blackfeet Indian village, instead of Two Medicine. We were delighted. They were going to the village to paint Julia Wades-in-the-Water. We watched in amazement as they brought to life on canvas the wonderful character of that withered but beautiful elderly lady. I wish I had kept those Great Northern Railway calendars with all the marvelous portraits of the Blackfeet people.

Rumble at the entrance lodge
Bill Treacy
(Glacier Park Hotel 1946-49)

On a quiet August Sunday, some of the wild crowd from Cut Bank spent an afternoon of music and beer in The Grill at the entrance lodge. By 8 p.m. they were looking for trouble and became abusive and unruly when asked to leave.

They lined up in front of the laundry dock and defiantly told the house detective, "Make us leave!"

Bill Treacy

All available forces of Glacier Park male employees were called from their dorms. A "high noon" confrontation rapidly developed. The house detective foolishly brandished a gun, which accelerated the tension. Boys on both sides were holding broken beer bottles, pipes, bats, and sticks.

My brother, Steve Treacy, was the golf pro at the entrance lodge that summer. He had recently returned from serving as a fighter pilot in the South Pacific. With the help of some other Second World War veterans, Steve separated the pistol from the excited house detective. This action calmed the troops on both sides. Everybody dropped their makeshift weapons. The boys from Cut Bank headed for the parking lot and drove off in their cars, and a catastrophe was averted.

I was always proud of my older brother for coolly defusing this explosive situation.

I was Don Hummel's PR man
John Dobbertin
(Glacier Park Lodge 1962-63)

Summer of 1962 started out as a real bummer. Wrapping up my sophomore year at the University of Michigan, the good news was I had been named editor of *Gargoyle*, the campus humor magazine. The bad news: my summer job—it would have been the third year—as a cub reporter for the *Battle Creek Enquirer & News* (Battle Creek, Michigan) vanished in the depths of the Kennedy recession.

What was a 19-year-old guy to do? Well, load up a station wagon with two fraternity brothers, a large tent, canoe, something to eat and drink and take off on the brand new Trans-Canada Highway. We headed for Banff and Jasper and the third week of June cruised down toward Glacier.

Whoa! Who are those two good-looking ladies hitchhiking? Of course, we gave them a lift. Turned out they were working for Glacier Park, Inc.

"Hey, you guys should go on down to East (we soon learned this was code for Glacier Park Lodge) and you can work there for the summer," the ladies told us, adding: "A lot of kids they hired either never showed up or when they got here found out it was darn hard work and left."

Don Hummel

And so we went to East. Two of us—yours truly and Doug Piper—took employment with Glacier Park, Inc. George drove the car back to Michigan. Piper scrubbed pots and pans in the kitchen at Glacier Park Lodge, preparing him for his future job building nuclear power plants. I started out in the laundry.

It was a happy enough place to work. However, the hours grew longer every day. What did those housekeeping people do with the endless hamper loads of linen and towels? Six days a week, eight full hours a day wasn't cutting it. We were asked—for no additional pay—to return to the laundry for evening hours. The issue really wasn't about money ... it was about our "free" time. And that's where this ditty started:

"We work in the dark in Glacier Park
For Hum-mel, Hum-mel,
H-U double-M E-L!"

After about a week of this, there was a general rising of the laundry troops—mostly coeds. So two of them and yours truly were elected to go see Glacier Park, Inc. president Don Hummel. He was most gracious, and the evening hours were eliminated.

It could not have been more than two weeks after I started in the laundry, and shortly after the laundry revolt, that the public relations director for the company was summarily fired. Upon hearing this, I immediately made my second visit to Don Hummel's office.

"I understand the public relations position is now available," I said.

"That is true," Hummel said.

"Well, sir, I can do that job," I said.

I explained to him I was a journalism major and had two summers' experience as a reporter, and several years before that working on a weekly teen page for the *Battle Creek Enquirer & News*.

Hummel looked me up and down, smiled and said: "The job is yours."

I telephoned home for some dress shirts and suits, and the adventure began. During the summer of '62 I spent a lot of time looking through old files, photos—all of the work the Great Northern Railway had done to

John L. Clarke operated a studio in East Glacier Park where he did animal sculptures from wood. Stories about Clarke, a deaf, mute Blackfeet, provided just the material John Dobbertin sought to publicize Glacier. Courtesy, Joyce Clarke Turvey

attempt to keep the name Glacier Park and the lodges—in the public eye. The summer was so far gone there wasn't much I could do to gear up the publicity. We did all we could.

By the time I returned for the same job in 1963, I had taken the one course in public relations (one-half credit) offered by the University of Michigan. Good news upon arriving at East in early June: my digs would be a private room in the chalet overlooking the new swimming pool.

George Plumer had taken the job to both manage the Glacier Park Lodge and head up advertising and public relations. George warmly greeted me and immediately said: "I don't know a blooming thing about advertising or public relations. I hope you do." And that was the beginning of a great working relationship.

George and I shared a very capable secretary, Donna Wilcox, who, if I recall correctly, was a coed from Texas. I had thought a lot about what should be done to start moving Glacier Park, Inc.'s public relations program forward. First, communications with the employees needed to improve and Hummel agreed to a weekly newsletter.

So we started *PEN*, or *Park Employee Newsletter*. We published every Tuesday. It wasn't fancy, but we made every attempt to keep it interesting. In addition to items from the hotels, we included a page of what was happening in the world. It was amazing how fast we all disconnected from world events with no television, radio or newspapers.

Then we made it a point to connect with all convention co-ordinators upon their arrival at the headquarters hotel. First thing I would do is volunteer to be certain their important speeches were written for news releases—including, of course, the fact of where they were meeting. We established terrific working relationships with United Press International and Associated Press and would telephone the releases to them (no faxes in the Dark Ages). The result was a steady flow of news stories all datelined "Glacier Park." All of them moved in the western states, and several made the national wires. The convention co-ordinators loved the publicity. Good publicity, happy customers.

One of the major conventions of the summer of 1963 was the regional seminar of state trial judges held at Many Glacier July 18 to 20. Keynote speaker was U.S. Supreme Court Justice Tom C. Clark.

Justice Clark really appreciated the article I drafted on his speech to the group. The news release, and several others on this convention, made the national wires. It also didn't hurt that Justice Clark was inducted into the Blackfeet tribe at a special ceremony at Many Glacier. I received a very nice, handwritten thank-you on U.S. Supreme Court letterhead from Justice Clark, and that now hangs in the Davenport, Iowa, law office of my daughter Judy.

I started looking for good feature stories with photos that we could also put out to UPI and AP. Blackfeet artist John L. Clarke was a fixture just up the road from Glacier Park Lodge. Over the two summers I really got to know John and took bundles of photos of him. He was 82 in 1963 (died in 1970). The release, with photos, on John appeared all over the country.

The experience in the two summers working for Glacier Park, Inc. were a super boost for my career. How lucky can one guy be?

[Editors note: Don Hummel's Glacier Park, Inc. owned and operated the former Great Northern Railway hotels in Glacier from 1960 to 1981, when GPI was sold. It is now owned by a division of Viad Corp. of Phoenix, Arizona.]

Glacier Park Hotel staff "mugwumping" at Glacier Park Station, awaiting the arrival of the next Great Northern Railway train.   Courtesy, Ginny Mouw

"Mugwumping" with movie stars
Kay Schwenk Ek
(Glacier Park Hotel 1952-54)

My summers were 1952, '53, and '54 at the entrance hotel (Glacier Park Hotel). We all thought that our hotel was the BEST, since we gave the first impression to those entering the park [from the east]. I remember being surprised when meeting some employees from Many Glacier Hotel that they felt the same way—that we just didn't understand that the best place to work was Many Glacier.

I don't know where the Many Glacier employees danced the night away, but for those of us who worked at East Glacier it was Dusty's, where the cowboys and Native Americans gathered and purchased their beer with silver dollars. The evenings often ended so late that the following day would involve a nap after serving breakfast, and a nap after serving lunch to be prepared for serving dinner—and so it would go day after day, night after night.

In the early 1950s a specific talent was not needed to get a prized job in Glacier Park. It was "who you knew" or who recommended you. I was delighted to get a call to say that there was an opening in the laundry. Work there was not bad. We had time to visit with each other as we dutifully ran the mangle or folded the white linen.

Early in the season, however, I was asked if I would like to be transferred to the dining room. This news was exciting and was the beginning of a great adventure serving guests. We always had to be groomed and dressed in our maroon dresses and our little white starched cotton aprons and hats (pinned to our hair). As I recall, the inspection of our uniforms was quite thorough.

Movie-making was a big adventure for those of us on the entrance staff in those years. We had the pleasure of watching the cast and crews filming a couple of westerns. The most notable star was Ronald Reagan. The film was *Cattle Queen of Montana*, with Barbara Stanwick and Lance Fuller. It was great fun watching the filming on our day off and serving those charming people in the dining room.

I had met Ronald Reagan the year before when we were "mugwumping"—that is, sitting with our mugs (faces) on one side of the wooden fence and our "wumps" on the other side, waiting for the train to come in. It was great fun to meet passengers arriving at the park or just passing through, and that was the case when I met Reagan. I was very impressed with him and the time that he took just to visit.

Another movie, *Dangerous Mission*, featured Victor Mature, Piper Laurie, Vincent Price and Dennis Weaver. We invited them to go to Dusty's with us. Some of the crew did, and Vincent Price came to one of our parties.

I got into trouble when I was invited to play *Scrabble* with Dennis Weaver, Piper Laurie and Victor Mature's double. The problem was that we played (very innocently) in one of their hotel rooms.

The hotel manager was angry when he saw me being escorted through the lobby and back to the dorm by the handsome double. He warned me of the trouble that I could have gotten into with those Hollywood types (and maybe, in particular, with this one).

I've kept in touch with numerous employees from my era. One of my roommates, Rosellen (Finley) Doherty, was the "Indian Girl"—greeting guests in the dining room in full Indian attire. Her father, Charles Finley, was a vice-president of the Great Northern Railway who, when visiting, would arrive in his own private railroad car.

Rosellen once brought a horse into the dorm. "Horse in dorm," she announced (a variation on the more common warning "man in the dorm.").

Another of my roommates, Mary Ronning (nicknamed "Sarge") worked at the entrance hotel for five summers. She was in charge—new employees in the dining room thought she was the boss, as she ordered waitresses and busboys about. She loved giving them a hard time, but later they would learn that her underlying personality was soft and sweet.

We might have forgotten some of the employees whom we worked with, but nobody forgot Sarge. She led us in song with her ukulele, and she was the kingpin for anything fun. She was my roommate and cherished friend until her death in 2008.

Sarge's sister Carol was the nurse at the entrance in 1947. She married the front desk clerk "Dusty" Hanson. Their meeting was an instant attraction, and by Christmas of 1947 they were planning their wedding for May, 1948. They recently celebrated their 60th wedding anniversary by taking their three children and the children's spouses to Glacier.

A couple of the friends whom I keep in touch with recall disasters in the entrance dining room. Mary Shepherd Phillips recalls, "We had to carry those large trays with many dinners and all the little dishes piled up, and it was such a trick to carry them on one's shoulder. Once I took a full tray through the swinging door. It caught the tray closing, and the whole thing went down with a terrible crash. I thought I would be sent home on the next train." Mary says that she never had to work that hard again in her life.

Actor Dennis Weaver poses with sisters Peg, left, and Kay Schwenk.
Courtesy, Kay Schwenk Ek

Michaela Walsh of New York City (who became famous for starting Women's World Banking) treasures the memories of her days at Glacier Park, but recalls another fiasco in the dining room. Once at lunch she spilled boiling soup down the back of the manager's wife. The scalded matron screamed, leaped out of her chair and raced from the dining room. Michaela thinks it must have taken her days to dry out the huge corset she wore.

The cherished memories of those great and wonderful years in Glacier Park will live with me forever. Living in St. Cloud, Minnesota, for a number of years, I shared my love of Glacier with Bishop George Speltz, now deceased. He often went to Glacier during his summer vacations, and always referred to it as "God's Country." I must go there again.

East Glacier in the 1940s
Ginny Leach Mouw
(Glacier Park Hotel 1940-42, 1946-50)

People who worked at Many Glacier Hotel always seemed to feel that it was the best place to be in the park. I concede that you have a wonderful view as you are in the midst of the mountains with a lake close at hand and Grinnell Glacier in sight. The only advantage, as I see it, is that you don't have to spend a lot of time hitchhiking, sometimes not at all or at other times only one way. At the outset, that is where I wanted to be.

June Pearson, the friend who talked me into applying, was a waitress there. It would have been nice to know someone when I arrived. It was pretty much understood that one needed some kind of pull to get a job, and I knew no one. The only thing I could think of was to have my grandfather, who had been a freight claim agent for the Soo Line, write a letter of recommendation.

What can I say? It worked. I arrived for an interview, the letter from my grandfather clutched in my hot little hand. The procedure was that you simply lined up and went to the first hotel manager who was free to talk with you. In my case that was Fred Sayles for the Glacier Park Hotel. I was happy to get a job, happy with the location and I never regretted my initial placement.

One big advantage was the village itself and the residents, many of whom went out of their way to make us feel welcome, and a few of whom joined the employees in a lot of their activities. Jay Staley, an outrageous Texan, and Lyle McMullin from the Glacier Park Transport Company took it upon

One of the benefits of the entrance hotel was its golf course.
Great Northern Railway collection, Minnesota Historical Society

themselves to introduce the newcomers to the local customs and traditions.

The restaurant across the tracks operated by the Lutz family was always open to us. Buzz Lutz and his dad were also Glacier Park employees, and Buzz did most of the baking for years after I was there. It was a fun place to congregate.

Then there was Dusty's, that dingy bar down the road which we were not supposed to frequent. There was a general store operated for many years by Leona and Brownie, who were especially friendly and helpful to the hotel employees.

We had the only hotel golf course and that was another plus. You could always spend a few hours hiking to Dawson Falls or hunting fossils at Two Medicine Falls. It was the only place where I found fossils were plentiful.

The activity that was the most fun was going down to the railroad station to greet the incoming passengers (always referred to as "dudes" in those days). Anyone who wasn't working at 11:30 a.m. was always there when the Great Northern's Empire Builder arrived from the east.

Ginny Mouw

The Blackfeet Indians were there in full regalia, beating their drums and singing. We watched the passengers disembark and then head up the walk to the hotel. The path to the hotel paralleled by a spectacular floral display, tended by Herk, the gardener, and his staff. It was simply breathtaking. These are some of the things that made working at the Glacier Park Hotel such a delight. I never wanted to trade places with anyone. Let's just say that the place where you worked was simply the best place to be. Whether it was Many, Lake McDonald, Glacier Park Hotel or one of the chalets, you were just happy to be in your own little niche.

Gearjammers earned their nickname missing shifts in their Red buses. Here a Model 54 bus is eastbound at "the Loop" on Going-to-the-Sun Road.

T.J. Hileman photo, Great Northern Railway collection, Minnesota Historical Society

Chapter 4

Gearjamming down life's highway

A crank and a prayer
William Hays
(Glacier Park Transport Company 1930s-1940s)

My father, Howard H. Hays Senior, operated the Glacier Park Transport Company from 1927 to 1955. These were significant years. They saw the completion of Going-to-the-Sun Road, the construction of the Prince of Wales Hotel and Chief Mountain International Highway linking Glacier and Waterton parks, and the selection and purchase of the Red buses which are still in service.

When my father made his first visit to Glacier, he saw it as a wonderland with almost unlimited appeal, so he bought into the transport company and became its operator at the beginning of the 1927 season. He immediately recognized that the quality of the bus drivers was critically important to the success of the company and he broadened their role. He and his general manager, Fred Noble, trained them to be well-informed guides in the parks, knowledgeable about geography, history, geology, trails, plant and animal life and hotels. As part of the training program, he produced a *Drivers' Manual*, a truly remarkable volume of information about the park.

Howard Hays

I began working for the company in the summer the Hays family arrived at Glacier—about two hours a day—doing whatever the office employees could dream up for a 10-year-old. In later years, I washed buses, greased cars, ran errands for the mess hall, served as transportation agent at Sun Camp (Going-to-the-Sun Chalets) and drove one of the Cadillac touring cars. And I had two younger brothers who came down pretty much the same trail.

Over the years I very much enjoyed my association with the gearjammers and, indeed, was proud of it. My being one of the bosses' sons didn't seem to turn them off at all. The jammers of that day recognized the importance of their role. They aimed at a high standard of service and they had a wonderful esprit de corps.

Gas monkey
Bill Sterrett
(Glacier Park Transport Company 1928-32)

My first year working for the Glacier Park Transport Company was as a "gas monkey," since I was too young to obtain a Montana chauffeur's license. My main job was pumping the gas that kept the big Red buses running.

Bill Sterrett

I was responsible for transferring gasoline from the bulk storage tank near the railroad siding to the pumps at our garage in East Glacier. We used a special electric pump to accomplish the transfer.

One exciting day I neglected to watch the pump and the garage tank overflowed. An ocean of gasoline filled the entire courtyard where the buses were parked. For a few hours it was strictly no smoking around those parts, and everyone walked gingerly to avoid making sparks that might ignite the petrol.

The Glacier Park Transport Company at Many Glacier
Jack G. Chamberlain
(Glacier Park Transport Company 1952, 1954)

For years the transportation agent at Many Glacier Hotel was the one and only Sid Couch. He got the buses off on time at the hotel and also was the official "dorm boss." If you were a slugabed or a laggard, Sid would admonish you in colorful language (especially if others were within earshot).

The transport company had a large garage, gas pump, employees' dormitory and parking lot at Many Glacier. The wonderful Mr. and Mrs. Porter staffed the dormitory (the present Upper Dorm), which had its own kitchen and cafeteria. They taught school for nine months each year in Idaho and cooked at the gearjammer dorm in the summer. Their sumptuous food, friendliness and knowledge of the flowers and natural history of the park was a real blessing. The dorm was a two-story, totally wooden structure. Each of the upstairs sleeping rooms had a "fire escape"—a knotted, two-inch-thick rope, 20 feet long, tied to a wall stud and coiled under the single window. The front room or lounge was stocked with books and games (used especially on stormy days).

Although Sid Couch taught accounting, he was legally blind (20/200). He always wore thick, "Coke bottle" glasses but never missed a thing. He claimed that he could memorize eye charts at the Department of Motor Vehicles. He would get a student to go with him on the day of his driving test to tell him the letters on the eye chart, which Sid then memorized.

He always had three things at Many Glacier—a valid driver's license, a chauffeur, and a three-piece brown suit. He was a wonderful, proud, humorous man.

In the early 1950s I was a biology student at Occidental College in Los Angeles. I was looking for a mountainous retreat from the heat, the newly growing crowds and the smog. A friend introduced me to Sid Couch and I was hired for the summers of 1952 and 1954. In both summers, I reported to East Glacier, where I was assigned a red and black limousine—a 1931 LaSalle in '52 and a 1930 Lincoln in '54. These vehicle assignments were made by a huge Blackfeet Indian, the longtime chief mechanic for transport company: Gene Kracaleea. He simply gave me a map and told me to go to Many Glacier to be under Sid's tutelage.

My title was "assistant mechanic." My job was to make sure the buses were gassed and lined up in the morning in the parking lot for the gearjammers. I also was to chauffeur Sid and others to and from the hotel some 500 yards away and to drive VIPs to Babb or to the Swiftcurrent Motor Inn. I occasionally had the job of rushing clients who had overslept to board a bus which was already en route.

Sid Couch, center, with Many Glacier bellmen.
Ray Djuff collection

I remember well once tending to a bus that was low on oil and changing the fluid but not the filter. The very next afternoon, Gene Kracaleea drove the 50-odd miles from East Glacier to Many to have words with me.

"Oil and filters are always changed together!"

The drivers feared the guy, but my visits to the Blackfeet Indian reservation town of Browning enlightened me about his life in Montana. I found him eventually likable and understandable by summer's end.

In addition to my other jobs, I volunteered to take the weekly trash from the dorm to the open pit dump, at that time just a mile down the road toward Babb. As a young biologist, I wanted to observe the bears that came to feast on the garbage. I would go alone in the early morning or at dusk so as to study their appearance and movements as closely as possible. I was lucky, I guess, as I had only benign meetings with bears. [The dump has since been closed.]

I played hours and hours of cribbage with the drivers and with Sid.

Sid played only bridge in Los Angeles and only cribbage at Many. Few people could beat him. I did, maybe once or twice during the entire summer, and his face would get red for hours. When he and I teamed up as doubles, forget it.

At night, we often ended up downstairs at the hotel lounge where many gearjammers and myself would dance until closing. Then we'd go off on foot to the Swiftcurrent Lake campground with leftover food from the kitchen. We would build a bonfire and sing and party for hours. Each morning, as Sid made abusive remarks about our haggard appearance, we swore that "tonight we will go to bed early." Of course, we never did.

All in all, it was the best of times. It was rather like a momentary sidestep from the more pressing plans of education, careers, etc. We were up high in the mountains with glorious air and fabulous scenery, with natural endorphins flowing all the time. Lasting friendships were made, great loves sometimes developed, and some ended in marriages. A fabulous time. A fabulous place.

Backing out of an avalanche
Tom I. McFarling
(Glacier Park Transport Company 1950)

The transport company had rules. One was that no new gearjammer could carry passengers over Going-to-the-Sun Road until he had first deadheaded over the Logan Pass. I was at Many Glacier Hotel when I was told to deadhead over to Lake McDonald. It was a beautiful morning, so I put the top down on my bus, No. 95, before I left.

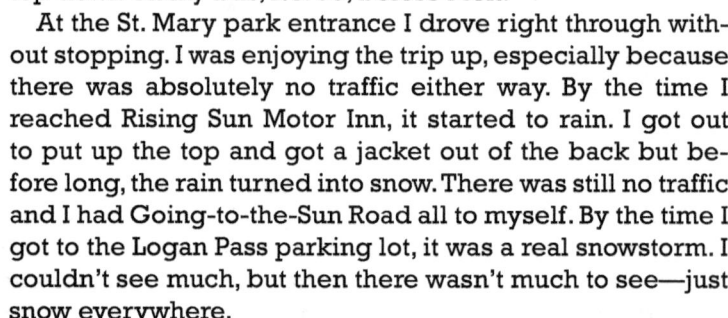

Tom McFarling

At the St. Mary park entrance I drove right through without stopping. I was enjoying the trip up, especially because there was absolutely no traffic either way. By the time I reached Rising Sun Motor Inn, it started to rain. I got out to put up the top and got a jacket out of the back but before long, the rain turned into snow. There was still no traffic and I had Going-to-the-Sun Road all to myself. By the time I got to the Logan Pass parking lot, it was a real snowstorm. I couldn't see much, but then there wasn't much to see—just snow everywhere.

According to GPT Co. rules, I was letting No. 95 have its cool-down idle run when the ranger came out of his building to inquire what the hell I thought I was doing. I replied I was deadheading over to Lake McDonald Hotel.

He said the road had been closed since daylight and he was getting ready to go down himself; but now he was going to try to reach the entrance by radio to make sure they let no one else come up. It seems that

Snow remains at Logan Pass, elevation 6,646 feet, well into the summer, with scenes such as this typical of late June. Bob Anderson photo, courtesy Lola Anderson

late snows had been extra heavy and there was still a very deep snow pack. It had been snowing all night and morning. With fresh snow on top of the old, there was an extreme danger of new snow sliding and even of an avalanche.

When he came back, he said the entrance gate had reported that it had not let anyone through all morning. I guess they had not even seen me come through.

He suggested I turn around and he would follow me back down to St. Mary. I thought about that, but decided that I had set out to deadhead over to Lake McDonald and that's just exactly what I was going to do. With that, I got into No. 95 and headed west out of the parking lot.

Clouds and fog were so thick I could hardly see anything at all. After a short distance the clouds and fog seemed to thin a bit and I could almost see into the valley. It was quite a sight so I stopped to take a picture and rolled the window back up. Then I heard it.

It sounded like a freight train right in the front seat beside me. I feared what it was, held my foot on the brake and waited. All of a sudden, there was the flying, tumbling, sliding snow mass right in front of me. I honestly thought the force of the slide would cover me or push me and the bus over the side. I do not know how long it took, but finally the snow stopped sliding down and across. Then silence—nothing but the rumble and echo from below.

The snow covered the road ahead and was over the front bumper, the radiator and the hood back to just where No. 95's windshield was. I didn't know what to do but I knew I did not want to stay where I was. There was only one way I could go and I was not about to abandon No. 95.

I slipped into reverse, said a prayer that by moving back I would not dislodge or disturb the snow again, and eased back about five feet. I was afraid to back any further without knowing exactly where the back wheels were so I opened my door and looked back and down to the side of the road. The haze and returning fog and clouds were so dense I couldn't even see the back of the bus. All I could do was to look straight down to the side of the road at those two layers of rock stacked there as a guard rail.

I thought I could judge where I was on the road by whether those rocks moved away from me or closer to me as I backed. I tried it and, soon found that by backing eight to 10 feet at a time I could judge pretty well if the rear wheels were in about the middle of the road.

Strangely, I did not really have any fear for myself. My whole thought was "How can I keep No. 95 safe from being knocked over the side by a new slide." Only by trial and error, luck and Divine guidance did I manage to get No. 95 up that west side of Going-to-the-Sun Road in reverse.

I don't know how many hairpin turns to the right or to the left there were or how much time it took. Even though the snow on the hood and windshield was not melting [the bus had no heater], I was ringing wet with sweat and totally out of breath when I heard the horn of the ranger's truck behind me.

He walked up and asked if I knew there had been this big snow slide. I told him I knew as I had been in it. He didn't believe me and walked down the road to see where it was and what damage, if any, it had done to the road. He was gone a pretty good while.

When he came back he said he could see where the front of the bus had left its mark in the side of the snow bank and asked how I got from down there to where I was. I told him I had backed up the road. He said he would never have believed it if he had not seen where I had been.

He wanted to go back to report what had happened and said there was a snowplow on the way up to open the road. He suggested I should leave No. 95 there and go back with him, but said I would stay with No 95. He left muttering to himself.

I wrapped one of the blankets around my shoulders as I was getting pretty cold. Soon I heard a sound from down the road. I figured it was the snowplow working from the other side. I waited a bit and started down again. You can't guess how slowly I went and how I listened for another avalanche.

When I could see the deep snow on the road I waited for the plow to break through. The driver made several passes through the snow bank, wide enough for me to get No. 95 through. In a few minutes I was on my way down again. After all, the transport company had its rules.

When I got down to flat ground, I started to breathe a bit easier. When I pulled into Lake McDonald Hotel it was late in the afternoon. I never told a soul how far I backed No. 95 up that road. Only that ranger, whoever he was, and I know for sure. I don't know if he ever told anyone. I hope not as I always wanted to keep that as our secret—just between me and No. 95.

Deadhead races
Dr. James W. Monson
(Glacier Park Transport Company 1952-53)

Gearjamming was the only job I've ever had where it was more fun to work than to have a day off.

I was in dental school at the University of Minnesota and belonged to a professional dental fraternity where several of my friends, who had driven buses in previous years, wouldn't stop talking about it. When Fred Noble, the transport company manager, came to St. Paul, Minnesota, on his annual hiring trip, they introduced me to him and I was hired.

James Monson is reunited, during a stop in the St. Mary Valley, with the bus he used to drive along the same roads. Courtesy, James Monson

When we arrived at the park, we were assigned buses (mine that first year was No. 88) and we started washing and waxing them. It took a couple of days to do that. It's amazing how much surface there is to polish on a bus. We also had to take our Montana driver's tests.

The buses had four forward speeds and reverse. Like all trucks and buses of that time, they had to be double-clutched while shifting. What that meant was that to go from one gear to another you had to first depress the clutch, shift into neutral, momentarily let the clutch out, and then depress it again to shift into the next gear. Shifting up was easy enough, but downshifting required that the engine be gunned while in neutral to match engine speed to the rolling speed of the bus. It was not easy at first, but came with practice. The bus engine had a governor that limited the speed in fourth gear to about 45 m.p.h. and in third to about 20 m.p.h. Brakes were mechanical, which were almost useless for stopping a loaded bus or one going downhill. We were very careful to control our speed going downhill by using the engine as a brake. We downshifted from fourth to third gear for all descents. The speed would hold at about 22 m.p.h. no matter how steep the hill. The tops of the buses were open, so people could stand up if they chose. For bad weather there was a canvas top which was stored in a well at the rear of the bus. We called the buses our "big red convertibles."

The drivers came from all over the country. There was a group from Minnesota, a group from Williams College in New York, some from Salt Lake City and some from California. Drivers didn't wear uniforms during my time as a gearjammer. We were required to wear a white shirt and tie and decent slacks. If it was cold we could wear any outer clothing we chose. Also optional were aviator-style sunglasses and leather driving gloves that completed the image of the dashing bus driver.

Fred Noble

The Glacier Park Transport Company was separate from the Glacier Park Company, which ran the hotels. Howard Hays was the owner of the transport company and Fred Noble was the manager. Each hotel had a resident transport agent who was our boss while we were at that hotel. At East Glacier and Many Glacier we had dormitories with a cook and mess hall. At Lake McDonald we slept in a tent and ate in the hotel employees' mess. At the Prince of Wales Hotel in Waterton Lakes National Park we had a water-front cabin and were allowed to charge our meals at a local cafe.

We lived a very nomadic life. At our transport company compound at East Glacier, we had a room where we could leave things, but most of our time was spent on the road. There was a locker in the back of the bus where we kept our clothes and our sheet blankets. When we arrived at any of the other destinations, there were cots available but there was no bedding. We used our sheet blankets and the lap robes from the bus to make up our beds. Often we would be away from East Glacier for weeks at a time.

The "new" Red buses are lined up outside the Glacier Park Transport Company garage in East Glacier about 1937. Courtesy, Dan Hays

Our schedules were determined by the lineup. The rule was first in, first out. Since there might be more buses at a place than were needed that day, the ones that were there the longest went to the head of the line. The first buses out went on the longest and most preferable trips, those over the Going-to-the-Sun Road which were the most fun and the most lucrative tips-wise, so we all wanted those. At East Glacier and Many Glacier, there was a lineup board on which our bus-number tags were hung in order. At the other places the lineup was kept in the agent's head. Sometimes if there were too many buses at one place or if they were needed at another, we had to deadhead to the other place. If we were deadheading from Lake McDonald or West Glacier to East Glacier, we went by way of Highway 2, which formed the southern border of the park. It was not a route that we ever drove with passengers and we usually deadheaded in convoys. We had some great races over that road.

It was absolutely verboten to pick up hitchhikers while deadheading. Of course, the hotel employees were often on the roads with their thumbs out. They were our friends, so how could we pass them up? One day, as I was returning empty to Many Glacier from the Prince of Wales, I picked up a couple of Many Glacier employees. I was very careful. I let them out just short of the U.S.-Canadian border and picked them up again on the other side so I wouldn't be reported. Unfortunately, I was on the road between Babb and Many Glacier when along came Sid Couch, the Many Glacier transportation agent, in his car (with one of the drivers driving). Sid was almost blind, but he always saw what he wasn't supposed to see. He remarked, "Who was that up there with Monson?"

Strangely enough, I never heard a word about it from him.

We were given a lot of training about the history of the park, the scenery, the Indians, the animals and the flora. We kept up a fairly steady commentary as we drove. My first bus didn't have a PA system, so I just shouted. The second one had a microphone that hung around my neck. A lot of what we said wasn't always completely factual, I'm afraid, but we tried to make it entertaining. We stopped often to let people take pictures. Sometimes with a congenial group we could get a songfest going. The group tours were the most fun. When the people had been together for awhile, it was easier to establish rapport with them.

It was the best job I ever had.

FDR wheels up Chief Mountain
Bill (Deacon) Trimble
(Glacier Park Transport Company 1961-66)

In 1961 I spent my first summer in Glacier having learned of the bus driver position from a fraternity brother, Van Price, who trained new drivers. Our transport agents included two who had been there for many years, Ino Belsaas at Lake McDonald and Bob Haase at Many Glacier. The young agents that year were Jimmy Nichols at Glacier Park Lodge and Bob Jacobson at the Prince of Wales.

Bill Trimble

The buses were still in remarkably good shape, thanks to the mechanics Breck Stevenson and Louie Anderson. Breck was known to growl about drivers, such as the one who got a little too close to the wall along Going-to-the-Sun Road and bent the right running board to a 45-degree angle. And Louie would complain when a driver failed to check his gas with the dipstick and ran out miles from the station. Both men lived in East Glacier all year and worked on the buses during the winter.

At the beginning of the season, each driver had to wax his bus, a job that was undertaken with enthusiasm. As summer rolled on, the daily bus washing wasn't always so much fun if the driver was in a hurry to meet a girlfriend. By far the worst job was the end of season steam-cleaning on the rack outside the garage at East Glacier. Some drivers would negotiate with the gas boys to do some of those tasks for them.

I worked as the transport agent at Many Glacier the last few weeks of 1962 and in 1963 was the agent at Glacier Park Lodge. In 1964, I was hired as the transport manager. Being 24 years old and single, I was more than happy to return to Glacier Park with a full-time job.

Hiring the drivers, training and supervising their behavior was a new experience for me. The majority were really good guys who didn't cause any problems. I always worried a little when a few showed up for lineup in the morning with bloodshot eyes and sunglasses. I knew they'd had a rough night.

Some were better than others when it came to giving tours, explaining the history of the park, geology, Indian legends, etc. Among the best were Dino Natta, Neil Scott, Jim Shore, Roger Tointon, and Dick Hicks, to name just a few.

One driver, however, had a little trouble relating the story of Chief Mountain. After telling the story of how Indians climbed the mountain for their vision quests, the driver was to end with the names of others who climbed the mountain in more recent times. Among the most well-known was Henry L. Stimson, who later became President Franklin D. Roosevelt's secretary of war during the Second World War.

President Franklin Roosevelt sees Glacier Park from the back of an open Cadillac during a one-day visit on August 5, 1934.

National Park Service

In this driver's version of the story, Franklin Roosevelt ended up climbing the mountain. When another driver subsequently learned of this, he came into my office laughing and wanted to know how Roosevelt was able to climb the mountain in his wheelchair.

Needless to say, some remedial training was implemented immediately.

The bus I was driving yesterday
Bill Schade
(Glacier Park Transport Company 1961-62; 1999)

My father, Fritz Schade, worked at Glacier Park in the 1920s while he attended college and medical school. He was a bellman at Many Glacier Hotel and he encouraged me to work at Glacier while I was in college. I was a gearjammer the summers of 1961 and 1962.

It's not the splendor of the park I remember most, not the crisp coolness of those early summer mornings in the open bus. It's not those repetitive trips up and down curving roads next to steep drop-offs on Going-to-the-Sun Road, nor all those trips to fetch passengers at the train station at West Glacier. It's not even the sounds of straining engines and grinding gears.

What I remember most is the fun of interacting with my passengers, all different, but all coming to see the wonders of the park and to have a good time. Although Glacier's staff trained gearjammers to deliver appropriate narratives along their routes, I never could resist lacing my daily presentations with jokes.

My gearjamming summers were many years ago, so some of the jokes lodged in my memory aren't quite politically correct these days.

Remember the island in St. Mary Lake along the Going-to-the-Sun Road?

"It's called Paradise Island," I'd confide to my passengers, "because no woman has ever set foot on it." The men would laugh and some of the women would make theatrical groaning sounds, but most of the tourists seemed genuinely amused by the corny joke.

All jammers recall how nervous some passengers became as we wound along narrow roads with steep drop-offs. I figured a little humor would ease the tension and used two jokes to accomplish this.

On the west side of Logan Pass, I would point out an old yellow road maintainer parked in a valley so deep it looked like a yellow speck.

"That's the bus I was driving yesterday," I said, implying that the vehicle had tumbled over the edge.

Further along the route, I'd say "If this makes you nervous, do what I do while I'm driving. Just close your eyes. I do and it helps."

While driving to Many Glacier Hotel, I'd feel compelled to tell passengers that the park staff had been diligently searching for a little Indian boy named "Falling Rock" who'd become lost in the park. Then, just around the next bend shortly before arriving at the hotel, I'd point a yellow warning sign "Watch for Falling Rock."

"See, we're still looking for him."

A jammer's journey
Bill Yearout
(Glacier Park Transport Company 1967, 1969)

I was a junior at West Virginia University and radical change seemed everywhere—except in my corner of the world. Amidst the noise of Vietnam, Lyndon Johnson, Martin Luther King Jr., Bob Dylan and Janice Joplin, I was intent on finding my own message. Postcards of Glacier Park and Red buses captured my imagination and appealed to my appetite for distance, beauty and adventure.

In March 1967 I applied for and was selected to fill one of the coveted gearjammer positions. I had no clue of how my life would be forever changed. As one of several early arrivals at East Glacier, I was instructed to report immediately to the mud lot (later to become the dust lot) to prepare Red buses for a summer of service. These early arrivals forged a special bond with one another and a unique relationship with our boss, O.A. (Pappy) Gamble. He was an imposing figure—a tall, lanky, old cowboy with a decidedly cranky demeanor. To break the drudgery of working in the mud lot, Bill Rixon, Al Giles, Tom Ewald, Bryan Timbers and I hitchhiked to nearby Browning to enjoy our first Montana rodeo—strongly enhanced by rain, more mud, and a number of locals intent upon making Great Falls Select a very popular and profitable beer.

Within a few days, the remaining gearjammers were in camp. Official gearjammer training commenced with driving practice, followed by cramming for the required Montana commercial license, studying/rehearsing the infamous jammer tour spiels, and shadowing the veterans, followed by exams and, for several applicants, dismissals.

We quickly learned the value of providing good tours, getting good tour assignments and providing some extras, such as unauthorized side trips to the Waterton buffalo paddock. We also came to recognize certain tour companies and their escorts as genial guests and good tippers while others were predictably nasty and cheap.

Bill Yearout, left, and Bryan Timbers in 1967.
Courtesy, Bill Yearout

The summer of 1967 was shaping up to be everything a kid could hope for—new friends, fresh ideas, great beauty, plenty of adventure plus an exciting job. I loved the idea of being in an international peace park, and hikes or pub crawls in Waterton provided a great chance for me to get to know something about real, live Canadians.

Glacier Park Lodge was headquarters for Glacier Park Transport Company and Glacier Park, Inc., football games and campfires. Lake McDonald was the most quiet of the four gearjammer overnight spots and home to Ino (you don't love me no more) Belsaas the beloved transportation dispatcher there for many years. In contrast, Many Glacier was a hot spot and well known for its employee entertainment.

When foul weather and cranky passengers were encountered at the same time, gearjammers were fairly certain to have a less-than-perfect day in paradise.

One morning I drove nine travel-weary passengers from Lake McDonald to Many Glacier via the Going-to-the-Sun Road. It was a dreary day for weather. The median age was at least 100 and there must have been six cameras, three hearing aids and 14 bags per passenger.

I was informed that this morning was expected to be the highlight of their entire trip and there would be consequences if the weather didn't clear, if the photo ops were less than postcard perfect, or if the upcoming lunch was nearly as unsatisfactory as breakfast had been.

The visibility continued to decline as No. 109 climbed upward to Logan Pass. Upon reaching the Garden Wall, one or two passengers were showing faint signs of enthusiasm (or nausea—my memory is a little fuzzy on this one), when one of my very powerful contact lens severely scratched my eye, then popped out.

Unable to see much more than the lines on the road, it now seemed like a good time for a real shift from monologue to creative dialogue. With survival instincts (humiliation avoidance) in overdrive, I was soon "creating" slopes loaded with goats (totally out of the question in 1967), mountains and formations where none could be seen, glaciers where none had been for eons.

Upon arrival at Many Glacier, my passengers provided the ultimate reward—an especially rousing ovation which my parents, who had literally just arrived from West Virginia, where there to witness.

Michele Koons **Julie Helgeson**

Later that summer, Michele Koons and Julie Helgeson were fatally mauled by grizzlies on the same night by separate bears in savage attacks that occurred many miles apart. Michele and Julie were well liked by all and jammers dealt with frequent queries by detail-hungry visitors for the remainder of the summer.

One morning, I departed the Prince of Wales Hotel in my bus with a particularly full pouch of what was supposed to be company mail. Upon our arrival at the U.S.-Canada border, U.S. officials inspected the pouch, found an assortment of undeclared women's apparel and seized me, my bus and passengers. Officials from the transport company and hotel company were summoned to the Chief Mountain port of entry to bail me out. In spite of the highly suspicious circumstances, my boss, Mr. Gamble, accepted without hesitation my denial of any knowledge of the pouch's contents. The whole deal was an innocent error, the responsible parties fessed up and I was set free with my bus and passengers.

The perfect adventure ended with much the same sad emptiness as it has for thousands of employees over the years. Each day of my final week, our ranks methodically thinned, often without a chance for goodbyes, until a final few simply disappeared from paradise, some perhaps forever.

A mountain goat licks salt from the leg of Lou Griskey. Courtesy, Lou Griskey

The leakiest Red bus
Lou Griskey
(Glacier Park Transport Company 1977)

Before beginning my senior year at Loyola University of Chicago, I decided to spend the summer of 1977 working in Glacier giving tours and driving a bus for the summer. My season in Glacier turned out to be one of the most memorable and important experiences of my life. In addition to learning about fauna and flora, geology and park history, I experienced great weather, wonderful people and lessons for a lifetime.

Among the many people and experiences of that summer, there is one person who I continue to remember, and who taught me some important things about facing life's ever-changing fortunes and making the most of a less than perfect situation.

Ned DeGarmo was a jovial type, always ready with an understated witty remark or a comedic interpretation of some current event. At the same time, he was a man in transition. He had left a job he didn't care for in Columbus, Ohio, and was springing toward uncertain prospects when his Red bus run finished in September.

I sensed that beyond his good natured and friendly comportment, he was someone who had an awareness of the pitfalls that life can bring even when one had done everything prudent and watchful to avoid them.

Ned, at 33, was older than the rest of the gearjammers. When I met him on my first day at the jammers' lodge, I respectfully referred to him as "Mr. DeGarmo." When he asked me to dispense with the formalities and just call him Ned, I told him that "I wouldn't dream of calling a man of your years by his first name."

The Red buses we were assigned to drive all came with their idiosyncratic problems. My bus (No.88), for example, had a bad clutch which eventually gave out as I was dropping off passengers at the St. Mary Visitor Center. I was lucky that it happened there and not as I was approaching Logan Pass.

Many buses had old canvas tops that leaked, sometimes so badly that passengers opened their umbrellas inside the bus.

No bus was leakier than Ned's. He brought this to the attention of the transportation chiefs from Day 1. All of his complaints were flatly ignored. The leaky top cost him some tips from passengers, I'm sure, but Ned seemed more frustrated by the ineptitude of the company's chieftains than with the loss of beer money. He was determined to get their attention.

One rainy afternoon, a group of four Red buses stood near the horse corral in the Many Glacier parking lot. We were preparing to pull out to pick up passengers at the hotel for a run to Lake McDonald Lodge.

Three drivers were helping Ned bail water from the interior of his bus. It was to no avail. Ned shook his head and, with a whimsical grin, looked over to one of the horses as it was dipping its nose in the watering trough.

Without hesitation, Ned ran over to the trough, picked up a bucket and filled it with water. Then he came over to his bus and poured it over his seat. He went back repeatedly and with the help of the other three drivers, filled the bus with water until he had a trough of his own.

We then raced down to the hotel with Ned in the lead and lined up in front an array of silvery-haired passengers eagerly awaiting their adventurous drive over the Logan Pass.

The Many Glacier dispatcher, Mark Nave, came out in his elegant manner to assist the passengers. He reached out gracefully to open one of the doors of Ned's bus. Water cascaded out, gushed over Mark's penny loafers and splashed onto his khaki trousers. The passengers gasped and howled at the spectacle.

Ned had made his point. It could hardly be ignored.

I often wonder whether Ned found fortune in his quest following that summer in 1977. I'm sure that wherever he went and whatever he did, he made the best of it. And I'm sure that people who came in contact with him were amused and happy for the experience of spending some time with Ned DeGarmo.

The bellmen and the buses
John Hagen
(Many Glacier Hotel 1970-80)

The Red buses were a constant source of interest and fun in my summers as a bellman at Many Glacier Hotel. Their arrival from the other hotels were difficult to predict. The bellmen developed sharp ears for the sound of buses driving up the hotel front. It was a point of honor for us to pop out the door and whisk up the parking cones to greet incoming tours without being prompted by honking horns.

I have droll memories of arrivals in rainy weather in the mid-1970s. At that time, the canvas tops of the buses were very old, and in dire need of replacement. They leaked so badly that passengers sometimes would arrive with umbrellas hoisted inside the bus.

Unlike the haphazard arrivals, departures of the buses were ceremonious and highly choreographed. The red-coated transport agent would oversee a "lineup" of buses—sometimes 10 or 12 of them at a time—pulling onto the portico at fixed intervals to load luggage and board passengers. Then the agent would bid the tourists adieu and send them on their way.

The bellmen often sought to enliven the departures of the tours with little touches of their own. Some liked to step into the role of the transport agent and send buses down the road with fantastic tales about the driver: "Your driver today is a student from Germany. Let's greet him with a

Many Glacier bellmen hustle to unload a Red bus.   Tessie Bundick collection

chorus of *Deutschland, Deutschland uber alles!*"

The buses' running boards lent themselves to a ritual known as the "bellman sendoff." Four to six bellmen would leap on the running boards, grip the roof, and energetically rock the bus from side to side as it was just beginning to roll, while waving and grinning at the passengers. We would leap off again after 20 or 30 feet, as the bus slowly gathered speed on the uphill grade near the Annex.

These sendoffs occasionally were elaborate. Sometimes a bellman would fly dramatically off the running board of a bus and roll down the hill to the Annex, while rescue workers rushed out with a stretcher. At other times, bellmen would sit on a luggage cart impersonating the Three Wise Monkeys as the buses set out.

Another harmless prank was repeated hundreds of times over the years. As a Red bus rolled on or off the portico at about 5 m.p.h., a bellman would slap a rear fender and then hop around on the tarmac holding his foot as if the bus had just run over it. Sometimes, the tourists would hear a "whump, whump, whump" and see multiple bellmen hopping and hobbling around behind a departing bus which had seemingly mangled them all.

Tour escort Carl Bentley is abducted from a Red bus by "cowboys and Indians" in 1976.
John Hagen photo

The single most memorable prank that I can remember involving the buses occurred in 1976. That summer, one of our former room clerks, Carl Bentley, had gone to work for a tour company as an escort. One day, when Carl and his group arrived at Many aboard the Red buses, they received a wild western greeting.

The buses with Carl's group made the usual stop on the frontage road to await removal of the parking cones. Just then, a party of wranglers dramatically came riding over the hill. At the same time, several Boston Tea Party-type Indians rushed upon the scene, dressed in colorful Hudson's Bay blankets and Taiwanese headdresses from the gift shop.

One of these warriors was Chip Smith, a 290-pound football player from the University of Nebraska. Chip ripped open the door of the lead bus, snatched Carl out like a sack of potatoes and tossed him onto the back of a horse. Then the whole party of cowboys and Indians rode madly over the hill again, leaving the drivers and tourists agog.

Cleaned and polished Red buses are lined up in the morning outside the garage at Many Glacier Hotel for the day's assignments, circa 1940.

Herman Rusch photo, Ray Djuff collection

Gearjammers make an inconspicuous exit
Bill Lloyd
(Glacier Park Transport Company 1959)

We had a layover at Many Glacier after depositing our tour groups at the hotel. Four of us gearjammers sat on the front porch. Two of the guys were law students at Columbia University, another was in medical school at Rice, and I was an army veteran and a history student at Penn State University. We were free for the rest of the day. No trips until tomorrow. What to do? We'd taken most of the half-day hikes around Many.

Four off-duty waitresses joined us. They shared our dilemma—how not to waste this day off. I know it wasn't my idea, but someone suggested a bridge tournament. Bridge was not my strong suit, but you had to love the company.

One of the gals suggested the hotel lobby. That was immediately vetoed by the jammers. Too many tourists hanging around asking unending questions. The men's dorm probably was not a good idea.

Angie (I do remember one name) piped up, "Why not the girls' dorm? The matron is away this afternoon."

The jammers decided that the girls' dorm had a lot of promise, with adult supervision away. One volunteered to bring refreshments. The gals did a reconnaissance and gave us the all-clear.

We convened on the second floor, moved beds against the walls and set up two makeshift tables. Jake (I remember another name), our refreshment guy, showed up with an ice bucket, eight glasses and a fifth of Jack Daniel's. One of the gals filled some jars with water.

We were all set.

But you probably know how this will end.

The party progressed quite well. Eight people can do a lot of damage to a fifth of bourbon. The gals seemed more interested in bridge than us.

Then Angie happened to look out the window.

"Holy mackerel," she exclaimed. "It's the matron and the hotel manager."

Ever the calm, cool dude (I was a veteran, right?), I checked the view. Yes, it was who she said. The matron and the manager were slowly walking up the path to the dorm. Both had zero-tolerance for escapades like this. We didn't have much time and our exit was blocked. One of the gals opened a window and pointed to the downspout.

"We've used this in times of trouble," she said.

Sliding down the spout was a bit scary, but our motivation was high. The raw fear of being fired in the middle of the season provided us with a lot of adrenalin. Luckily, we all got out in time and scampered down the path into a thick grove of pines.

"I left the rest of that bourbon," said Jake. "I hope the gals hide it in time."

We found out later that it was discovered and disposed of after a fairly stern lecture on the values of temperance and, in the park, of abstinence.

One-passenger Wilson
Don Perry
(Glacier Park Transport Company 1954-59)

Early that summer of 1954, they were filming a movie, *Cattle Queen of Montana*, starring Barbara Stanwyck and Ronald Reagan in Glacier. The cast and crew (and equipment) were based at the newly opened St. Mary Lodge.

One of the new drivers took a run from East Glacier to Many Glacier Hotel carrying a single passenger, a little old lady. I believe the driver's last name was Wilson. He was a pre-med student at Case Western Reserve in Cleveland. He was a very nice person, but didn't always seem to concentrate well on the task at hand.

Sid Couch (my high school teacher who got me my job) was the transportation agent at Many. Wilson was more than one hour late arriving there with the little old lady. Sid called Fred Noble, the general manager of Glacier Park Transport Company, who said he was about to send our chief mechanic, Gene, to look for the missing bus. Then Sid called again and told him that Wilson had finally arrived with his very hungry passenger.

The next day we got the whole story. Our normal rest stop on the east side run was at the Blackfeet Indian Craft Shop at St. Mary junction.

When Wilson approached the junction, he noticed a lot of activity in front of the lodge. The cast and crew were loading to go out for a day of shooting film. They appeared to be a little behind schedule. Wilson thought that his single passenger would enjoy stopping for a while to watch the commotion, so he parked right beside the front porch of the lodge.

Nothing was moving. Then Barbara Stanwyck walked out onto the porch and in a very loud voice that could probably be heard throughout the entire junction yelled, "Let's get this *@#&% show on the road!"

Everyone started jumping. Wilson thought the little old lady might faint. In those days language like that was not all that common in public. It was such an interesting stop that Wilson lost track of time.

Brian Kuhn worked as a seasonal ranger in Glacier Park in 1986 and 1987 as part of the park's bear management team. Courtesy, Brian Kuhn

Chapter 5

Bear country

A mummy on St. Mary Ridge
John Hagen
(Many Glacier Hotel 1970-80)

One summer evening, Bob Horodyski arrived at Glacier too late to find an open campsite in the park. He therefore pitched his tent at a private campground on St. Mary Ridge. In another tent there slept a nervous man who was new to Glacier, but well aware of the presence of bears. In the dead of a moonless night, this man felt a call of nature and stumbled off to the outdoor privy.

While in the outhouse, the man heard the sound of heavy footfalls. With a pounding heart, he looked out through the cracks in the door and saw a large, black shape stomping past a couple of yards away.

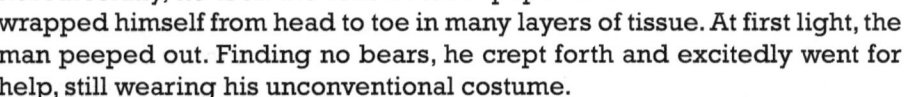

The man was afraid to come out and remained in the outhouse until dawn. Dressed only in underwear, he soon began to shiver with the cold. Resourcefully, he took the rolls of toilet paper and wrapped himself from head to toe in many layers of tissue. At first light, the man peeped out. Finding no bears, he crept forth and excitedly went for help, still wearing his unconventional costume.

Seconds later, Bob Horodyski awoke to the sound of gruesome yelling at the doorway of my tent. Looking out, he recoiled at the sight of what appeared to be an Egyptian mummy, thickly wrapped in pallid bandages, hulking over him in the dawn.

"There's a bear out here!" the mummy was shouting.

Fully awake, Bob scrambled out of the tent and followed the apparition.

"Where did you see the bear?" he asked.

"Right in front of the outhouse," said the mummy. "A grizzly bear as big as a truck."

Bob examined the soft earth in front of the outhouse and discovered a set of hoof prints. The "bear" was a Shetland pony belonging to the campground owners and now stood innocently grazing in the shadows.

Battle on a mountaintop
Don Loeffler
(Glacier Park Hotel, Many Glacier Hotel, Sun Camp, 1940-42, 46-48)

One summer I was substituting for a fire lookout on the top of Apgar Mountain. He had to return to his home town of Seattle to register for the draft prior to the Second World War. Before leaving, he showed me the routine—including how to deal with a pesky bear that came around once in awhile.

This particular bear was attracted to the foodstuffs that were hanging suspended from the lower level of the lookout tower. Sure enough, the first night I was by myself and Mr. Bear came a-calling.

As instructed, I grabbed the cast iron frying pan and quietly crawled out on the catwalk. When Bruno stood up and began clawing at the door to the provisions, I whacked him on the noggin with a mighty blow that they probably could have heard clear down at the ranger headquarters.

He let out a loud bellow and took off on a run down into the woods. I never saw that bear again.

A grizzly endeavor: Relocating bears in Glacier Park
Brian Kuhn
(Glacier Park seasonal employee 1986-87)

In the summer of 1987, I was a member of Glacier Park's bear management team whose job it was to keep grizzly-human confrontations to a minimum. This was done by patrolling the trails and monitoring activity in the backcountry.

Occasionally we had to relocate a problem bear. One relocation involved taking a trapped cub and its loyal mother to a remote backcountry area in the Pinchot Creek drainage. It started out simple enough. Brian Jenner and I were to pull a tooth from the 250-pound mother grizzly's mouth. This is routinely done so that the age of trapped bears can be determined.

We had used a drug called M99 to immobilize both of them. This drug relaxes the bear to the point where it is awake and can see, but cannot move. Therefore, the first thing I did was to remove my name tag, just in case I ran into this bear again under different circumstances.

I had a very uneasy feeling while working with both hands in that grizzly's mouth. The drug decreased her respiration so when she did take a breath, it was long and deep. The feel of that hot, bad breath on my hands and face was really uncomfortable.

After completing this routine workup on the bears, we prepared to relocate them. Our first task was to have two rangers flown to the release site, as the helicopter didn't have enough power to fly both bears and rangers at the same time. Next, according to the plan, the bears, dangling in nets beneath the helicopter, were flown in while we waited. This is where the plan and reality took quite divergent paths.

Ranger Jenner and I were to be dropped off at the head of the Pinchot Creek drainage in a heavy rain, low clouds and a temperature of about 34 degrees. Jenner and I sat in a cluster of subalpine firs, trying to get shelter from the elements and watched Murphy's Law come true as the clouds descended. We waited for what seemed like hours, though in reality it was probably 30 minutes.

The pilot finally called to let us know that he was on his way with the bears, asking for the conditions in the valley. We told him things didn't look good with clouds on the ground and visibility at 10 feet or less. When he reached the Pinchot Creek drainage, he tried to head up in our direction. Then he informed us that he had come as far up the drainage as the clouds permitted. He set the bears down on a landing spot only about 100 yards away. We were to bushwhack down the drainage until we met the helicopter and the bears, administer the antidote drug and get out of there.

The bears had already been drugged for close to a couple of hours, a long time for a bear to stay immobilized under the influence of this drug. The problem was that the effective time for this drug varies somewhat from bear to bear. It was possible that the bears could begin to awaken at any time. We needed to get to them to give them the antidote and release them from the net as quickly as possible. We did not want them to awaken on their own all tangled in the nets.

The terrain was rugged and thick with brush. I couldn't count the number of headers and complete somersaults we executed coming down those slopes. After 15 minutes of such travel, we still couldn't even hear the helicopter below us.

Brian Kuhn

A few thoughts began to race through my mind as we continued racing down the drainage at full speed. Wasn't this drainage chosen because it was very good grizzly habitat? Hadn't we earlier released two grizzlies here? Were they still enjoying this prime habitat? With the dense fog, had the pilot gotten confused and flown up the wrong drainage? What if these bears woke up before we got to them and somehow got out of the nets? Their mood would not be pleasant.

We kept heading down the valley with no sign of the helicopter just as our supervisor decided that the pilot should fly back to West Glacier to pick up two more rangers who could bring the bears back up. My first thought was: Is this guy crazy? We can't see 10 feet in front of us, we are running at full speed in the direction of two grizzlies and he wants to wake them up, perhaps before we can get to their location. I much preferred the thought of running full speed toward sleeping bears than wide awake, grumpy bears.

Just as the helicopter was lifting off to get more rangers, we broke through the bottom of the clouds and spotted him. I almost screamed into the radio, "Don't leave us!"

We told the pilot that we had him in sight and would reach him in 20 minutes as we continued descending and falling. When we finally reached the helicopter the pilot pointed out the bears for us and we headed cautiously in their direction, making lots of noise and then throwing small rocks at them to see if they were awake.

We made our final approach with a shotgun trained on the head of the sow just in case she woke up suddenly and wanted a piece of us. Thankfully, they were still under the drug. After rolling both bears out of the nets, we injected the antidote. Within moments both bears were up and moving. They soon moved off into the brush and we moved back to the helicopter and returned to West Glacier. What a day.

The late-night walk
Liz Gehring Coddington
(Many Glacier Hotel 1956-59)

In 1957, the garbage dump at Many was moved way up north. The grizzlies got so hungry they came down to the hotel to feed by the kitchen garbage cans.

Liz Gehring Coddington

One night I worked as a cashier in the lobby until 11 p.m. My three roommates called me on the phone and asked me to stop at The Grill and bring them ice cream cones. I ordered four cones (one for me) and headed up the darkened driveway to the dorm.

As I came past the kitchen, I noticed people just standing in the road, and I soon found out why—two grizzlies were at the kitchen garbage cans and two more were coming down the hill to join them. Every time someone moved, the bears growled and advanced on them.

We stood there for about a half hour, literally inching our way past the bears. I had ice cream melting down my arms. By the time I got to the dorm there was no ice cream left in the cones, but I was covered.

Another night the same summer, the Many Glacier and Swiftcurrent employees had a bonfire party down at Swiftcurrent. On the way home, my date and I were walking down the long dark road past the rangers' house when we heard a deafening roar.

Looking to see what could be making such a horrendous noise, we saw about 10 grizzly bears fighting over the food in the rangers' garbage cans. My date got so scared he ran all the way back to Many, leaving me the dust.

Think twice before kicking
Don Loeffler
(Glacier Park Hotel, Many Glacier Hotel, Sun Camp, 1940-42, 46-48)

The Glacier Park Hotel Company hired a Marine Corps veteran in 1946 for the position of night watchman and fire guard at Many Glacier Hotel. His sole job was to circle the hotel and dorm looking for fire. I think this was a condition imposed by the hotel's insurance company.

Once in a while he would (probably under the slight influence of John Barleycorn) borrow one of the many bear skins which graced the hotel lobby railings, get down on all fours, and proceed on his rounds. He was never really aggressive in his posture when wearing the bear skins.

About half of the tourists he came across were scared, while the other half were very excited about seeing a real live bear up close.

Omar Ellis, the hotel manager, was well aware of this charade and told my Marine friend that it was "OK," as long as he knew that he stood a good chance of being shot by an overly eager park ranger.

One night, down in The Grill, the bartender was bragging to me that he had just kicked the bear-costumed night watchman in the butt while out on the boat dock.

I thought that was rather strange.

I pointed out my Marine friend, who was standing over by the bandstand talking to a couple of waitresses.

The bartender turned ashen and had no trouble shaking cocktails for the rest of the evening.

Campsite 91 and the dazzled macaroni bear
Rolf Larson (with help from Sylvia Geshell)
(Many Glacier Hotel 1975, 1977-80)

It was one of those calm, still summer evenings in Glacier Park's Swiftcurrent Valley. A bright yellow glow exploded above the dark slopes of Mount Wilbur. The vivid color of the sky intensified the deep silence of a day's end in Swiftcurrent valley. It was as if time was standing still—or perhaps just a momentary aura of calm before a storm.

Friends were gathering at the Swiftcurrent campground after their day's activities. One had climbed a nearby peak. A couple of others had spent the day fishing. One had searched for an elusive wildflower with camera in pack.

Bill (we will call him), had just returned to Campsite No. 91 with supplies from Kalispell; enough staples for a week. Bill decided to try baking brownies. With enthusiastic help from friends, in no time, eager hands dug greedily into a delicious tin of steaming treats.

Having soon gorged themselves, the celebration continued with a newly acquired case of Canadian lager. Just about that time Larry Burton and Sylvia Geshell arrived, ready to cook a few hamburgers before everyone headed to Many Glacier Hotel for an evening of summer fun. When dinner was done, Larry suggested Bill place his new box of food and the brownies inside his van while they all went to the hotel. Bill insisted they were just fine on the camp table. He carefully covered his brownies with foil.

"You're making a mistake," Larry warned. But Bill assured him there were no critters within a hundred miles and headed off unconcerned.

Several beers, many dances, bad jokes and hours later, Bill made it back to his campsite. Seeing his supplies untouched, he continued partying at an adjoining campsite. Eventually, he crashed for the night.

Though the night's celebration was over for Bill, another equally enthusiastic celebration began a couple hours later, when a local of the bear community discovered the banquet Bill had left on the camp table.

Not long after sunrise, most everyone in the campground was awake and watching the spectacle of a black bear squealing with delight as he tossed bags of macaroni into the air, biting cans of food open and spreading flour everywhere. That is, everyone but Bill and his fellow campers at Campsite No. 91 who were sound asleep.

Trying to control the crowd as well as tranquilize, or at least scare off the bear, a couple of rangers were rather busy for a while. Able to control the onlookers long enough to get a clear, safe shot at the bear with a tranquilizer gun, they rudely interrupted the bear's merriment. The bear, however, did manage to escape.

Once again, Bill found himself on the road to Kalispell for supplies. This time he bought enough ingredients for two giant batches of brownies.

"He'll never come back here," Bill said of the bear, "I'm sure the memory of that tranquilizer taught him a lesson he won't soon forget."

"Answer me this," Larry said, "if you went somewhere and got a free meal, wouldn't you be likely to return later to see if you could get another handout?"

"Naw, he won't be back. The dart made sure of that," Bill answered confidently.

"I wouldn't be so sure," Larry cautioned.

Bill was right. The bear did remember that shot. But he was also wrong. That night the bear dragged the box of supplies into the brush before feasting. He was especially fond of the brownies.

Now came the ranger's ultimatum: "Either you properly store your food, or...." The list was long. Bill swore up and down that he would be careful. The rangers then parked a bear trap a little beyond Campsite No. 91.

Bill again went to Kalispell for supplies. Upon his return, he fixed a simple dinner—with brownies. The presence of the nearby trap, baited with salmon, made Bill feel much more secure. Finding himself once again invited out for the evening, Bill resolved to return early to clean up and properly store his supplies.

After several hours, Bill returned to the campsite tired and extremely relaxed. He felt a warm reassurance, looking over at the dark, smooth silhouette of the bear trap. He also vaguely remembered something about having to do something with his food, to hide it or something; that was it, hide it. He couldn't see any good spots to hide it, and he didn't particularly want to grope around in the dark, so he grabbed a large box he had been using to store wood, setting it over his smaller food box on the camp table. He felt rather clever.

"That should outsmart him. That doesn't look like food to me."

With one last look at the bear trap, Bill crawled into his tent.

What Bill didn't realize was his corner of Campsite No. 91 was becoming the nightly social event for that bear. On arrival the bear immediately discovered the treat left out for him. This feast definitely merited a return gesture on his part, a token of his esteem. What more could that bear have done than to just go over, friendly like, and sit himself down with the box of treats. Leaning against the tent opening, he lifted the large box lid to discover eggs, bread, sugar and many other delights inside. That bear must have felt much gratitude for such a gesture on Bill's part because he cozied himself right up to the tent opening.

Bill never did quite figure out what it was that got to him first about that bear, whether it was the movement, the noise from his breathing, the crunching of eggs or if it was the stifling odor. Maybe all of them combined. What Bill did know for certain, though, was that when he awoke, what he found was his new bear friend right at the entrance of his tent.

For the next four hours Bill looked on as the bear alternated between sending a look of affection his way and meticulously picking his way through the goods, occasionally popping the top off a can to enjoy its contents.

The rising sun seemed to break the bear's concentration. He soon grunted a breathy farewell and sauntered off. Though utterly exhausted (and perhaps still a bit hung over), Bill could neither sleep nor enjoy the morning's beauty. His nerves would have no part of trusting his eyes to shut. When discovered by friends, dark bags were firmly set beneath haunted eyes—along with the remains of the feast strewn all over the campsite.

"What happened to you? Are you sick?" Larry asked.

"It was that darn trap," Bill mumbled.

"Trap? What trap? What are you talking about?" a friend coaxed. "What happened to your box of food? Why is it in front of your tent?"

Bill paused, trying to collect his thoughts.

"The trap," he continued, "it didn't work."

The rangers were baffled by how the bear had made it through the campsite without being lured into the salmon-baited trap.

"I have a theory," Larry offered, "Would you like hear it?"

There was something in the tone that bothered the rangers, but what else could they do? They resolved to listen with careful consideration to an ex-park ranger.

"If you really want to catch the bear," Larry responded, "It might be wise to open the trap door so the bear can get into it."

This was followed by an explosion of laughter from Larry as he wandered away. That laughter that trailed away with him would have made a horse proud.

The rangers popped a look of surprise like children experiencing a jack-in-the-box for the first time.

The day the meat came in
Bill Wanser
(Crossley Lake Camp 1924-38)

We had plenty of smoked ham and bacon in the early days at Crossley Lake, but lettuce and fresh meat were such a joy to have—for a brief time every four weeks or so.

There was no refrigeration in camp. Once a month a 10-horse pack string would come in with perishables from the Park Saddle Horse Company staging area at Many Glacier. Then the guests and the camp help greedily indulged in rare roast beef and fresh salads.

It was late August one season during the 1930s. Our tent camp was about to close for the season. On this particular day we expected a large crowd of horseback dudes—maybe 30 or 40—plus the pack string with raw meat and lettuce. My mother, who managed the camp, prepared us for a busy working day. Her admonition to me (at age 11) was that I was to work at the woodpile, carry baggage, and shine shoes. I was not to hang around with Diamond Dick—my most admired, tall-in-the-saddle cowboy guide.

Sure enough, about four in the afternoon, we heard a "Hoorah" and Diamond Dick hove to with a party of schoolmarms from Many Glacier. Close behind came the pack train, bearing fresh meat and other good stuff.

This welcome sight produced The Bear Problem. It seemed that whenever fresh meat was in camp, the bear could smell it from miles away. Then the bear would come at night for a try at the standing rib roast in the cooler shed built above the creek. The bear would come by means of a well-worn path through the willows. We knew this bear because she sported a white triangular patch of fur on her chest. We called her Josephine.

Diamond Dick showed up with a whispered proposal that I fetch some flypaper from the commissary. He suggested we might provide Josephine with a bit of excitement.

In those days, our fly prevention program at Crossley Lake consisted of

Not all bears look alike. Distinctive markings such as a white chest triangle can set individuals apart.
Chris Morrison photo

sticky adhesive on sheets of paper some 12 by 12 inches square. We also had little ribbons of flypaper to hang from the poles of the tents. I fetched both sheets and ribbons. Then, in the dusk, without anybody knowing, Diamond Dick and I spread the sheets along the path. We also dangled an occasional ribbon off the overhead limbs.

That night, we waited out behind the woodpile with great excitement for Josephine. Sure enough, she came bouncing down the trail and we heard her snuffling around the cooler. Diamond Dick and I figured, "A-ha! Josephine has a new set of shoes."

The next morning, we eagerly peered up the trail to see how many pieces of paper were gone. Every single sheet was still in place. Josephine had outsmarted us. She had neatly straddled the path all the way through the willows.

The moral of this story is that prudence dictates that one should never try to stick a bear with something designed for a fly.

Millie and Ema (Ma) Perkins were the hostesses extraordinaire at Granite Park Chalets from the mid-1930s to 1948. Courtesy Millie Perkins, Ray Djuff collection

Chapter 6

Chalets, tent camps and motor inns

The Bakers invade Crossley Camp
Bill Wanser
(Crossley Lake Camp 1924-38)

Once upon a time in the early 1930s, an incident came to pass that stamped an indelible impression upon my young mind. By pure happenstance, an end-of-the-season, just-before-the-snowballs-flew, late-arriving horseback party came in from Many Glacier. They were scheduled for an overnight stay at our tent camp at Crossley Lake on the North Circle Tour.

We understood by the grapevine that the very, very rich, influential, well-to-do Baker party was due in. Further, we were instructed to give our very best and that some spit and polish would go a long way in not only the tip department, but also as a word-of-mouth for advertising the Park Saddle Horse Company.

But as September got closer and the snow line crept along the top of the peaks, no Baker party came, so we started the arduous, week-long process of folding up camp.

My mother, Berith Wanser, two waitresses, a cook, and I (bellhop) had to dismantle 18 tent cabins. Each tent had a double bed, a 3/4 bed, a small stove, wash basin, a portable potty, towels and bedding—all of which had to be carried to a permanent, rat screen-lined "commissary" building for permanent storage during the winter. Plus the dismantling of the main dining and kitchen tents, the laundry and the teepee.

Wood chopping (my job) seemed like an endless chore, but the wood pile had to be sufficient for the following summer to re-establish the camp.

So with this seemingly feverish folding up camp activity, we hardly expected any more dudes from Many Glacier. Then late one afternoon, during the final days before saddling up and heading for civilization a loud "hoorah" echoed up the trail, and into camp rides the very, very rich, influential Baker family.

What to do. My mother, I recall, was about in tears. She explained that the

Crossley Lake tent camp was one of the stops on the North Circle Tour, which stretched between Many Glacier Hotel and Upper Waterton Lake.

T.J. Hileman photo, Great Northern Railway collection, Minnesota Historical Society

newly arrived guests would simply have to catch as catch can, eat with the help and overnight by doubling up with the cramped quarters available.

Then what started as an overnight stay developed into four or five nights, with the Baker family pitching in and chopping wood (hooray), carrying mattresses, washing dishes and helping with the task of dismantling camp—and thoroughly enjoying every minute.

When they left, all of us stood by to wave them off down the dusty trail. Mr. Baker leaned down from his horse with a sizable tip in his hand. We refused to accept. (He later mailed it.)

The story doesn't end on the shores of Crossley Lake, but a week or so later, at a farewell party at the entrance (East Glacier) with very important dignitaries present to give the Baker party a proper sendoff. The Secretary of the Interior, head of the park service, the Glacier Park superintendent and our boss, George Noffsinger, were in attendance as the question was asked, "Mr. Baker, of the parks in the western United States, which did you enjoy the most?"

He replied, I'm told, that the best time they ever had was at Mrs. Berith Wanser's Crossley Lake tent camp.

Swiftcurrent porter-bellman
Mac Willemssen
(Swiftcurrent Motor Inn, 1967; Many Glacier Hotel 1968-70)

In the summer of 1967, I worked as a porter-bellman (PB) at Swiftcurrent. As was the case with my fellow PBs, I was enticed by the description that we would be doing "men's work" relative to the upkeep of the cabins and motels and also have a chance to earn tips as bellmen. Once we got to Swiftcurrent, we found that reality did not reflect the advertising.

The reality of our job was that "equal opportunity" had arrived early in Glacier and we were essentially maids-in-blue jeans for the summer, making beds, hunting for dust kittens and generally doing what, until then, most of us considered "women's work."

The illusion of earning tips as bellmen also quickly vanished. We found most of the guests at Swiftcurrent had little inclination to tip a summer employee to show them where their cabin or motel might be located. In fact, after about two weeks of futilely running ahead of cars to show where their accommodations were located (since most cars were too full to add one more person to ride along), one of our artistic employees drew a map of Swiftcurrent showing each numbered cabin and motel unit. A descendant of that map is still used today.

In those days, the cabins were the bargains of the national park system: $5 for a single bedroom and $7 for a two bedroom. They were heated by wood-burning stoves. One of our duties was to chop wood for every cabin and then clean the ashes out of the stove. There was no electrical heat backup, so if you were a guest and could not get a fire started, you curled up in your blankets and awaited checkout time.

Since I believe the statute of limitations in Montana has run for "fraudulent wood piling," I can finally describe one of the great scams of the summer of 1967. Glacier Park Inc., which owned Swiftcurrent Motor Inn, bought wood by the truckload and had it dumped in a pile the size of a house.

Swiftcurrent Motor Inn employee Ken Hallock by the woodpile. Courtesy, Mac Willemssen

Someone in the GPI management team thought it would be a good idea to know exactly how many cords of wood were in the pile. As PBs, we were told that an additional duty would be to pile the wood into an orderly rectangular mass so it could be exactly measured. Each piece of wood was a semicircle approximately 12 to 15 inches in length and about one foot in diameter. This semicircular shape facilitated orderly piling.

It took us PBs about 60 seconds to realize we had a Herculean task and about another 60 seconds to devise our remedy. We decided to construct a two-layer veneer of neatly stacked wood on all sides and the top of the helter-skelter pile. Working very feverishly and, I might add, in what was considered to be record time by GPI management, we came up with an orderly, measurable pile of wood in about three days. Our achievement was given a nod of approval by none other than Don Hummel, the owner of GPI, on one of his inspection trips.

As a postscript, during the summer of 1968, as the wood pile dwindled and the "veneer" literally and figuratively wore off, GPI management became convinced the inexorable weight of the winter snows had destroyed the beautiful, orderly pile of wood.

Granite Park Chalets and Ma Perkins
Dick Schwab
(Many Glacier Hotel 1947-52)

The Granite Park Chalets have been my favorite place in Glacier since I first hiked there in 1947 and stepped into the enchanted world of Ma and Millie Jean Perkins.

Fairly soon after arriving in Glacier I began to hear of this place high up in the mountains and accessible solely by horseback or foot. What intrigued me above all in the reports about the chalet was its Shangri-La isolation, and that all food and other necessities had to be carried in by pack animals from Many Glacier Hotel. Occasionally, strings of mules heavily loaded with canvas packs, and accompanied by two or three wranglers, filed out from the Many Glacier for this destination over on the other side of Swiftcurrent Pass. It reminded me of a Marco Polo caravan. When I got there myself, Granite Park turned out to be even more magical than I had imagined.

Ever since the first time I rounded the corner and saw the chalet perched on its high mountain shelf along the Garden Wall trail, I have been filled with admiration for whoever it was who had the daring to select the site— the small compound of rustic stone structures amid snowy mountains, steep chasms and valleys, richly watered alpine meadows, bright flowers, and glistening streams and falls.

The luminous spirit of Ema (Ma) Perkins, who managed Granite Park

Ema (Ma) Perkins, center standing, and her daughter Millie, serving at right, put on dinner for guests at Granite Park Chalets. Ray Djuff collection

from 1935 through 1949, filled the chalet. The moment Ma came out to greet you with open arms, she won you over for life. No one who has had the experience can forget the image of that short, lively white-haired lady casually clad in jeans and a shirt with the sleeves rolled up, walking toward you with her smiling, round face and bright eyes radiating hospitality and humor. It did not take long to recognize we were in the presence of an extraordinary person.

Ma and Millie Jean's (Ma's daughter) dinners were legendary. The food at the chalet matched the best home-cooked food anywhere in the country. Prepared on a huge, old range, the meals were succulent and hearty accompanied by oceans of coffee and served on the heavy Blue Willow ware. The bread and pastries came fresh and steaming from the oven. Dessert was often a sublime wedge of pie made from wild huckleberries. You were feasting like royalty in the middle of a remote alpine wilderness.

Evening was the most enchanting time of all at Granite. After dinner, we repaired to the front porch to chat and joke, or strolled around the chalet, watching the stunning sunset turn the sky and mountains all conceivable miraculous and brilliant colors. As darkness fell a campfire was kindled, when weather permitted it, and we gathered to talk, sing, and tell stories.

The two chalets at Granite Park, with the main building, right, featuring the "cribs."
T.J. Hileman photo, Great Northern Railway collection, Minnesota Historical Society

Ma, Millie and the other employees, after having cleaned up the dishes and put the kitchen in order, joined us and brought popcorn, hot chocolate, tea or coffee. I don't think any of us ever had any better times than around that campfire. On the most magical of nights, the sight of the perfect white and gray form of Heavens Peak, standing like eternity in the moonlight across the valley, would take your breath away.

On stormier or colder nights we would gather in the cheering heat of the big stove in the lobby. It was not long before Ma had us hypnotized with the power of her personality. Part of her genius was in knowing how to coax the best out of everyone present. Anyone who could was inspired to make some contribution—a tune, a poem, a ghost story, or at least a spirited participation in the singing and word games. But whether she intended to or not, Ma was inevitably the soul of it all. Magnanimity and irrepressible impishness were the hallmarks of her character. She had natural dramatic flair, and a puckish expression played around the corners of her mouth.

Sooner or later we got her to draw on her repertoire of poems by Robert Burns, which she recited flawlessly in an animated and expressive brogue. She was an incomparable storyteller, and it was not long before, by popular request, she was in the middle of a tale.

Then came the high point of the evening. Ma read everybody's fortunes in the tea leaves. She adopted the manner of Madame Arcati at a seance. Her voice became hushed and solemn. There was many a significant pause and a worried look. It was a perfect performance. Ma was one of the shrewdest students of human nature, and she could size up someone in an instant.

After the fortune-telling, we all trooped off to bed. At that time there were still two rows of small log rooms, called "cribs," forming part of the chalet complex. They were rugged, log, lean-to structures with doors to each chamber opening toward the chalet.

None of the sleeping quarters anywhere in the chalet was heated, and it got frigid at night at that altitude. Ma and Millie Jean provided us with their latter-day "warming pans," which were unique to Granite Park so far as I know. They were medium-sized stones that had been absorbing heat on the stove of the lobby during the evening. Ma and Millie wrapped up one for each of us in thick newspaper so we would not get burned, and off we went to our rooms. They removed the dread of having to brave an icy bed.

Each of the rooms was lit by a single candle. Normally the moment you blew out the candle you were asleep. Before you knew it there would be a cheerful voice calling out, "Good morning. Time to get up." and you could hear the sound of a pitcher of steaming water being set down just outside your door. That was another luxury—the feeling of warm soap and water from the washbowl on your hands and face as you re-entered the waking world of Granite Park Chalets all refreshed, and began to smell the dazzling odors of breakfast being made in the kitchen. Ma, Millie, and the rest of the crew had been up well before dawn to get everything ready.

Ever since 1947, when I was literally bowled over by Granite and the remarkable people there, I became a great advocate of the chalet, hiking there whenever I could, urging everyone who would listen not to miss the experience, and sometimes recruiting visitors to go there. You could count on something exciting happening and being welcomed as if you were the only person in the world.

A guest wrote this completely accurate salute: "To 'Ma' Perkins, Millie Jean and Granite Park, a trio incomparable, inseparable, and indomitable." That says it.

Egg white facials
Bill Wanser
(Crossley Lake Camp 1924-38)

One time I left the Crossley Lake tent camp on my "top horse" to look for some lost saddle horses out on the flats toward Canada. About a mile from the camp, I found that I had forgotten my lunch so I turned around and headed back.

At the time of this story (around 1930), many young ladies believed that egg whites had beneficial cosmetic properties. On this particular morning, all the men had left the camp and the female employees had put on "egg white facials."

Thus, as I galloped unexpectedly into the camp, I found all the cooks and waitresses sunning in a semi-topless state, with ghastly white faces. A chorus of screams arose as the ladies flew to their feet and ran for the jack pines.

Sun Camp adventures
Don Loeffler
(Glacier Park Hotel, Sun Camp, Many Glacier Hotel 1940-42, 1946-48)

My first glimpse of Sun Camp (as the Going-to-the-Sun Chalets were called) was from the bow of the launch *St. Mary* in 1932. By that time, the road from St. Mary Chalets to Going-to-the-Sun Chalets was finished, but the approach was much more spectacular by water.

My dad felt that our family would enjoy this approach while he gave us a detailed dissertation on his wanderings through those rocks and rills. He was entitled to do so, since he really knew the territory.

The road over Logan Pass was not finished at the time of my first visit. However, work was progressing well. The noise from dynamite detonations echoed up and down the lake.

I remember how much fun my brother and I had throwing small rocks down into the water in front of the dining room, until we got caught by our parents. We then proceeded to see how close we could walk to the edge of the cliff without falling off until, we were again apprehended and sent to our rooms.

Many years later, in 1941, I was hired to work at Going-to-the-Sun Chalets.

There was an interesting character in residence at Sun Camp by the name of Gus. As a youth, he had put in a stint as a gandy dancer, a laborer in a railroad maintenance gang, with the Great Northern, and then had ended up employed by its subsidiary, the Glacier Park Hotel Company. He was a likable chap, full of stories.

He would hold court nightly down at the beer parlor. I would sit at his feet and listen to the wonderful and exciting tales of the past as if he were some mystical guru. We employees held him in high esteem. He was not a mountain climber, but he could fix almost anything. His stories of the construction of the Going-to-the-Sun Highway were legendary. I should have taken notes. We never could figure out how he could open a bottle of beer with his thumb.

Gus told me about a small mountain tarn less than a hundred yards off the road just about at the turnoff to Sun Camp. I was very interested in this information since people rarely swam in the frigid waters of St. Mary Lake. I eagerly investigated Gus's swimming hole. Sure enough, there it was—small, cozy, hidden, and most important, not ice cold. I led a contingent of employees (mostly female) to the secluded spot after swearing them to secrecy.

The Going-to-the-Sun Chalets, also called Sun Camp, were built at the narrows on St. Mary Lake. The chalets were razed after the Second World War.
Great Northern Railway collection, Minnesota Historical Society

Cy Stevenson, the hotel company's chief engineer, stopped by one day and in the course of our conversation I happened to mention that I knew of a nifty little pond to swim in near Sun Camp. Cy said he was aware of it, and that it was the source of drinking water for the Going-to-the-Sun Chalets. He strongly suggested that I take my friends elsewhere. Gus's secret tarn now shows up on the topographical maps as Lost Lake.

One day I hiked around the upper end of the lake to Louis Hill's cabin on the south shore. What I found was not one cabin, but two. The prime structure was on a small isthmus almost directly across from Sun Camp. I surmised that the smaller cabin was most likely a guest house, which had almost rotted away. The high winds blowing down the lake had reduced the remains to ghostly traces. The privileged few who were fortunate enough to stay there had what I considered the best views in Glacier.

There is a delightful little hanging valley called Preston Park cradled between Mount Siyeh on the north and Going-to-the-Sun Mountain on the south. This Shangri-La setting persistently was used to perpetrate a hoax. Cy Stevenson (who probably started the whole business) first told me this mischievous tale: "Preston Park has been set aside as an amusement area complete with Ferris wheel, merry-go-round, shooting gallery, candy floss, etc., etc. It is a great place to visit when you get tired of looking at the glories of Mother Nature."

Cy almost had me convinced of the existence of this amusement park. From that time forward I did my best to sell the concept to first-timers to the park. I almost had a couple of dishwashers convinced, until they asked me, "Where do all the visitors park their cars?" They had me cold. I later learned that this duo had sold the idea to a couple of waitresses who they took on a hike up to Preston Park. They returned dog-tired, but without any stuffed animals.

Tales of St. Mary Lodge
Steve Berg
(St. Mary Lodge 1960-67)

I was born in St. Paul, Minnesota, and grew up across Summit Avenue from the Black family. Hugh and Margaret Black had operated at St. Mary since the early 1930s. Lucky Black, fifth of the six Black children, was my close friend and classmate. Because of my relationship with Lucky, his parents hired me to work in the laundry at St. Mary Lodge in 1960. Lucky and I turned 16 that summer.

My pay was $100 per month (or $125 per month for college-age employees) plus a bonus paid at the end of the season to those who worked satisfactorily and stayed to their departure date. About 125 employees ventured west for an unforgettable summer with the Blacks.

A disproportionately large number of employees were Catholic, reflecting Margaret's preference, although a few Lutherans snuck in from time to time, provided they had sound Catholic references. Each Sunday, the Catholics left their jobs with impunity to attend mass, requiring Protestants and unbelievers to attend to the tourists. The potential was there for a religious revolt, but all was forgotten by powwow time Sunday night.

We worked six days each week. Days off were spent hiking, visiting the swimming pool in Waterton, Dusty's Bar west of East Glacier and, of course, the notorious Babb and Harwood bars in Babb.

Staff powwows, informal get-togethers over a bonfire at St. Mary River and the old St. Mary Chalets dock, were popular, this being the apogee of folk music and guitars. The Blacks hosted several employee parties: a talent show, Sadie Hawkins dance and, late in August, a Christmas party in their home.

The summer of 1964 was my most memorable, because of the flood. Warm rain was unceasing. Divide Creek inundated the lodge and motels. Power and sanitation facilities were erratic. After the June flood, the goal was to open by July 4, and we met it with one day to spare. Camaraderie

St. Mary Lodge in the late-1950s. Mike Roberts photo, Ray Djuff collection

was at its height as everyone on staff helped pull the Blacks out of a tough position.

There was a family atmosphere at St. Mary in those years and some degree of in loco parentis. However, Hugh and Margaret were referred to as Mr. and Mrs. Black, not Mom and Dad. There was nothing corporate about St. Mary. Planning was pragmatic. People who could fix things, I not among them, were held in high esteem.

Hugh and Margaret complemented each other in their skills and personalities. The six Black children, their cousins, and many friends of both groups, returned annually, as I did, but new employees were not excluded from the fun.

The Blacks were blessed with loyal, ageless senior managers who acted as links between them and their employees. Like NCOs in a military unit, these managers, often a husband-wife team, were the glue to the success of this operation. And successful it was.

[Editors note: The Black family sold its St. Mary operation in 2008. In 2011 it was acquired by Glacier Park, Inc.]

Climbers get a bird's eye view of Many Glacier Hotel in 1926.
Great Northern Railway collection, Minnesota Historical Society

Chapter 7

Showplace of the Rockies

Glacier hard to imagine without Ian Tippet
Tessie Bundick
(Many Glacier Hotel 1972-73, 1976-80)

It would be hard to imagine life without Glacier Park and it would be equally as difficult to imagine Glacier Park without Ian B. Tippet. To me, he is as much a part of that beautiful place as Mount Wilbur or Stoney Indian Pass.

I first met Mr. Tippet in his office at Many Glacier Hotel in the summer of 1972. I had arrived, fresh from a Red bus ride, out of East Glacier, to take up my post as a Many maid. He welcomed me, handed me the key to my dorm room, looked out over the top of his glasses, and asked if I had brought white, hospital-type shoes to wear on the job.

I assured him that I had not forgotten this seemingly indispensable bit of uniform attire and went up to meet my roommate, thinking all the while what an interesting gentleman was the manager of this lovely, old hotel. And, indeed, he turned out to be a most interesting boss.

Trained at the finest schools in Europe, he was really the best in the business. And it certainly was to his credit that he took young college students as raw and as green as a dining room salad, and turned us into a passably good staff.

Ian Tippet

We worked hard at our hotel duties and rehearsed long, unpaid hours to entertain the guests, but we also played with bursting energy, as well, with all the unbridled enthusiasm of youth. We pulled many pranks on each other and participated in parties until the wee hours like there was no tomorrow.

I'm sure there were moments when Mr. Tippet thought we considered Many Glacier and environs our private summer camp and the guests incidental to our fun. Most of the time, he graciously looked the other way when some employee breech of conduct reached his ears and eyes. How often his impeccable British sense of the rightness of things must have been upset by the roughhouse hijinks of American university students.

I'll never forget how we, the Annex maids of 1972, would decide to indulge in an extended break during the morning and enjoy a giant cookie and soda at the snack counter operations. Laughing and talking in our uniforms as the minutes ticked by and beds went unmade, we would shamefacedly return to our dust mops after Mr. Tippet, who could show up at the most inopportune moments, would sweep through the St. Moritz Room, spy our party, and say, in passing, "This is not a country club for employees."

It probably did not seem always apparent to him, but his staunch work ethic, sense of pride and his notion of "aggressively doing one's job" did wear off on us. Everyone admired him and was affected by him, in one way or another.

A harassed-looking tour escort, on being told that a certain troublesome couple had been assigned to a room with a door which would not latch, responded: "That's OK. The bears can go in and hug 'em."

One freebie
Rev. Jim Singleton
(Many Glacier Hotel 1977-79)

It was 1977 at the front desk at Many Glacier. Mark Bazan, Tony Settles, Rick Taylor and Jim Singleton were managing the rush.

Amid the confusion, Mark became upset with a guest (perhaps it was in defense of a foreign exchange student working with us that summer, who occasionally made the guests impatient, and of whom Mark was protective). In his Utica, New York, fashion, Mark told the guest off with notable curtness.

An hour or so later, Mr. Tippet came by the front desk. The unhappy guest had stormed off and reported the incident to him, and we feared for Mark Bazan's future.

But Mr. Tippet said, "I've always said that over the course of the summer, each employee may have one freebie with a guest. There are times when we will lose our tempers. One freebie for the summer."

For the rest of the shift, Mr. Tippet would walk by, holding up one finger and repeating to us, "One freebie."

Baggage sagas
John Hagen
(Many Glacier Hotel 1970-1980)

Hotel work is fascinating because of the variety of tourists you encounter. This fascination is enhanced by the array of baggage the tourists bring. Ancient, peeling black leather valises that might have come off the *Mayflower* arrive side-by-side with aluminum cases that look like they were designed for the set of *Star Trek*. Elegant leather satchels, military duffle bags, battered steamer trunks and bags festooned with colored tape pour out fantastically from the luggage compartments of buses and tourist vehicles.

In recent years American luggage has emphasized wheels, but the Japanese put wheels on their luggage decades ago. In the 1970s Japanese tours would come to Glacier with suitcases wheeled in the most amazing fashion—wheels on the bottom, wheels on the sides, wheels jutting out at dramatic angles, wheels hinged and swiveled—wheels, wheels, wheels. These bags sometimes had long, retractable leashes and could be led around like dogs.

Bellmen of my era were very partial to suitcases of a sort we called "stackers." These bags [from the 1920s to 1950s] were hard and square-sided. They could be laid flat and propped over the front ends of our

Bellmen at Many Glacier Hotel jokingly pretend to use luggage as a football for a field goal kick.
Courtesy, John Hagen

luggage carts, with other stackers piled on top of them. This allowed us to maximize the number of bags transported on a cart—16 to 18 bags, which was useful when we were working an 80-bag tour.

"Stacker" bags had been popular in earlier decades, but by the 1970s they were heavily outnumbered by Samsonite luggage, which had slick, curved sides, making them treacherous to stack. Now and then a bellman would stack Samsonite imprudently and the stack would topple, sending bags to the ground with a crash. At such times we would fantasize about bellmen subbing for the gorillas who smacked and stomped on Samsonite suitcases in television commercials of that era.

The luggage of group tours sometimes totaled a couple of hundred bags arriving in the afternoon and going out the next day. Moving all those bags through Many Glacier Hotel's rambling halls required good teamwork. This was especially true in the Annex, where there was no elevator or freight lift. The bellmen would form human chains to hoist the bags to the upper Annex floors. The staircase was doglegged, with two short flights between each floor. The bellmen would stand one above the other and pass bags up through the open stairwell.

Due to the lack of an elevator, bellmen form a chain on the staircase of the Annex of Many Glacier Hotel to get the luggage of guests to upper floors. Courtesy, John Hagen

This sometimes was a challenge when luggage was cumbersome and heavy. Care was required to be sure that the upper man had a firm grip on the handle before the lower man let go. Once or twice a bag was dropped and went plummeting down the stairwell like an anvil, cracking open in the basement in a shower of underwear.

The bellmen engaged in jocular commentary while chaining the heavier bags.

"Brace yourself! It's another sewing machine," a colleague might grunt from below.

The legendary bellman Chris (Wizard) Vick was famous for his fantastic remarks about such suitcases and their owners.

"Oof! Somebody brought along his own tombstone," he might indignantly exclaim, or "Somebody brought her chopped-up husband."

This would set the crew laughing so hard that they would almost drop the bag.

Unlike the Annex, Many Glacier's main wing had a freight lift—a creaking, lurching, ancient cab suspended on greasy metal cables. The lift was run by means of a pushbutton and a crank (which had an "up" and a "down" position, and a brake to be applied when reaching a floor). Gentleness was required in applying the brake, for sudden braking could throw a cable off the wheels in the shaft. Then the maintenance crew had to remount the cable (a task which they heartily disliked, and which might be postponed for several days while the bags had to be run up and down stairs).

One morning while I was riding the freight lift, an alarm clock in a suitcase abruptly went off. I initially thought that this sudden jangling was an alarm in the cab itself. I glanced up fearfully at the cables, afraid they might be about to part and drop me down the shaft. A split second's reflection reassured me that the lift was too old and crude to have any sort of built-in alarm.

When tours checked into the hotel, the first order of business was to mark room assignments on baggage tags. Occasionally tags were marked incorrectly and bags were delivered to the wrong room. When owners called to complain that their suitcases had not arrived, we would have to hunt for the missing bags. Lost bag searches usually were concluded in short order. You'd start by checking for the most probable mistakes. A bag missing from Room 50 likely could be found in Room 150, or in an adjoining room (48 or 52), or in Room 56 (a "0" hastily scrawled on a luggage tag could be mistaken for a "6").

Sometimes, however, the bag would not turn up in any likely room. Then we would have to run a systematic search of the whole hotel. Many Glacier had over 200 guest rooms, so a search of this sort was grueling (especially if it occurred at night, when guests had started to go to bed).

I remember a couple of harrowing after-hours searches of this sort—going room-by-room down shadowy hallways, tapping sheepishly on doors, being peeped at suspiciously over door chains, being snarled at by dogs, requesting people to check their closets for a misplaced bag. On one of these searches we found the bag, sitting undiscovered in a closet, in approximately the 199th room.

Guests were protective of their bags—a natural tendency that was occasionally carried to extremes. No memoir of baggage in the 1970s would be complete without recalling the following episode.

Colonel and Mrs. Truman (not their real names) were an elderly couple who stopped at Many Glacier for several days. The front office manager thought that they had overstayed their reservation and wanted the room for other guests. When the couple could not be found at midday, he instructed the bellmen to move their luggage out of the room and store it.

This was a serious mistake, both as to the length of the reservation and as to the treatment of the bags. When the couple returned and found their belongings gone from the room, they were irate. Ian Tippet, our manager, cautioned everyone in the aftermath that one never moves bags without the owner's permission.

What made this episode distinctive was that the couple did not calm down. The colonel must have been a ferocious martinet in his army days. All through the afternoon and evening he marched back and forth from the front desk to the bellmen's desk to the manager's office, bawling people out, in company with his pugnacious wife. The two were absolutely implacable; no apologies could appease them. Finally they retired for the night. A brief peace descended over the lobby.

Then a terrible cry rang out. The colonel came tramping down the main staircase, shouting in a thunderous voice that must have been heard throughout the hotel: "MRS. ... TRUMAN'S ... YELLOW ... BATHROBE ... IS MISSING!"

I was unfortunate to be the single bellman on duty that evening. My heart sank on hearing the colonel's voice. I hustled into the bellmen's closet and there on a hanger (oh, blessed relief.) was Mrs. Truman's yellow bathrobe. I handed the bathrobe to the colonel, who bawled me out a final time and tramped back to his room.

I turned to Mr. Tippet, who was standing manfully nearby.

"What a relief," I said. "I was afraid they'd flushed the bathrobe down the toilet, just for an excuse to bawl us out."

"I thought the same," Mr. Tippet said stoically. "I thought that they had destroyed it."

A touch of class
Ian B. Tippet
(Many Glacier Hotel manager 1961-83)

The summer season years at Many Glacier Hotel from 1961 through 1983 were a unique, never-to-be forgotten periods, where the outlook was "how can we make the guest's memories of the place so far more meaningful," when we were challenged by no elevators, only half the guest rooms with lake views (everyone wanted lake view and nobody wanted to climb stairs), clanging and banging steam pipes as boilers were started early morning and closed down late in the afternoon, fiercely hot rooms some days and bitterly cold the next, depending upon weather, lake or wind conditions, thin bedroom walls, and many other challenges.

The recruitment of music, drama, or theater majors would be the answer:

For 22 consecutive summers Many Glacier Hotel employees produced full-scale Broadway musicals on the St. Moritz Room stage. Here's the cast in 1979's production of *You're a Good Man Charlie Brown*.　　　　　　　　　Rolf Larson photo

these employees would work hotel jobs by day and have music or theatre assignments in the evening. I went about starting to notify every single music and drama department at every college or university in the United States that Many Glacier Hotel needed talented individuals as summer seasonal employees.

My hours as company human resources vice-president were long. I was often at the office by 4 or 5 a.m., would go home for dinner at 6 p.m., and then be back at the office until 10 or 11 p.m. to handle the vast amount of mail that started to come in. It took up to two hours some days just to slit open the envelopes.

From 1957 until 1961 I had "played" a bit with the hiring of talented students for all of our properties, but when made general manager at Many Glacier Hotel in 1961, I was determined to go "all out" with a program that would be unique within the national park system.

Personal letters were sent with each contract. Twenty-five thousand completed applications came to me every winter for all of our historic hotels and lodges. I wanted to also catch students majoring in culinary arts, accounting, hotel and restaurant management, and history and geology (the latter for bus drivers or tour guides). Standards became higher and higher as the years progressed.

A summer calendar for Many Glacier Hotel was drawn up, a long board done by a professional artist, for the wall in the long hall to the dining room where all guests would see it: "Many's Months of Madness." The names of all employees who celebrated a birthday during the season would be appended. All the events for every day of the season were appended. . . . It went something like this:

Monday night: Hootenanny
Tuesday night: Movie
Wednesday night: Community Sing
The Thursday Serenade
The Friday Skit (Departments in turn on stage in the St. Moritz Room)
Saturday night: Big Dance Night
Sunday night: Concert Night

The calendar was full, even before the first day of the season.

Conscientious, dedicated committees headed each event. At least a master's degree (or PhD) candidate directed the Broadway musical for the season, and a conducting major from schools such as Eastman or Julliard conducted the orchestra. Dedicated theatre tech students worked late at night on costumes, lighting, set building, sound systems, program assembly, and the multitude of other responsibilities.

Twenty-seven Broadway musicals were performed in 20 seasons at Many Glacier as the highlight of the summer. The final Broadway musical, *Kiss Me Kate* in 1983, had 60 performers on stage and 46 musicians in the orchestra, plus masses in all of the tech support. We rented costumes from New York costumers.

The Monday Hootenannies and the Thursday Serenades (the latter hosted by myself and an employee) were the "star" weekly events, filling the lobby with audiences so great that the National Park Service became somewhat concerned about numbers of guests on balconies. The Saturday Night Dances massed in the St. Moritz Room (the hotel had its own mature Hotel Dance Combo). A string trio played in the hotel lobby in the afternoons.

The Thursday Serenade Series over the years proved to be the class weekly presentation of countless musicians and actors, from opening performances of the Many Glacier Singers to cello performances, woodwind quintets, brass quartets, string trios, soprano, bass and tenor soloists, dramatic readings, and cuttings from such exciting operas as *Porgy and Bess*, with tenor voice on the lobby floor singing to his loved one—a soprano—on the first lobby balcony, with light and sound going back and forth.

In 20 seasons, every form of entertainment of high-class variety was included in the Thursday Serenade Series. Thinking back, it was a brilliant series.

I was fortunate to have Professor Roger L. Stephens as my assistant hotel manager. Stephens was director of 12 of the 27 major Broadway musicals, enhancing them with his brilliant talents. Employees felt they were in summer school—not only working in a hotel position, but gaining more experience in their anticipated careers.

A student had to be majoring in voice or have a wonderful singing voice to secure a position as a waitperson in the dining room. We sang at the end of the first, then the second guest sitting. Thirty-seven voice majors/waitpersons raised a sound that has never been heard since at Many Glacier's Ptarmigan Room. It sends shivers down the spine and brings tears to the eyes.

Music and drama in those years kept employee morale high, and contracts of employment completed. It's amazing and very hard to believe that between 1961 and 1983, there were seasons that saw zero employee turnover from start to finish. The quality of the employees was unbelievable, both in their hotel role and their talent role. We were dealing with America's best young people. I was blessed to have been at the helm of it in those earlier years and we gave joy to thousands of guests.

Room guest calling switchboard: "What's the weather like this morning?"
Operator: "Cloudy, I'm afraid."
Room guest: "Are the mountains still there?"
Operator (dumbfounded): "Yes, sir—I assume so."
Room guest (acidly): "I mean, can you still see them?"

Hootenannies
Sean Williams
(Many Glacier Hotel 1978-81)

When I first spotted the ad—a half-page photo of Mount Gould—with its invitation to spend a summer playing music (and working) at Many Glacier Hotel in the Rockies, I was enchanted.

I was in my first year of college as a music major at UC Berkeley. I rushed back to my dorm and asked a friend for a letter of recommendation. He kindly wrote one and had the entire dorm sign it as a petition. According to Mr. Tippet's offer of employment, it won me the job (and thanks, Dwight, wherever you are). And for four summers I found my "voice," matured as a human being, and met both my dear husband (Cary Black, bass player in the house band) and my best friend forever, Gloria Hatch (then known as Tib, who worked first as a maid like me, then as Mr. Tippet's secretary).

I packed up my banjo and guitar and got myself out to Montana from

There was never a shortage of guitars at hootenannies. Courtesy, Laura Chihara

California to begin what was unquestionably the most important developmental experience as a musician and performer that I could have hoped for.

Yes, I had a job ("relief maid," which meant the 5 a.m. to 2 p.m. shift, no tips, and virtually no contact with the rest of the housekeeping staff). But the really extraordinary "work" at Many Glacier was the combination of musical rehearsals, performances, and opportunities to learn stagecraft.

In front of transient hotel audiences night after night, I completely lost any sense of stage fright that I'd brought to Glacier. I learned about timing, covering up mistakes, polishing an act and interacting with other performers. I learned what to do when the sound system failed. I had the chance to expose audiences to a wide variety of musical styles and to gauge their reactions.

Best of all were those glorious moments of musical collaboration—performing Faure's *Pavane* on cello, guitar and flute because it was the instrumentation we had on hand, for example. Watching a talented singer-songwriter perform *Dust in the Wind* with a full complement of chamber players was transcendent. And playing *Stayin' Alive*, one of the great disco anthems, as a bluegrass tune complete with hot dancers Ellen Rockne, Tib Hatch and Bonnie Brown in overalls was a highlight of my first summer.

In the years since, I have held Many Glacier in my heart as the perfect—perfect—model for how to support young musicians. To this day, the skills I use in my daily life as a professor (for every lecture is, in fact, a kind of performance), and in my other moments as a performer, stem from the experiences I gained in those four short summers.

If Mr. Tippet had not had the profound wisdom, generosity, and willingness to generate a staff of performers and nurture them year after year, I strongly believe that all of our lives would be dramatically different. To Mr. Tippet and all the musicians of Many Glacier, I offer my sincerest thanks.

One evening at Many Glacier, the lobby balconies were crowded with people awaiting the start of an entertainment program. A hotel bellman started along one balcony, pulling a rollaway bed. A lady across the lobby abruptly sang out: "That's not fair. You hafta sit on a chair like everybody else."

Music in the mountains
Don Loeffler
(Glacier Park Hotel, Sun Camp, Many Glacier 1940-42, 46-48)

Ever since Glacier Park Hotel was opened in 1913 there has been music in the air.

My own first contribution was at Glacier Park Hotel in 1940. I was billeted in the employees dorm, where I ran across an old acquaintance from our Central High School days in St. Paul, where we both had played in the band. He asked me to sit in on the piano once in a while so that he could dance with a waitress he had just met. Talk about a win-win situation. The band liked my piano playing and I soon found myself at the keyboard almost every night after doing heavy-duty work all day. (Who needed sleep at that age?)

After a couple of weeks, however, my boss, Cy Stevenson, began transferring me from one facility to another and by the time I was assigned to operate the hydroelectric power plant at the Many Glacier Hotel, I knew I had hit the "big time." All the employees told me that Many was the place to work. Within 24 hours of moving into the employees' dorm there I could see why. There was a good band playing down in The Grill, lots of pretty girls and last and probably least, the food was better.

When the drummer in the band decided that he would rather be a bartender because the tips were good, he asked me to take over, which I was only too glad to do. The musicians were excellent and it was a thrill for me to be performing with them. Orville Fleming was the violin player and leader. Dave Mathews was on alto and tenor saxes. If I had known then that he would soon be touring with the Harry James band, I would have paid more attention to his great solos. Sonny Lyons, who was five foot two and weighed about 110 pounds, was on the piano. He was a talented player who sat on an assortment of books and pillows to give him the right keyboard height.

The double helix staircase which used to stand in the Many Glacier lobby created an opening in the floor and allowed sounds from The Grill to waft up into the guest rooms overlooking the lobby. The band had to play its last few sets pianissimo, so as not to disturb the guests who had retired. We played *One O'Clock Jump* at about 11 p.m. In spite of our consideration for the guests, hotel manager Omar Ellis was still on our case. Once I recall him coming down the stairs holding an alarm clock in his hand. He proceeded to the bandstand and cut the music in the middle of our closing selection.

The band used the Duke Ellington composition *Prelude to a Kiss* as its theme song. We slightly adjusted the lyrics of the beautiful melody called *Moonlight in Vermont*, changing it to "Moonlight on Grinnell," but maintaining the melody line. I almost had my girlfriend Barbara convinced that we had composed that song, but she got wise to us in about a week.

The Many Glacier dining room was always filled with singing. Several of the waitresses and busboys had fine voices. Periodically they would put down their trays and assemble at the big stone fireplace at the north end of the dining room and burst forth in well-known songs. Even today, after all these years, when I hear the melody *Jean* I am transported to Many Glacier Hotel.

Fiddler on the Roof
Clark Bormann
(Many Glacier Hotel 1973)

In 1973 at Many Glacier Hotel we performed the musical *Fiddler on the Roof*. I played the role of the young revolutionary from Kiev. We performed 13 shows in 14 nights, which even then seemed a killing pace. It was a stressful experience.

One night, after a very long day with the bellman crew, I got backstage, put on my makeup and dressed in most of my costume before I stretched out on the floor for a quick nap before my entrance. This was a big mistake. I was suddenly and violently shaken awake by another actor who said they were ad-libbing and awaiting my entrance. I jumped up, hastily buttoning my vest but forgetting completely about checking my prayer shawl before I raced around the corner and up to the stage.

The line they were waiting to deliver, and the one which first acknowledged me was, "Say, you're not from around here."

This time, however, the circumstances permitted the speaker to say,

"Say, you're not from around here. Around here we don't wear our prayer shawls around our ankles."

I followed his gaze and saw, to my horror, that that was exactly where my prayer shawl was—around my ankles.

I don't remember what happened after that inauspicious beginning.

Now presenting: the Ptarmigan Room
Karen (Koller) Bohnert
(Many Glacier Hotel 1977-78)

I started at Many Glacier as a maid in the summer of '77, and for the month of June I did my duty in my little denim apron. I eyed the dining room staff with envy. Everyone knew they made more money and got one and a half whole days off each week.

But there was something more, something almost magical about the Ptarmigan Room. It always seemed to me that when you approached the room from the lounge, it opened up before your eyes much like a stage appears as the curtains open at the beginning of a play. This play was, of course, a musical.

You could tell by the colorful costumes, the romance of the huge stone fireplace, the way the "actors" and "actresses" swept back and forth across the "stage," and by the stupendous backdrop of the valley—not to mention the singing and dancing during the dinner hour.

One day Mr. Tippet called me into his office and told me that because I had done such a "mah-velous" job as a maid, I was the first person to whom he would give "the opportunity to turn down a job in the dining room."

What? Trade in my polyester nurse's dress for a red cotton dirndl and white blouse? Trade in making a couple thousand beds and cleaning hundreds of toilets for serving prime rib and fresh strawberries? Trade in a view of dust bunnies under beds for a view of the lake and the valley? I couldn't say "I'll take it" fast enough.

So, I began as an understudy, following some of the best wait people around for a couple days, and trying to pick up as many of their tricks as I could. I learned the best way to mix the hot cocoa, how to fold dinner napkins, how to de-bone a trout before serving it, and when to tell the broiler cook to fire my steak.

But probably the best piece of advice I received was from a cook who warned me: "The chef is gonna be watching you like a hawk. When you screw up he's gonna yell at you. Just stand there and say, 'Yes, sir. Yes, sir.'"

I thought it rather odd that he had to tell me that—until I didn't stir the soup correctly one evening. The chef came flying over to me, screaming and ranting and making such a scene that I was reminded of some Jerry Lewis movie and almost laughed. But I remembered my friend's

Many Glacier Hotel's Ptarmigan dining room in 2010. It has since been renovated and the false ceiling removed. Ray Djuff photo

advice, and, casting my eyes downward, I said "Yes, sir. Yes, sir." and humbly stirred the soup as he instructed. Having asserted his authority, he left me alone the rest of the summer. I was learning that unique characters existed behind the scenes as well as on stage.

As an actor in this play I learned that timing was everything. The faster you reached your breakfast tables with that pot of coffee, the happier everyone was. And if you could present the check right after your co-workers sang the Rice Krispies song, your tip went up. At dinner you had to time things just right and really hustle so that you could get your entrees served before it was time for the dining room chorus to perform. Our accompanist par excellence was Rob Rhein. When he started playing, it meant "Get your butts to the front of the room 'cuz it's time to sing."

Long before there was *Tony and Tina's Wedding*, there was the Ptarmigan Room. It must have been one of the early forms of participatory theatre, with the customers influencing the nuances of story line and dialogue.

The wait staff usually recited their lines without a great deal of variety, but the customers were a different story—you never knew what they were going to come up with. My favorite was the time Bill Rollie waited on a retired couple who wanted to talk about their travels. The woman told Bill,

"Last year George and I took a trip around the world. Next year I think we'll go someplace else."

"Such as where ... Mars?" Bill speculated when he got back to the sidestand.

They say a good actor can recite the same lines every night and still make them sound fresh and spontaneous. If my stint as a waitress is any indication, I'd make a lousy actress. As the summer went on I got tired of asking people what they wanted to drink with their meal, in spite of changing inflections, word order and rephrasing the question ("And to drink ... , How about a beverage?" etc.).

Twelve hour days eventually wore on all of us, and even the occasional snarfed fruit, nap between meals, and lunch off didn't entirely restore our mental health. We turned to humor to get us through, improvising on our regularly scripted lines.

Impatient guests who didn't think their food was coming fast enough were told, "You know, I do only have three hands."

When you go on a hike and can't seem to go slow enough to enjoy it because you keep racing along at dining room pace; when you think the alpine glow on Grinnell Point looks like a scoop of orange sherbet; when the star above Swiftcurrent Peak reminds you of the cherry on top of the cottage cheese; well, you know you've spent too many hours in the dining room.

But there's a good side to that—it makes you finally willing to leave. And so, as the last guest was seated on the last meal of the last day, we all applauded.

Yes, we were glad to be done with waiting tables. But it was more than that: a production this good deserved a standing ovation.

The rowboat race
Ray Kinley (as told to John Hagen)
(Many Glacier Hotel 1919, 1922-77)

Among the Many Glacier bellmen during the 1920s was Whitey (so called because of his "cotton top" blond hair). Whitey was a varsity rower at a prominent eastern college. He had been the champion sculler on Lake Charles and liked to boast about the fact.

Some friends of Ray Kinley's impishly told Whitey that Ray was also a champion oarsman and he was bragging that he could beat him in a contest. Whitey hardly believed this was true, since Ray had lost one hand in a train accident. However, the bellman rashly agreed to race Ray across Swiftcurrent Lake and back in Captain William Swanson's rowboats.

The lake that year was very low, and Ray's friends had noticed a sunken log peeping up out of Burch's Bog, near the icehouse. The boat crew obligingly towed this log around to the Many Glacier boat dock.

Then, the night before the race, Ray's friends placed eyescrews in the bottom of one of Swanson's rowboats. Replacing the boat in the lake, they wired the heavy, water-soaked log to its bottom.

Next day, a huge crowd gathered for the race. Whitey confidently took his place at the oars of the boat which was wired to the hidden log. Ray boarded another boat alongside him.

As the race began, Ray shot out ahead of Whitey, who was amazed to find himself almost dead in the water.

Then Ray pretended to be rowing frantically to hold a narrow lead, pulling alternate oars with his one good hand. However, he had no trouble keeping ahead of Whitey, whose labors were nullified by the enormous drag of the log.

Finally, Whitey decided to throw in the towel. Seeing the point of the hoax, he made no more boasts about his rowing prowess.

Mr. Tippet and the bed-making contest
Pat Wontorski
(Many Glacier Hotel 1976-80)

To spice up another day of room cleaning, we in housekeeping decided to hold a bed-making contest. We found five or six rooms in a row on the third floor—all with unmade single beds—and rounded up a houseman with a stop watch.

As the reigning bed-making queen (my title was earned during the 1976 Many Glacier Olympics) I was to be the officiating judge. Someone had unearthed the old red fur-trimmed Miss Many Glacier robe from a closet somewhere, and it was decided that I should wear this over my maid uniform. I was also sporting some kind of festive head gear.

To mark the official beginning of the contest, a houseman dropped a washcloth off the balcony into the lobby. Perhaps this is what caught Mr. Tippet's attention—perhaps the noise level increased as the contest went into full swing. I must have been immersed in my royal role because I didn't hear those familiar footsteps racing up the stairs.

All of a sudden there at my shoulder was Mr. Tippet, demanding to know, "What is going on here?"

Gesturing to my colleagues with a bouquet of plastic roses, I explained, "We were just having a little bed-making contest, and since I won last year...."

Mr. Tippet stared in the direction I had indicated with an uncomprehending expression. When I turned around, I discovered that all the hotel room doors were closed, and that there were no maids or housemen in sight.

There was an uncomfortable silence. Mr. Tippet then inquired, "Why are you wearing that regalia?"

I quickly responded, "I'll take it off."

He replied, "Then go pack, and be on the next bus out of the valley—the season is over."

Nothing like ending the season with a bang.

The choir boys
Mac Willemssen
(Swiftcurrent Motor Inn, 1967; Many Glacier Hotel 1968-70)

Although Many Glacier Hotel was famous for its musical productions in the 1960s, manager Ian Tippet also took great pride in his flag football team. Once each summer, Mr. Tippet's "Choir Boys" would take on Glacier Park Lodge's football team at East Glacier.

Mr. Tippet also worked as personnel director for the hotels, and this status allowed him to stack the deck a little. In 1965, a first-year Glacier Park Lodge employee named John Slater led the team to a convincing victory; the next year he was head bellman at Many Glacier and turned the tables on his former teammates.

In 1967 I worked at Swiftcurrent Motor Inn and became the ringer on the Many Glacier team; for the next three summers Swiftcurrent was a pleasant memory as Mr. Tippet deemed it in the best interest of the company to have me work at Many Glacier.

In 1967 John Slater could not work in the park. The game with Glacier Park Lodge was postponed a week because the original date was the Sunday after the "Night of the Grizzlies." (See page 70.) Mr. Tippet spent that day contacting and consoling the families of the two girls who were killed and the young man who was badly mauled.

When we finally did have our game, the Choir Boys scored a touchdown on the opening kickoff. Unfortunately the Glacier Park Lodge team dug in and it was a see-saw battle from then on.

I do not remember the score, but we lost by less than one touchdown and on our final play, Roger Stevens was "tackled" just short of the goal line.

The most vivid memory of that game, however, was the spirited rivalry between the Many Glacier and Glacier Park Lodge (GPL) cheering sections.

I must admit that lining up as middle linebacker with your fans yelling "GPL, GO TO HELL" got the adrenaline going.

More surprisingly, however, was realizing that at least one voice chanting that cheer had a very distinct British accent, Tippet's.

Christmas at Many Glacier
Carol Repulski Dahle
(Many Glacier Hotel 1970-75, 79-80)

My first summer at Many Glacier, I heard varied stories about the upcoming celebrations. Some said we celebrated Christmas just so we could celebrate New Year's Eve a week later.

The New Year's Eve celebration was a costume party for the employees, a feast fit for a king and queen with enough dancing, laughing and singing to set the moon and raise the sun.

In 1970 my roommate and I found a couple of large boxes, some black and white paint, and we went to the festivities as a pair of dice. One couple went as a brick and a bricklayer. Six housemen went as a six-pack of beer. By 1972 the New Year's Eve celebration was cancelled due to the employees having "too much fun."

Needless to say, we perennial employees were initially saddened, but there's generally a silver lining to every cloud. In this case, the silver lining was the increased focus and attention on the Christmas celebration.

An integral part of every Christmas celebration is, of course, the Christmas tree. For many summers arrangements were made to go outside the park to get a tree for the lobby. But one summer there were some legal and technical obstacles that could not be surmounted, and we found ourselves without a tree the day before Christmas.

John Hagen, Harvey Barkowsky, and I (there were others I've forgotten . . . sorry.) just knew we had to come up with an idea that would put a Christmas tree in our lobby. I don't remember who had the initial idea, but with my knowledge of a sewing machine and John's artistic talents, we took two double-size bed sheets and sewed them together end to end. John sketched a beautiful 10-foot Christmas tree complete with decorations, and then John, Harvey, and I stayed up all night into the next morning, painting and painting and painting.

After stitching a hem so a rod could be inserted and the tree hung in the lobby, the sun came up as guests were filing through the lobby on their way to the dining room for breakfast. As they looked refreshed and ready for a new day, we looked bedraggled and worn out. However, their "ooohs" and "aaaahhhs" as they appraised our "sheet" tree was music to our ears.

One of my more poignant memories is being in the lobby getting ready to begin the Christmas program, and hearing the brass ensemble playing Christmas carols from the balcony, organized and directed by Terri (Saunders) Stone. It was magical and unforgettable.

The friendships made during our summers in Glacier were intense. With Christmas in the middle of those months, it seemed as though we

Unable to procure an evergreen tree for the lobby, Many Glacier Hotel staff perform before a drawing of a tree for Christmas in July. Courtesy, Laura Chihara

packed 12 months of living into three months of summer.

Many of us knew even then that moments like these would not happen again, and these were the memories we would be holding in our hearts 30 and 40 and 50 years hence.

The tip bowl
Susie Mieras
(Many Glacier Hotel 1970)

I had the very illustrious job at Many Glacier Hotel of being the general cleaning maid. I worked by myself, starting at 5 a.m. But soon after I arrived, so did the lobby porters, so I wasn't working solo for long. And then the front office staff reported for their shifts.

But my job involved a single glaring problem. Every one of the maids received tips. In essence, I too was a maid. The only difference was that I cleaned toilets where the others cleaned rooms. So I decided to put a dish in the ladies' room of the main hallway.

Susie Mieras

Lo and behold, at the end of the first day of my experiment I found $10 in that dish. And at the end of the second day, there was money actually spilling over. My friend, Karen Hudak at the information desk, helped me to find a substantially bigger crystal bowl. Together we printed out a lovely sign that said, "Thank you very much."

For one solid week I was raking in the bucks. It seemed too good to be true and it was. The president of Glacier Park, Inc. came to Many Glacier at the end of my profitable week. His wife discovered my money-making scheme and went straight to hotel manager Ian Tippet.

I was called to the manager's office. Very politely, I was told to kindly remove my bowl and not to place it in any restroom again. But, boy, did I have a good thing going for that one week.

Why Many Glacier's radiator pipes clanked
Ray Mann
(Many Glacier Hotel 1980)

Lewis the boilerman at the Many Glacier Hotel had daily battles with his steam management.

There was the daily, early morning banging of the radiators and pipes. Lewis was adamant about waking up the guests every morning with his own personal call. Since the boilers were high pressure steam and operated at about 175 p.s.i. (pounds per square inch) and the hotel radiators ran at about 60 p.s.i., he would bypass the regulator by pulling down a long, three-foot handle in the boiler room. This would allow the high-pressure steam to race through the hotel causing rapid expansions and contractions in the whole system.

Cy Stevenson, chief engineer for the hotel company, tried to stop this behavior, but couldn't be at Many Glacier all the time. Lew respected and feared Cy, but not to the extent that the opportunity to "alarm" guests each morning could be missed.

I also recall the steam in the cold water lines quite vividly. The first thing I saw and heard was a first floor toilet hissing and yelping with each flush. I think this went on for some time.

Cy solved the problem by phone. Lew had been "injecting" steam, at 175 p.s.i., into the cold water lines.

I can't recall the details exactly, but he accomplished this by using the old steam-driven water pumps, which predated the boilers, and were installed when the hotel was built. They were used to keep water in the boilers if power failed by using the steam to pull water from either the lake or the domestic supply.

I don't think many people knew of these pumps. They were actually quite beautiful pieces of work. Lew was able to open one of his many "secret" valves and send the steam through the water lines. It was ingenious, in a demented way.

As I recall, Cy Stevenson spoke to Lew by phone and his subsequent screwing of valves and mutterings brought everything back to normal.

I befriended Lewis as much as one could. I think his life had been hard and he responded with pranks (which actually were dangerous at times) as a way of balancing his life with the world. Lew certainly might have been considered a strange sort, but he was never mean.

Interacting with tour escorts
John Hagen
(Many Glacier Hotel 1970-80)

In a passage in *War and Peace*, Tolstoy describes squads of soldiers taking on collective temperaments—cheerful, sullen, hopeful or cynical— through the influence of the leading personalities in each group. Anyone who has experience with group tours has seen the same dynamic at work. Some groups are jolly and resilient; some are petulant and morose. And more often than not, the group's temperament reflects the personality of its escort.

As a bellman at Many Glacier Hotel for eight seasons, I dealt with hundreds of escorts. My notebooks are full of descriptions of their personalities—"a big, bluff, good-natured escort who molded the tour in his own image;" "a sober, rotund little minister leading a melancholy tour;" "a placid old fellow who absolutely couldn't be hurried, although his people hadn't been fed and the dining room was about to close."

When a tour bus pulled up to the hotel, the first order of business was to whisk the escort in for a quick conference at the front desk. The front office manager, the escort and the head bellman would huddle over a tentative list of rooming assignments and make any necessary changes. Some changes were made to split up incompatible roommates. Most of them, however, involved the perpetual issue of stairs.

Many Glacier had no guest-accessible elevator in those days (just a creaky, untrustworthy freight lift in the main building, and no lift of any sort in the Annex). Most guests had to climb one to three flights of stairs. If several tour groups were in the hotel, the front office would divide the prized first-floor rooms among the tours. Each escort could reassign the rooms within his tour if people needed a first-floor room for reasons of health.

These rooming conferences were sometimes tests of character. Most of the escorts were pleasant to work with and were fair and efficient in resolving problems. A few, however, were querulous, abusive and unreasonable in trying to obtain more first-floor rooms at the expense of other tours.

Sometimes an escort of this sort would assemble his tour group around him for support. The escort might bluster demagogically, "This is a luxury tour and our people all are promised first-floor rooms" and a chorus would thunder, "No stairs! No stairs!" Then the hotel personnel would have to show their mettle and stand their ground as courteously as they were able.

A rooming conference which I smile to recall involved a flamboyant and good-natured Italian escort. Perusing the list, he directed a switch in two pairs of roommates ("Put these people together. They alla time complaining."). Then we pointed out that because the hotel was full, a few of his group's rooms were on fourth floor.

"Can Mrs. Palumbo climb three flights of stairs?" we inquired. "Of course!" he replied, with a magnificent, hip-handling gesture. "She ees a BEEG woman."

After the rooming conference, the following order of business was the tour talk. The escort would gather his group in the lobby, where a bellman would instruct them on dining room hours, boat cruises, evening programs, baggage procedures and the like.

Sometimes the escort's personality helped to shape the course of the talk. My notebook records a fellow bellman relating afterward: "I felt like the emcee on a kids show. The escort announces: "He-e-ere's Steve!" and the people all shout in unison: "Hi, Steve!"

Tom Francis does a luggage count with a tour guide.
Courtesy, Sid Francis

My own most memorable tour talk was given to a Japanese group, none of whom spoke English but the escort. I would speak a sentence in English and pause for him to translate into Japanese. After each translation, the group mysteriously broke into uproarious laughter. I would say something unremarkable ("The dining room is down the hall"), the escort would translate, and the people would guffaw. I suspect that the escort was making jocular remarks about the lederhosen which we bellmen wore ("Ridiculous-looking person in shorts and suspenders says, 'The dining room is down the hall.' ").

After finishing the tour talk, the bellmen would distribute keys to the guests. This process sometimes posed another test of character for the escort. If guests protested an upper-floor room, there was nothing to do at this point unless other guests were willing to switch with them.

Escorts could err by being too passive, as well as by being too aggressive. Sometimes officious tourists would inappropriately try to take control. My notebook describes "Mrs. Smith, a brass-faced woman with the air of an army sergeant-major" engineering room changes after the keys were passed out, while the escort stood by silently.

"The Joneses shouldn't go to third floor. The ladies in 104 will be delighted to trade with them," said Mrs. Smith, as she brusquely collared those ladies. They looked anything but delighted.

"We're going as ordered," muttered one, as another member of the group consolingly patted her on the back.

Very occasionally we met an escort who tried to manipulate the staff with bribes. One escort, who'd failed to book Red buses in advance and found none available, demanded of the transportation agent: "All right, who do I pay off?" Another habitually kept dollar bills in his fist and pulled them out, like a magician pulling out handkerchiefs to try to get special favors (e.g. additional first-floor rooms). This may have been standard procedure at some hotels in New York, the escort's home base, but it cut no ice at Many Glacier.

My most memorable escort story dates from a tumultuous evening in 1980. A group of employee-actors was putting on a lobby performance of cuttings from the musical *Sweeney Todd*. This drama has a macabre story line, involving a barber who cuts the throats of his customers, grinds their bodies up and bakes them into pies. The employee-actors probably omitted the most ghoulish parts of the show, but the audience was ill at ease.

Suddenly a hideous scream rang out. A woman came charging down two flights of the main staircase into the lobby.

"Help! Help! He's going to murder me." she cried.

Everybody assumed at first that this commotion was part of the performance, but the woman took refuge behind the front desk and we saw that she was genuinely terrified.

The woman was a tour escort. She had become romantically entangled with the charter bus driver (not a Glacier Park employee) assigned to her tour. That evening she had attempted to break off the relationship. The driver, she said, had then declared that he was going to "put her in a pine box." Moreover, she told us that the driver had a gun in the bus.

We telephoned the rangers for assistance and sent several robust employees to the parking lot to guard the bus. A carload of rangers arrived within a few minutes and briefly arrested the driver. The driver protested that he had been misunderstood, and that his statement had been: "We're both going to end up in pine boxes, anyway." After extensive parlays, the rangers let the driver go, but took the precaution of confiscating his gun.

Amid all the staged and real-life shrieking and running about, the hotel guests were shaken and glad to wander off to bed. I finished my evening bellmen's duties and went off to bed myself.

As a department head, I had a "crow's nest" room on one of the fourth floor balconies high above the lobby. The hotel was quiet, dark, and peaceful as I got beneath the sheets.

Then a woman's scream rang out below me. I can hear it still, protracted and desperate: "AH-H-H-H-H!" I leaped out of bed, assuming that the driver was attacking the escort.

I pulled on my pants and rushed out on the balcony. Looking down,

I saw a hysterical woman leaping about in her nightgown on the balcony on third floor. She was flailing the air overhead with a pillow. She was not the escort and her consternation had nothing to do with the driver. She was an ordinary guest whose room had been invaded by a bat.

Reflecting upon the escorts, I'm impressed again with the power of leaders to influence the mood and temperament of groups. For good or ill, the conduct and character of leaders tends to impress itself on the lives of those for whom they are responsible and to shape their characters, too.

A winter at Many Glacier
Tracey Wiese
(Many Glacier Hotel 1999-2000)

Sometimes, just getting across the Swiftcurrent Falls Bridge against the howling wind was the toughest part of the day. A few times I had to go hand-over-hand across the bridge rail just to keep upright. Wind defines Many Glacier in the winter time.

My husband and I spent the winter of 1999-2000 at Many Glacier. I was the hotel winter keeper and he the National Park Service ranger. It was a mild winter as far as snow depth and cold temperatures, but the wind was truly an experience. Near our cabin we had a maximum of four feet of snow, but the wind got hold of it and blew it around so that often there was just a skiff in front of the cabin and about 12 feet piled up at the back. On really windy days we could literally watch the drift grow until it reached the peak of the roof.

Often times the bridge over Swiftcurrent Falls would be blown free of snow and we would walk, carrying our skis, to the other side of the bridge. Between the winter keeper's cabin (Chalet H) and the bridge sits the gearjammer dorm (Chalet I) which is perched on the brink of the falls, taking the full force of the wind as it drops off the mountains and speeds across the lakes. We referred to the few yards in front of the jammer dorm as "the washing machine."

The wind hit that building and ricocheted off causing the air, and anyone caught in it, to bounce every which direction. Carrying skis was like having long, skinny sails for the wind to grab and I felt like a rag doll bouncing back and forth. Watching each other go through the "washing machine" was always good for a laugh and almost as much fun as doing the agitation cycle oneself.

Early in the winter season I wandered all over the hotel learning my way around the labyrinth of floors and rooms. I also made a concerted effort to check out every weird noise that I heard while all the lights were still working so that none of them would come back to haunt me later in the dark of winter. Wind vibrating the shutters or rattling a loose board can take on a

Snowdrifts to third floor rooms at Many Glacier Hotel require the building to be dug out before opening each summer to avoid meltwater from damaging the interior. Ray Kinley photo, John Hagen collection

whole new dimension when wandering around the old hotel in the gloom of a gray winter day. Usually, after checking the hotel to make sure that the warm room was still warm (where the computers and phone system are stored) and that the shutters were in place and that no corner of the roof had blown off, we would continue on skiing.

The wildlife in Many Glacier is just as amazing in the winter as it is in the summer, and even when we didn't see the animals themselves their tracks were left behind in the snow to let us know who was in the neighborhood. We got to know the travel patterns of the wolverines that frequented the valley and a couple of times I was lucky enough to spot one.

One of my favorite wildlife sightings was not outside at all, but inside the hotel. I was walking down the darkened basement hallway and just where the light shines down the stairs from the lobby to the entrance to Heidi's Ice Cream Parlor, a pine marten darted across the floor and disappeared into a utility closet whose door had come slightly ajar.

It was weeks later when I met the pine marten again. This time it was in the electrical room, walking on the pipes that hang from the ceiling. I made my best pine marten imitation sounds and it stayed and watched me for several minutes trying to figure out what I was saying before disappearing into the ductwork behind the walls. The hotel must have been like a giant playground to the little marten, who left signs of having checked out nearly every floor.

Many Glacier in the winter time is a world apart from its summer identity. No hikers or horses, no traffic or tourists, just the sound of the wind and the tracks of the resident wildlife as they eke out a living in the cold and windy valley. I feel truly lucky to have had a chance to experience a Many Glacier winter.

Flooding in Glacier can happen at strange times and while it's typical in early June, at the beginning of the tourist season, this scene at Many Glacier Hotel occurred in November 2006 due to a late season storm.

Courtesy, U.S. Geological Service

Chapter 8

Glacier's dragons: floods and fire

High water in June 1964
Malcolm R. Campbell
(Many Glacier Hotel 1963-64)

Before first light on the morning it begins, dorm supervisor Ray Kinley is shouting like a banshee down the hall of the Many Glacier Hotel dormitory.

"The hotel is flooding. Get your lazy selves out of dreamland, gentlemen."

We step outside into the cold rain, pull our coats around us, and follow him down the long steps to the main door of the hotel. Hotel manager Ian B. Tippet and the professional staff are in the lobby already, haggard and barely recognizable in old clothes, bathed in the unreal glow of flames from the stone fireplace.

The power is out, the phones are out, the water is out, except for the lake which is in—a living creature from the Lucerne and St. Moritz rooms past the lake level guest rooms, down Stagger Alley to the laundry room.

There aren't many of us, the skeleton crew that arrived several weeks ago to shake out the winter cobwebs before opening day. The work was ahead of schedule, until now.

We rescue braided rugs, heavy when wet, and beds, mattresses, chests of drawers, pictures off the walls, the piano from the St. Moritz Room stage. We move slowly and methodically in the cold and the wet, and the gray light.

Hypothermia is a real danger. Tippet is everywhere at once, moving purposefully and quickly, as is his custom, and in spite of the protests, he regularly sends us upstairs into the lobby to be wrapped in blankets and force-fed hot coffee.

We are constructing history. Reports are coming in, well-intentioned and mostly true, that conditions at Lake McDonald, Two Medicine, and St. Mary are worse than those here in the Swiftcurrent Valley, and that through a wide, 14-county area, towns, bridges, livestock, dams, the Great Northern mainline, and families, whose faces we'll see later in the newspapers, are down, out, broken, undercut, missing, ruined and swept away. "Nature turns outlaw" the *Missoulian* headline says.

As June 8 flows into June 9 and 10, a discovery is made, and that is that mortal men have no words left for describing the scope of events such as these, for they have already spent their words on small things.

The lake level rooms are explosions of mud. Tippet wastes no time mobilizing cleanup and repair crews that often work past meals and sleep. He looks tired but attacks each task with single-minded precision and no complaint. He keeps asking us if we're all right.

The road between Many Glacier and Babb is washed out above Lake Sherburne. The only uncontaminated water available comes from the artesian well down at the caretaker's cabin. The lakes are brown and high. The county health department flies a nurse into our isolated compound with enough typhoid serum for everyone. Most of the staff is at East Glacier, the hotel company headquarters, waiting for the roads to open and wondering, as we are wondering, if there will be a 1964 season.

At night, we sit on the front porch of the dorm talking to Ray Kinley while he tells fishing stories and ties flies. He remembers other floods, but this is the worst.

"Tippet will get us open," Ray says. "He's the one who can do it, don't you know."

When the hotel opens with a bankers' convention on June 18, I exchange my sodden, mud-caked dungarees for lederhosen and a white shirt, and prepare to carry luggage, clean ashtrays and pronounce the names of glaciers and mountains on demand.

I walk into Tippet's office. "The buses are here, sir."

He looks at me over the tops of his glasses and says, "Very good, Mr. Campbell."

Tippet is tall and lanky and when he sits at his desk, he leans out over his work and more or less envelops it. Today he is impeccably dressed, ready once again to assume his duties as the perfect host.

The great flood of 1964 at East Glacier
Howard Olson
(Glacier Park Lodge 1959-65)

I worked part-time or full-time from 1958 to 1965, most of the time for Cy Stevenson as camp engineer in East Glacier. Working for Cy was an experience in itself. He was very good at organizing maintenance projects.

The flood of 1964 stands out as one of the more harrowing experiences. The first week in June we had about 12 inches of wet snow and that was followed by eight inches of rain. The damage was immense to the whole area, roads, and bridges washed out and people drowned

In East Glacier, the flood destroyed the reservoir that provided water for the hotel and town. The force of the flood waters changed the flow of the water so that the river diverted around the reservoir. This caused the new channel to follow the path of the water main (a 10-inch diameter pipe) and destroy approximately 100 yards of the water line.

Fortunately, there was a small stream of water that intersected the water line at a point where the pipe was intact. We decided that it might be possible to cap the water line at that point and connect it to a hose and pump the water from the stream into the 10-inch line.

Cy was able to rent a big diesel irrigation pumper from a company in Cut Bank. We made a slight excavation in the stream bed so that the water would pool and then placed our suction hose into this pool. The output from the pumper was another hose that we screwed into the makeshift cap on the main water line. We ran the diesel pumper 24 hours a day.

It was necessary to draft workers from the hotel to help to keep watch on the pumper. I would instruct them as to what they should do if something went wrong (mainly watch the gauges) and make sure the intake hose didn't suck air. We had this temporary system going for at least one month while the contractor repaired the reservoir and water main. The stream that we tapped for our water supply was almost dried up by the time repairs were finished.

The chlorinator was downstream from our temporary service so we injected a strong dose of chlorine into the line to keep everybody healthy. After the initial hookup to the pumper, we opened the main and flushed out some of the debris that had gotten into the line. Nevertheless, my assistant and I spent the majority of our time for the next two weeks cleaning strainers and flushing water lines.

Fortunately, the first convention at the hotel opening was a Jaycee convention. They were a partying group and quite tolerant of conditions. I remember getting a call to one of the rooms in the Annex and after cleaning the faucet screen, I apologized to him for the inconvenience and he said, "Don't worry about it, I've been drunk for two days and I don't need water anyway."

The fire of 1936
Ray Kinley
(Many Glacier Hotel 1919, 1922-77)

August 31, 1936, was my 45th birthday. That evening, I had been guiding a fishing party. For a couple of weeks a fire had burned on the slopes of Heavens Peak, away on the west side of the park. The west wind carried ash and debris up over the Continental Divide which sifted down all over to the Swiftcurrent Valley. Black ash floated on the surface of the water like burned newspaper, but it didn't hurt the fishing. The sun was a dull orange ball, all day long.

I got back to the hotel around 9 p.m. I had two lakefront rooms in those days, one for me, and one for my fishing customers. As usual, the rooms were full of employees. They would come by in the evening to bum box lunches which were left behind by the customers. Sometimes I wheedled extra lunches out of my fishing parties by telling them that "a group of very poor Indians" had been by begging for food.

I was going to shave before I went on duty as night clerk. I walked over to my window to pull the blinds down. Far away in the darkness, I saw two ominous glowing red spots, like dragon eyes. They were spot fires, high on the Continental Divide near Swiftcurrent Pass. The Heavens Peak fire had jumped the fire lines and blown over into our valley.

A few moments later, the telephone rang. It was Omar Ellis, the hotel manager.

"Ray, is there anybody down there with you?" he demanded.

"Yes, Mr. Ellis; there's quite a number of boys in my room, and some girls are next door," I answered.

"Well, send all the boys upstairs to their fire stations." Mr. Ellis ordered. "And send the girls to the dormitory."

The fire crews got their equipment. Some hauled the hose carts out of the sheds and connected the hoses to the hydrants. Others took down the standpipe hoses which hung in the hallways of the hotel, and ran them out onto the lakeside balconies.

As the Heavens Peak forest fire approaches Many Glacier Hotel, staff test and practise with firefighting equipment.
Courtesy, Donald Wheeler

The fire came with a rush. It blew down the valley from Swiftcurrent Pass to the hotel in less than an hour. A high wind was rattling all the windows. It was like the exhaust from a blast furnace. All around there was an eerie orange glow, as the fire reflected off the clouds of smoke overhead, and off the surface of the lake.

The wind shot flaming pine knots across the lake, like missiles from a catapult. They ignited trees on the lawn behind the hotel. Flying embers rained down on the building, but the hose crews doused them all.

The fire burned around Swiftcurrent Lake on either side of us. Across the water, Mount Altyn looked like a city lit up at night. The burning pine

Smoke rises from the August 1936 Heavens Peak forest fire just before it jumps Swiftcurrent Pass and begins its descent toward Many Glacier Hotel.

Courtesy, Donald Wheeler

trees were like street lights. Four of the old chalets on the mountainside were burned as the fire swept through. The other chalets by the falls were spared.

At the Swiftcurrent campground, the park service recently had built a fine [tent] museum. The rangers tried to protect it with hoses, but the heat was too intense. They had no more than gotten the hoses out when they had to give up and run for their lives. They piled into a car and never stopped until they got to the entrance station.

The fire destroyed the museum, and also burned down most of the cabins at Swiftcurrent. Some of the cabins, however, survived. The fire was moving so fast that it traveled in swaths and left objects unburned in between them. The wind blew the fire from cabin to cabin like a blowtorch. The heat was so great that the cast iron sinks were melted into odd shapes, like taffy. Close beside them, other cabins were left intact.

The guests at Many Glacier Hotel were evacuated in buses. Some protested and had to be compelled to go. The last bus left in the nick of time, as the fire was burning along the road.

The employees mostly were nonchalant, although one girl went into hysterics. When the boys weren't putting water on the fire, they were putting it on each other. When the danger was past, the boys trooped into the lobby, and stripped to their under shorts. They all were wringing wet. They wrapped themselves up in Hudson Bay blankets, and sat in a circle around the fireplace. It looked like an Indian council.

Next morning, the air was completely still. The smoke from the charred trees rose straight up all over the valley, like thin black pencils. There was an odor of burning pine. I can't describe the feeling of waking up to burned-over desolation, where it had been so fresh and green. It was as if we were in Dante-land—the Inferno, don't you know.

The great flood of 1975 at Rising Sun
Dick Bridegroom
(Rising Sun Motor Inn 1972-75)

The great flood of 1975 occurred just as the season was about to start. Employees were coming in, the store had just opened, rooms were being rented and the campground was open. My recollection was that it was a cool spring and winter snow was about normal. And then the rains came and came and came.

It rained for several days straight; Rose Creek started to rise moving from one channel to another channel. The creek was no longer a creek, but a raging river. By about 11 p.m. the river broke out of its newest channel and started a brand new course, this time going right through the camp store and new motel, across the parking lot and surrounded the coffee shop, creating an island. The employee cafeteria and recreation hall took on water and filled with stone and sand.

Dick Bridegroom

During the night we lost our phone, our electricity, our heat, our drinkable water supply and our plumping. The refrigerators and freezers, of course, didn't work and we couldn't cook on the stoves.

For most of us this was something new. I spent the night in the coffee shop stranded there when the river broke. By morning, when we could see what was going on, I was able to leave our new island and cross the new lake to high ground. Employees were dumbfounded and couldn't do much more than shake their heads with disbelief.

By late morning, it was decided that the employees were going to fight back and try to force the river back into its channel. We didn't have sandbags or shovels or picks or axes, so we decided to use our hands and dig out rocks and tree branches to start making a dam to force the water back into its channel. This was followed by dirt, sand and stone. By late afternoon, the river was back in its channel. We had five bridges at Rising Sun before the flood; by the end of the flood, all five bridges were gone. Going-to-the-Sun Road was impassable; the road fell into the river.

The first thing that we had to do to recover was to get some drinkable water. Luckily, we had a Glacier old-timer with us, Harold Hawley. He knew where a spring was down the road and a bunch of us went down and collected barrels full of water to bring back to the employees. Food was the next thing; we didn't have a stove to cook on, but we were able to barbecue and heat water over a fire. Since the freezers were out and things were starting to thaw, we were able to eat things that were meant to be sold to customers. So, there was some good out of the experience.

One of the funny things that came out of the flood was that the camp store manager was giving away food to the kitchen that he had in the coolers so it wouldn't be wasted, but what most people don't know was that he also was doing the paperwork to transfer the cost of the food from the camp store to the kitchen. In other words, passing the buck.

The flood of 1975 was an experience for everyone who was there. I will never forget it. Every time I go back to Rising Sun Motor Inn, I think of it and still see the damage that the river did. I can still see our dam that we built, the new channels the flood created, the remains from some of the old bridges that were never fixed, piles of dirt and rock that came out of the camp store and coffee shop, but most of all I remember these stories and the good times that I had that summer.

Trapper Creek Fire 2003: A lookout's view
Christine Baker
(Rising Sun Motor Inn 1970-72; park ranger 1973-85;
Belly River ranger volunteer 1986-87; fire lookout 1988-2004)

Being back at the Swiftcurrent fire lookout after a 10-year hiatus at Huckleberry lookout was like heaven in 2001. Oh, I loved my time at Huckleberry—the bears, the North Fork, the fire challenges—but I almost felt like it was retirement for me to be back at Swiftcurrent. Let the North Fork lookouts do all the heavy work—I'd just look out over all this beautiful, nonflammable scenery all summer and interpret for visitors.

Wrong! The 2003 summer would set me right. It would prove to be one for the history books, and would show us all once more just why those hard-bitten old park planners had decided back in 1936 to build a lookout atop—of all places—Swiftcurrent Mountain.

I drove home for lieu days [days off in lieu of paid overtime] that hot July weekend, all the while trying to ignore the nagging feeling in the pit of my stomach that I really shouldn't be taking leave. Conditions were heating up in Glacier. Temperatures were high and fuel moistures were abysmally low.

I had this wild card hunch that I might not be home again for a long, long time. It was nothing I could put into words or even share with my husband Bob, but I found myself boxing up double rations for my next pack trip. I didn't really know why—I just did it. As it turned out, those would prove to be the last four days off I would have for the rest of the summer.

When I returned to Swiftcurrent, Flattop Mountain was puffing here and there, but the smoke just wasn't that impressive. The lightning storm had planted its seeds, but nothing much was showing yet. I settled in, put a little extra care into my afternoon scans, and turned my attention to my revised lesson plans for *Beowulf*.

There was no mistaking it when the Trapper Fire decided to make its move. I was looking right at it when it did. That wimpy white column suddenly grew tall, turned to brown, then black. Then it was wider and moving. I remember calling the Fire Cache and trying to sound calm, controlled—but feeling that this was pretty darn outrageous and that they'd better get on the stick and do something.

"It's crowning!" I remember saying, and it was ... and moving fast.

A crowning fire is a big concern, kind of like that magic number "7" on the California earthquake scales. I kept telling myself not to panic. After all, this was in the middle of Flattop Mountain—there's just not as much that a fire can really hurt there.

Swiftcurrent lookout. Christine Baker photo

Granite Park Chalet was a concern, but the fire movement was toward the northeast, and Granite looked OK, at first. My real concern was Swiftcurrent Valley, and making sure nothing remotely resembling a spark would ever touch an east side fir tree. What was happening on Flattop was huge, but that fire had lots of bare rock and a couple of glaciers here and there to cross before it could even touch the east side. Surely it couldn't cross the Continental Divide?

I can remember using the word "surreal" a lot in my journal that afternoon. It didn't take too long before my vista towards the west was nothing but amber billows of smoke and embers. Visibility deteriorated to nothing, and I began coughing from the intense smoke.

I wasn't sure whether I should be concerned about that so I soaked a bandanna in water and took to breathing through it to filter some of the soot. That got old fast, so I discarded the bandanna and just coughed and took my chances.

By this time I figured the fire could be anywhere below me. I knew Chris Burke down at the Granite Park Chalet was moving fast to get hoses and sprinklers operating and that meant the fire was probably also moving southeast. I could only imagine what kind of chaos was going on down at Granite right now.

Many Glacier personnel were all ears as they listened to west side radio traffic. They needed to know just where the fire was and the potential threat to the valley. Time for them was crucial. Once the fire was on their side of the rock, the clock would be ticking. I couldn't tell them a whole lot because I was in a sea of smoke and flying debris. Bob Adams and Rachel Jenkins hunkered down to monitor their radios at Many Glacier Ranger Station all night, should an evacuation become necessary.

Night fell, and finally I could see the fire appear through the smoke as a thousand points of flame and torching trees. It was like looking at the Milky Way on a clear evening. So humbling. The sheer area of land that the fire had traveled over since that small white puff of smoke the afternoon before was enough to inspire awe. I remember just staring a lot in unbelief.

Sleep wasn't an option. This was history, and I was privileged to have a front row seat. I cradled my head on and off on my pillow just marveling at what was before me. My beautiful Glacier was growing, changing, undergoing those epochal upheavals that we so blithely spout are natural and destined, but to actually have them happen on our watch are so difficult and foreign.

All night I watched that glow. At times I wrestled with whether I should call Many Glacier, but the glow didn't travel, and I knew the wee hours and higher humidity of the morning would calm the beast of the Trapper Fire.

About 2:30 a.m. I saw four distinct spot fires north of me and east of the Divide. They were pinpoints, but they were there—fires on the east side. Still, their location was so remote, and they would have huge distances of rock to cross before they could ever ignite anything flammable. I sat glued to them until at last they disappeared. Gone? I couldn't be sure. But by 5 a.m. I felt more secure.

A month later, after weeks of watching the Trapper Fire have its way with my memories of Flattop Mountain and the Highline Trail, I hiked down from my lookout for the season, heading for a way-too-soon end to my summer and a begrudging beginning of another school year. I regaled in the switchbacks down to the tree line, gazing out over the pristine beauty of the Divide that we all have come to love no matter from what perspective we view it.

But then I came to the trees—those beautiful firs I have come to love—my friends and companions on my ascents and descents of Swiftcurrent Mountain—the ones that frame Heavens Peak in all my photos and that my kids have learned to take for granted. They weren't there.

Instead I saw blackened ghosts and charred ground cover. I hiked through a lunar landscape that I knew was both natural order and devastation.

I thrilled and mourned all at once. I don't think I will ever feel that again.

The evacuation of the McDonald Valley
Mary Grace Severson Galvin
(Lake McDonald summer resident 1936-)

On July 24, 2003, a Glacier Park ranger came knocking on the door of our in-holder's cabin just north of Lake McDonald Lodge. We were told that the valley was being evacuated. The Robert Fire was threatening West Glacier and the western entrance to Going-to-the-Sun Road.

When the ranger came, I was at the cabin with my daughter and two grandchildren. My husband Jim and my son-in-law were away on a hike in another part of the park. The evacuation order was mandatory and urgent, however, and we had to leave the valley without them.

We filled our small car with as many keepsakes as we could pack in it—not many, since we had to transport four people and a dog. Our neighbors, Mark and Linda Kuhr, were just leaving also, and they graciously shared some room in their bigger vehicle. Then we drove to the refuge of our Kalispell home.

Jim and Mary Galvin
Courtesy, Mary Galvin

Two hours later, Jim and our son-in-law returned from their hike to find the road blocked at West Glacier. A ranger told them that we had evacuated safely. Jim called on his cell phone and described the scene beyond the gate as "very, very scary—just black and red."

While we were in Kalispell, we volunteered at Flathead County's Emergency Co-ordination Center. There, the United Way provided evacuees with food and shelter. We were glad to be able to help some of the hundreds of travelers far from home who were displaced by the fires.

On July 27, we were thrilled to have the evacuation order lifted. We found sprinklers pouring water over our cabin. Glacier's superintendent Mick Holm had instructed district ranger Charlie Logan to sprinkle the in-holders' homes. We were deeply grateful.

Two weeks later, on Aug. 10, the Robert Fire blew up again. That night we were in bed when the evacuation order arrived with a knocking at our door. With no time to spare, we grabbed what we could and flew down the road. To our horror, we could see the fire raging down Howe Ridge toward our end of the lake. In some locations, the fire was cascading down the ridge wiping out every tree in its path, with the lake the only reason it was stopped. Kelly's Camp, across the lake from us, was greatly at risk. The firefighters did burnouts there to save the camp. More burnouts stabilized the fire. Deo gratias.

On Aug. 16, Jim and I were able to return to our cabin to stay. Needless to say, we did not bring back any of the treasures we had removed in

The Robert Fire threatens West Glacier, as seen from the north end of Lake McDonald in the summer of 2003.   Courtesy, Mary Galvin

the evacuation, only food and my laptop computer. At that point, only the cabins right around the lodge were safe to inhabit. Things were still too spooky to allow folks to return to the head of the lake or Kelly's Camp. It was very smoky, and we did not go outside any more than we had to.

The *De Smet* (the excursion launch) had been hired to carry firemen to Kelly's Camp each day. On the first day, the smoke on the lake was so thick that the *De Smet* got lost in a white out. Later they obtained a compass, so that they could make the trip without getting lost.

By early September, the fire had burned down to Trout Lake and all around the west flank of Mount Stanton. The fear was that it would climb between Stanton and Mount Vaught, and then sweep down across the Going-to-the-Sun Road.

On Sept. 8, however, the miracle that we had all been praying for arrived in the form of rain. We had about five hours of steady showers and accumulated three-quarters of an inch. It doesn't sound like much, but it had me dancing barefoot in the grass. The rain, though not a fire season ending event, decisively slowed the advance of the fire.

We unwrapped our boat from the space blankets it had been bundled into since the fires had started, and charged up the lake to see the big burn near Apgar. It was a devastating sight. It looked like a war zone. Miles of destroyed forest ran right down to the lake. It was the saddest boat trip we have ever taken.

After that we pulled our boat out of the lake and stored it for the winter. That was truly a season-ending event.

Evacuating the lodges: a general manager's diary (2003)
Cindy Ognjanov
(President and general manager of Glacier Park, Inc.)

July 23 – 10 p.m.: The phone is ringing—must be an emergency, otherwise they wouldn't be calling me this late. It's Colin Burrows, the manager at Many Glacier Hotel. He says, "There's a ranger in the lobby telling everyone we are under a voluntary evacuation order."

I tell him I'll find out what's going on and call him back. I hang up and before I can dial the phone is ringing again. This time it's Clint Davis from Swiftcurrent Motor Inn telling the same story.

I hang up and call the east side district ranger. Sure enough, the Trapper Creek Fire has come across Swiftcurrent Pass. If it decides to run ... well, anything could happen. I call Colin and Clint back and tell them to notify each guest individually that there is no immediate danger, but you never know. A handful of guests decide to leave.

July 23 – 11 p.m.: After numerous phone calls between my hotel managers and the park service, I call each of my division directors and tell them to come to my house immediately for a meeting. Within 10 minutes they are all there and around the dining room table we formulate an evacuation plan.

July 24 – 1 a.m.: I try to get a couple hours sleep. We will all meet at 4 a.m. so that we can be at Many and Swift by daylight. I call both hotel managers and tell them to do complimentary continental breakfasts in the lobby and be prepared to evacuate.

July 24 – 5:30 a.m.: We arrive and everyone knows where to go and what to do. I go to the front desk at Many and try to help with the checkout, which is already in progress. The warehouse trucks have backed to the kitchen and the crews are loading all of the perishable food from the walk-ins and freezers. The gift shop crew is also methodically packing—as soon as they are done loading the food, we will put all this in the truck, as well. The maintenance guys have been asked to take down all of the paintings.

July 24 – 6:30 a.m.: I go to Swiftcurrent. The same process is happening there. These two groups of people are a very efficient team.

July 24 – 8 a.m.: I go to the ranger station to receive an update on the status of the fire. It's not good. It is still moving, albeit slowly. I heard references to Heavens Peak [1936] —scary!

July 24 – 9 a.m.: All of the guests at Many and Swift have gone. I have called an all-employee meeting at Many. I give them the latest report on the fire and ask them to please go to their rooms and pack their belongings, then proceed immediately to East Glacier. I give them a time deadline to report to East. We insist they sign out when they leave the room and then sign back in when they get to East. My HR team is waiting for them at East.

July 24 – 9:30 a.m.: Same meeting at Swiftcurrent. Everyone is leaving—as we leave Swift we can see the fire in the pass. I am very pleased we have gotten everyone out safely.

July 24 – 11 a.m.: My cellphone has a message on it, so I stop on my way back to East and call my office. Unbelievable—the Robert Fire on the west side has exploded. We have until 3:00 this afternoon to evacuate Village Inn and Lake McDonald Lodge.

July 24 – 11:45 a.m.: I have notified everyone about what is happening on the west side. We unload one of the warehouse trucks, grab three more vans and off we go to Lake McDonald. Thank goodness for cellphones. While my husband is driving, I am on the phone trying to find out exactly what is happening. No one seems to know too much—only that there are fires out of control and on the move.

July 24 – 1:30 p.m.: I arrive at Village Inn. Thank heaven Lynn seems to have everything under control. I leave her to finish and go to Lake McDonald Lodge. Most of the guests are gone and all of the employees have started to pack. All of the directors start loading the truck with food, retail items and paintings. I call another all-employee meeting.

July 24 – 2:30 p.m.: I ask all of the Lake McDonald employees to do the same procedure as I asked of the Many and Swift folks. Even as I am talking to them, I am asking myself where in the world we are going to put all these people.

The Robert Fire burns toward the north end of Lake McDonald in the summer of 2003, threatening homes and accommodations. Courtesy, Mary Galvin

July 24 – 3:30 p.m.: We are past our deadline, but are not quite done—we have a couple more buses of employees to load. We also have five Red buses with no drivers and we can't find the keys. A bit of panic sets in, but we find the keys (in the trunk of my car). By 4 p.m. we are leaving Lake McDonald. As we leave, ash is falling like snow.

July 24 – 6 p.m.: We have arrived back at East Glacier and what a sight—there are employees everywhere. The cafeteria is overflowing, but what a beautiful spread the chefs have put out for all of these "fire refugees." The HR gals have done an amazing job of finding space for everyone to sleep. The Moccasin Room is fast filling up with mattresses. A tent city has sprung up over by the jammer dorm. The back lawn has its share of sleeping bags. Unbelievably, every single employee showed up and now they are all anxious to know what is going on.

July 24 – 7 p.m.: One more all-employee meeting. There are probably 500 people at this meeting. I report what I know (which isn't much) and then answer many, many questions.

July 24 – 10 p.m.: I am finally at home and can't believe what has happened today. I am sure that never before have four hotels (on two sides of the park) had to be evacuated on the same day because of two different forest fires.

Over the next few days emotions ran high. We had a big outdoor party and barbecue on the front lawn at East Glacier. We did everything we could to keep the employees happy and occupied. I knew we would get to reopen soon and I didn't want to lose them. Sure enough, two days later we were able to go back to Many Glacier and Swiftcurrent and we did so without losing a single employee.

The Lake McDonald and Village Inn folks weren't as lucky. It took 12 days before we could reopen, but were we ever happy when we were able to do so. For all the employees, it was like going "home." Five days later the Robert Fire burned its way the entire length of the lake in a matter of a few hours and we started the evacuation process all over again.

What a gut-wrenching time that was.

When we reopened Lake McDonald and Village Inn 10 days later, we did so with one-third the normal staff. Many of the young people decided to stay where they were rather than go back and take the chance of another evacuation. It was OK. The heavy smoke kept occupancy at an all-time low for the next four weeks, so we managed with our small group of employees. God bless them all.

[Editors note: The summer of 2003 was the worst fire season in Glacier in recent memory. Lightning strikes in July touched off the Trapper Creek Fire in the upper McDonald Valley, the Wedge Creek Fire just outside Glacier in the North Fork, and the Wolf Gun Fire in the Livingston Range. Meanwhile, backfires were set to save West Glacier and Apgar from the Robert Fire. It wasn't until heavy rains in September that the fires were snuffed.]

The Red Eagle Fire of 2006
Don Loeffler
(Glacier Park Hotel, Sun Camp, Many Glacier Hotel 1940-42, 1946-48)

The Blackfeet Highway between Cut Bank campground and St. Mary had been closed by the fire authorities, so we had to detour to Browning from Glacier Park Lodge, where we had been staying. The detour took us north on the Duck Lake road to Babb. We passed the Chewing Blackbones Blackfeet Indian campground, which had been completely taken over by firefighters.

This incident camp was a complete city with dozens of tents, food handling vans, first aid units, shower and toilet units, and even a media tent station for the fourth estate. Space was cordoned off for the water dropping helicopters.

Evacuation was proceeding at St. Mary Lodge and the highway to the south was closed at that point. The sheriff said the fire had jumped Highway 89 on Hudson Bay Divide and was burning eastbound into the reservation. The asphalt and even the guard rails were on fire.

We drove west on Going-to-the-Sun Road to Rising Sun Motor Inn. All the while, we hoped our long-standing reservations would still be intact. They were not. After realizing a computer error had been made, the reservation clerk made a room available in the motel—complete with a front row view of the fire. By this time the forest across the lake was burning intensely and presented a real threat if the firestorm leaped over the narrows to our side of the lake. A change in wind direction could cause this to happen.

While we watched the flames advance, a helicopter arrived in front of us. We worried it might be for evacuation purposes. It took off almost as soon as it landed and went down to the lake for a bagful of water to dump on the fire. By now the fire was advancing up the northwest slope of Divide Mountain. I went over to a wall-mounted fire extinguisher to make sure it was in good working order. It was. My wife Barbara said, "Thank goodness. I feel so much safer now."

Fortunately the wind died down and the fire did not jump the lake. We departed the next morning and drove over Logan Pass with the sun partially obscured by the smoke—giving the landscape an eerie cast.

[Editors note: The Red Eagle Lake fire was discovered on July 28, 2006, and roared eight miles out of the valley to the south side of St. Mary Lake. By late August the fire was largely controlled, thanks in part to several drenching rains. It was mapped at nearly 35,000 acres, about half of which was inside the park and the rest outside.]

Much has changed at Lake McDonald Lodge, but the atmosphere remains as homey and inviting as the day it opened.
Ray Djuff photo

Chapter 9

Lake McDee

Mama Frase of Lake McD
Carol Lindsay
(Lake McDonald Hotel 1952; Glacier Park Hotel 1955)

Some years ago I saw a newspaper story about the restoration of Lake McDonald Lodge. The architects claimed that the renovation was carried out with attention to the smallest detail, from the latches on the bathroom stalls to the weathered rocks in the dining room fireplace.

But I beg to differ. To be authentic, they would have had to resurrect one of the hostelry's most colorful characters—Mama Frase. In her heyday in the 1950s, Mrs. Frase personally hired or fired every employee assigned to Lake McDonald.

Who could forget Mama? You didn't need her picture, nor would you want one. She had only two characteristics worth noting—her size and an absolute knowledge of who she was, but that was enough.

She was built like Texas, her native state: colossal in every aspect except height. Her fleshy layers, tightly corseted, tended to escape unfettered in her limbs.

From her throne room, the dining room, this dowager queen greeted her affluent guests year after year as members of an exclusive club reserved for the rich and famous. How many others could command a staff of hundreds in a setting renowned the world over?

Mama Frase
Courtesy, Joanie Fandle Lyons

Mama had two weaknesses as far as I could see. One was a singular devotion to the head cook, and the other was a myopic attachment to her niece, who was employed as the dining room hostess. The hostess's long, dark hair and olive complexion were ideally suited to her role as an Indian princess [hostess, in appropriate costume]. Her lovely facial features, however, were usually overpowered by heavy pancake makeup and layers of mascara, while her southern drawl was evident the moment she spoke the words, "Good morning, y'all."

No matter; she could do no wrong in Mama's eyes.

Toward the rest of us, Mama was a tyrant—a female General Patton. Woe to the hapless waitress or busboy who displeased the aging monarch. Termination of employment was often swift and brutal: "The bus leaves for Belton in half an hour and I want you on it."

A withering stare from Mama could upset the delicate balancing act of the most accomplished waiter, sending a tray and its contents clattering to the floor. This might set in motion a dissonant counterpart to the romantic violin concerto in the dining room, as the bearer collapsed in tears in the kitchen.

Cleanup under Mama's watchful eye often lasted until 10:30 p.m., throwing evening rendezvous plans of the college-aged staff into chaos. We were called to account for every errant crumb on a chair or fingerprint on a salt or pepper shaker.

The summer parade of tourists continues. New faces greet guests in the storied, old lodge, but when a fully stacked tray rattles to the floor in an otherwise peaceful dining room, the ghost of a corpulent dictator smiles. And I remember Mama.

The fire brigade
Bonham Cross
(Lake McDonald Hotel 1939-41)

The forest fires in the summer of 2000 brought back memories of Lake McDonald Hotel's firefighters during my years there.

Male employees made up two fire brigades. One team operated a portable pump on large wheels called the P-stream, powered by a gasoline engine. Its range was limited by the reach of its hose to either nearby Snyder Creek or the shore of Lake McDonald. Hose Company No. 1 would connect its hose to one of the hydrants near the hotel and its adjoining cabins. It produced powerful water pressure, sending its stream a great distance.

I cannot recall how often drills took place, but it seemed to be often. Team members always knew before the day and hour of the fire drill, usually at 2 p.m. on a Friday. However, we had to wait for the alarm to sound before learning the location of the make-believe fire. When the alarm sounded, team captains rushed to the hotel entrance to obtain this information, then shouted its location as they ran to join their team members.

This was a timed event and each team fought to be the first to squirt water near the target. The P-stream's efforts were always notable, creating

Lake McDonald Hotel employees douse one another during a 1941 fire drill.
Bonham Cross photo

a sensation as we ran the hose to the nearest source of water, then push-pulled the wheeled pump as close as possible to the "fire."

The usual scenario was to send our rather weak stream in the direction of the other team while they were making every effort to dowse us. This turned out to be great entertainment for an audience of guests, tourists and fellow employees. Both teams became thoroughly soaked, and any team member who failed to appear was located and promptly dunked into Lake McDonald.

This event was reassuring, I think, to people using the hotel, its adjoining cabins and other buildings. I was never aware of a fire having taken place there.

During my tenure at the hotel, I used to go with Bob Cleland as he took garbage down to the incinerator, located south of Apgar. We could see not only the incinerator, but could get occasional glimpses of black bears on their way to sample any spilled food. The forest at that time looked like shrubbery because the trees came up only as far as our waists. Now, of course, it is a thriving forest again.

I missed a fire near the hotel in 1942 because I was in the process of joining the air corps at that time. The P-stream extinguished a fire, which started across the road at the laundry beyond the reach of hydrant hoses. Snyder Creek was close by and provided plenty of water for the portable pump to extinguish the fire before it spread.

When I heard about it, I was sure sorry not to have been there. Now, I always cross my fingers when I hear about forest fires in Montana.

Rough ride on the rails
Mark Hufstetler
(Lake McDonald Lodge 1978-83, National Park Service 1987-88)

Since its earliest days Glacier has had an affinity with the railroad that traces the park's southern border. The old Great Northern Railway built most of Glacier's hotels and provided sleek, opulent passenger trains to carry visitors to the Treasure State. The railway tradition has continued throughout the years, and today Amtrak's Empire Builder still shines the Burlington Northern Santa Fe's rails through Marias Pass, stopping at Glacier Park Station and West Glacier to unload eager vacationers.

Many hotel company employees use the Empire Builder to travel to Glacier. It's a link to and from a far removed outside world. Most Lake McDee employees have realized this, but a few have gotten carried away.

The life of a hobo can sound pretty exciting after six days of slaving away at Lake McDonald Lodge, and the freight trains headed to exotic places rumble along just a few miles away. So one summer day in 1982, Joe and Mark decided to break away. Bellman's uniforms were exchanged for tramp's clothes and the duo headed for the freight yards. After hitchhiking to Whitefish, Joe and Mark spent an afternoon at the yards interviewing professional transients. They received lots of advice: carry a big knife, don't let the railroad cops beat you up, block the door of your freight car open (if it should slam shut, you'd be locked inside). The perils, though, failed to shake their resolve.

The next evening found them back in Whitefish, nervously watching as an eastbound freight pulled into town. A flatcar hauling a semi-trailer squeaked to a stop in front of them; they scrambled aboard and hid between the semi's wheels. A moment later the train lurched to a start, and Joe and Mark were on their way.

It was a glorious way to travel. The adventurers enjoyed an unparalleled sunset as the train snaked along the Flathead River, the engine's whistle melodiously echoing from the canyon walls.

Soon it was dark, though. An increasingly cold wind assaulted the pair as they lay under a thin blanket. Pebbles on the roadbed bounced up and hit them. The semi, just inches from their heads, lurched back and forth with horrible crashes. Sometimes the train would stop at isolated sidings, and gruff men with flashlights would shuffle past. The idyll of the rails had turned into a frightening night.

The dawn brought some physical comfort, but also the realization that the train was hurtling through the eastern Montana prairies, moving further from Glacier. When the train finally slowed for a minute, Joe and Mark hopped off. They soon realized they had been deposited in Havre, Montana; the town's dusty, windswept side streets seemed hardly worth the trip, but at least they had gone somewhere.

Getting back home was now the main concern. After waiting vainly (and half-heartedly) for another freight, they saw the Empire Builder drifting into the station. The temptation was too great, and the duo surreptitiously slipped aboard through an untended door. The trip back to McDonald was made in grand style, sipping Cokes in the lounge car and watching the scenery unfold. They disembarked at West Glacier, a Red bus was waiting faithfully at the station and they caught a ride home. Maybe they really had found the way to travel, after all.

Midnight cruise aboard the *De Smet*
Patrick Springer
(Lake McDonald Lodge 1959)

This true tale of adventure took place in August 1959. The exact date escapes me, but it must have taken us until August to figure out all the details of the escapade—a midnight cruise on Lake McDonald aboard the good ship *De Smet*. And, as then, I take full responsibility for what happened, and the consequences.

The actors in this tale included our manager, Ian B. Tippet, then 29 years old and only a few years out of London Hotel School, our matronly housekeeper, Ruth Putney, and a soon-to-be man of the cloth, John Bell. There were a variety of dining room, housekeeping, and kitchen personnel, and gearjammers. Finally, there was the jazz trio, from Mankato, Minnesota. The bass man was Tom (Baby Huey) Martick, the drummer was Tom (Motor Mouth) Randolph, and I played the piano.

The band played nightly in the Stockade Room (McDee's bar) until about 9:30 p.m. At that point, the guests in the rooms above were prone to complain about the noise. The band then usually moved to the "rec hall" to entertain the less fussy guests and the employees.

On the night in question, however, we stealthily moved the band's equipment onto the *De Smet*. The boat captain, Neil Hart, had agreed (with some understandable hesitation) to take the entire staff out for a party. Employees brought aboard two kegs of cold beer, trays of food from a secret cache, the drum set, the piano bench, and the sheet music. Finally, a sturdy group came staggering up the gangplank with the piano and placed it on the upper deck of the boat.

My recollection is that, with the exception of Mr. Tippet, Mrs. Putney, and John Bell (the lookout man), every member of the Lake McDonald hotel staff was on the *De Smet*.

Everyone was hushed.

We poled the boat well away from the dock before gingerly starting up the motor. When we were well out on the lake, the kegs were tapped and the partying began. I went up on the top deck and seated myself at the

The MV *De Smet* on Lake McDonald in 1941. Harry Blakey photo

piano. The mountains and Lake McDonald were gorgeous in the moonlight, and our friends all were enjoying a marvelous time. We began to play our music with gusto.

Unfortunately, none of us was aware of how sound travels across open water. We soon found out.

By 12:45 a.m. everybody around the lake was wide awake and expressing their displeasure to the Park Service. Soon we saw ranger vehicles proceeding up the road from headquarters to the lodge.

Still, we had no idea that we were in trouble until a ranger with a bullhorn hailed us from the Sprague Creek Campground. He ordered the *De Smet* off the lake, with emphasis upon the word "immediately". The captain did as he was told and headed back to the hotel dock, while the merriment continued.

When we moored at the dock, we were met by a squad of rangers and by Mr. Tippet, in an indignant state. His initial impulse was to fire every employee on the boat – not being aware that literally every employee was on the boat. I instructed the rest of the staff to stay where they were, and got off the boat to talk the matter out with the authorities.

My chief negotiating point was that it would be impossible to run the lodge the next morning if everyone were fired.

I accepted responsibility for organizing the party. The upshot was that I alone was fired, and all the rest were allowed to leave the *De Smet* and go home to bed.

Doing the trapline
Mark Hufstetler
(Lake McDonald Lodge 1978-83, National Park Service 1987-88)

Employees have long argued the relative merits of their respective hotels, but in at least one facet Lake McDonald has the others beat: McDee, as it is known to employees, is the only location with a respectable number of bars in the vicinity.

While east side employees must be content with an occasional sortie to the infamous Babb Bar or downing a mediocre pizza at St. Mary, there are literally dozens of atmospheric watering holes within reach of Lake McDonald Lodge. For the large percentage of employees willing to tackle the Lake McDonald road after one too many beers, the night life awaits.

For a time, the favorite of these employee hangouts was the Belton Chalet. This transformation of an old Great Northern hostelry had bar trays full of peanuts, cheap beer and classic bartenders. It was a wonderful spot to spend cool, lazy afternoons listening to an aging jukebox and watching the trains roll past. The restaurant next door, with its homemade desserts and Great Northern sandwiches, was an equally alluring hideaway.

At night, though, if the motley hordes of McDee people stormed the aging wooden stairs, the atmosphere changed. The Belton was then remembered for dancing on tables, spirited peanut-shell fights, and moments of both humor and drama. One year, a middle-aged Lake McDonald Lodge chef disrobed before her kitchen crew in the Belton, and a few years later another chef picked a fight that came close to ending in gunplay.

The crowd that liked to dance would venture a few miles past the Belton and settle at the Dew Drop Inn. The Dew Drop is the quintessential Montana bar, with busy pool tables, greasy burgers and country music on the weekends. Here, the unsurpassed excellence of McDee's country swing dancers took form and was displayed to the bemused eyes of the local audience.

If there was a little more gas in the car, one could go on to Kalispell for a visit to Moose's Pizza and red beer were favorites in the dark, dusty confines of Moose's, as was carving your initials on the facility's tables and benches.

A few years ago, a Lake McDonald front desk crew contrived the ultimate method of celebrating all of this decadence: it was called "doing the trapline."

The object of the evening's work was to hit every bar between Lake McDonald Lodge and Kalispell in a single night, without throwing up in somebody's back seat. At the appointed hour, the adventurers gathered in the lodge's own Stockade Room for a farewell drink. They then piled into cars piloted by (relatively) non-drinking drivers, and were off.

The master list of bars for the route was carefully followed: Frieda's, the

Belton, the Dew Drop, Stoner's, the Packer's Roost, the Deer Lick, Dam Town Tavern, River Bridge Inn, Paul Bunyan's, the Blue Moon, and Moose's, to name a few.

When the crew was finally ejected from Moose's at 2 a.m., they staggered off to the nearby Blue & White Motel, where someone had earlier reserved a room in the name of Don Hummel (then president of the hotel company that operated Lake McDonald Lodge). After a short night, punctuated with many trips to the bathroom, it was back for a long day at work. No vows of sobriety, though: there was dancing at the Dew Drop that night.

Christmas at Lake McDonald
Janet Eisner Cornish
(Lake McDonald Lodge 1973-76)

Upon my arrival, for the first time, at Lake McDonald Lodge in early July 1973, I was surprised to learn the employees were preparing for a summer Christmas celebration. The festivities, scheduled for July 24 and 25, provided an opportunity for employees, far flung during the rest of the year, to share the holiday with their Glacier friends. I must admit that at first I found myself feeling a bit out of place. Growing up in a home where Hanukkah was celebrated, I wasn't sure what to expect or how to respond.

My concerns were short-lived. Although arriving nearly a month after most of the other employees, I was welcomed warmly. Before my first day was over I was happily immersed in the community of employees, performing in the evening's musical and comedy show, and joining my new friend, Leslie Kerr, for a hike before starting my first shift the following day. The gracious and genuine offer of friendship and camaraderie was overwhelming. The desire to share a celebration and gifts with my new-found friends followed naturally.

So, a few days before July 24, a tree appeared in the lobby, courtesy of the bellmen. We decorated its branches with a variety of home-made ornaments—paper snow flakes, pine cones, ticker tape from the teletype machine and a few special decorations brought by returning employees.

Hotel guests watched in amazement as we prepared for the holiday. Trips to town were directed to the purchase of leather strips, decoupage sealers, fabric and beads, while back at the lodge employees worked on crafting treasures.

Photographs, smooth stones, pieces of wood and pine cones were transformed into beautiful gifts, each one reflecting something of the place and the people.

On "Christmas Eve," the employees gathered in the lobby to exchange gifts and present a musical show to the guests, complete with carols and a reading of *The Night Before Christmas* by Mr. MacDonald, the gardener.

The staff at Lake McDonald Lodge gather in the lobby in July 1973 to mark "Christmas Eve," with Janise Peterson and Kirsten Cornish acting as Christmas elves handing out presents.

Leslie Kerr photo, Janet Cornish collection

Santa Claus was on hand to distribute the presents to employees and various holiday treats to the guests.

My experience as a concessions employee in Glacier National Park in the 1970s is defined in large measure by the friendships that were forged. Relationships were formed easily and quickly, yet had uncommon depth and intimacy.

Now, decades later, the friends that I made at Lake McDonald Lodge continue to be part of my life experience. Today, in the back of dresser drawers and tucked in between the pages of photograph albums, I hoard the treasures that I received from my dear friends—a jewelry tree made of a piece of driftwood, a small log with the words "Miss – Information" burned on its face, folded bits of paper with song lyrics and poetry, and a book of special knowledge that every front desk employee should never be without.

Pack rats versus the boat crew
Marit Hanson
(Glacier Park Boat Company 2008, 2010)

College students are not meant to feed themselves. Sticking a college student into a fully equipped kitchen and telling her to prepare a balanced meal is tantamount to giving a chimpanzee the keys to a Ferrari and telling it to take you to the mall.

Case in point: the summer after my freshman year of college I shared a tiny cabin in the wilderness of Glacier Park with four other college students. Our collective cooking wisdom amounted to a working knowledge of a can opener, and so if it had to be sautéed, baked, chopped or even boiled in water, we didn't make it.

We were tour boat captains working on Lake McDonald, one of Glacier's busiest lakes and meal times were 30 minute wedges placed like awkward bookmarks throughout our 12 hour workdays. We didn't have a glimmer of foresight among the five of us, so we never packed meals. Lunch was an apple from the fruit basket with a handful of trail mix, a giant muffin swiped from the counter, a swig of milk from the jug when no one was looking or, once, stick after stick of string cheese.

Dinner was a similar affair. We pawed at whatever was available, ravenously indifferent to its nutritional content. Several times my friend Ali and I treated ourselves by basting a chicken with butter and Frank's hot sauce, cooking it and eating the dripping meat straight from the pan.

It was during one of these cobbled-together meals that I first encountered The Creature.

It was the skittering that caught my attention. My hand, already grimy with salt from my Chex Mix dinner, paused halfway into the bag. I glanced up at the rafters in the corner of the kitchen, where the logs didn't quite fit the contours of the metal roof but there was nothing there. Just as I was about to turn back to my sodium binge, something poked its large, furry head through the hole in the roof. I froze. Unaware of my presence, the creature squeezed the rest of its body through the hole.

At a glance I might have mistaken it for a squirrel; its size, fur, and long, bushy tail were identical to those of that particular rodent. The other features, however, were hideously distorted. Its face was pointed and shrewd like a rat's, and its feet were naked and pink. The Creature began to scurry along the rafters against the wall, then suddenly it went rigid, spotting me. I must have been quite the sight: eyes bulging, jaw hanging slack, hands suspended awkwardly over the kitchen table. I don't know how long we locked eyes. Most likely it was less than a second, but I can't shake the image of an epic stare down, à la *The Good, the Bad, and the Ugly*.

The creature and I, sizing each other up, hands (or paws) fingering our holsters. I shot first.

A shriek tore from my throat—a thing of pure terror that ripped through at least three octaves before I ran out of air. It would have made Alfred Hitchcock proud. The squirrel-rat thing spasmed as if I had jabbed it with a cattle prod. Flipping itself around, it shot out the hole in the roof before I had time to refill my lungs, leaving me gawking, hand still poised over the bag of Chex Mix.

By the time my co-workers made it back to the cabin, I had become so paranoid that I had retreated to my room and was attempting, like a child warding off the bogeyman, to zip myself into my sleeping bag. My dramatic revelation, however, didn't have quite the effect I had hoped for.

"Oh, that. It's a pack rat," said Anna with complete calm.

"A pack rat?" I echoed.

"Yeah. They always try to move in at the end of the summer," she said, sighing.

Technically, it wasn't a pack rat, the term drawn from the rodent's habit of collecting odds and ends. The scientific name for it is a *Neotoma cinerea*, or bushy-tailed wood rat. Nocturnal by nature, the large rodent (at one to one and a half feet in length, it's the largest of all its subspecies) spends most of its time eating and gathering tidbits it finds attractive. It then stores its treasures in its midden, a shelter it makes by heaping debris, plants and feces into large mounds and gluing the whole mass together with its own urine.

Anna brought a trap back to the cabin the following day. It was a monster in its own right. The toothed maw of gray plastic was longer than my hand and could have snapped my wrist if I was stupid enough to trip the spring. Brett lathered the inside with chunky peanut butter, set it beside the fridge and assured me that the pack rat would soon be dead. Despite this I refused to spend more than five minutes alone in the kitchen for the next few days, convinced that at any second I might find myself face-to-face with the pack rat. Brett, Dan and Anna, seasoned veterans of critter killing, found my jitters hilarious.

Lying in our bedroom at night we could hear tapping of its claws as it navigated the rafters above our heads. We had put the food in the refrigerator and the cupboards, so it spent the majority of its time trying to figure out how to open the doors. Most of the time these efforts consisted of exploring the dark crevices behind the kitchen counter and banging around in the walls like a living, possessed pinball, though every once in a while it got creative and would attempt to steal our pots and pans for midnight jam sessions. After a few nights, I began wearing earplugs to bed.

Then, scarcely a week after the whole mess had begun, it was over. I entered the kitchen one night to find Dan seated at the table with a grin on his face so smug it would have made a cat sick. The pack rat was dead, he informed me, its head crushed in the jaws of the trap.

That night, Ali and I celebrated the defeat of the beast over cans of Pabst Blue Ribbon and triumphantly returned the fruit and bread to their rightful places on the kitchen counter. Later, as I crawled into bed, a wonderful sense of relief spread over me. Finally, I could drift to sleep without the lingering dread that I would awake to feel sharp, little claws digging into my sleeping bag. I was naïve, of course. We may have rid the cabin of one pack rat, but to the rest of its brethren, we may as well have put up a vacancy sign.

Two days later we found tiny bite marks on our apples. Then we saw the second pack rat had also tipped over the cereal boxes, ripped open the flat of muffins and gobbled up the top of a jumbo blueberry muffin.

Brett rebaited the trap with peanut butter and placed it next to the fridge. Word must have gotten out in the pack rat underworld, though, because this latest interloper was wise to our ways. Even after we added a chunk of cheese, it refused to go near the trap. This one was a lurker, choosing to slink behind the baseboards of the counter at night rather than bump about like the first one.

After about a week of this behavior, I began to have the sinking suspicion that it was studying us, laying low until it figured out all the nooks and crannies of the cabin and could use them against us when it came time for the inevitable face-off. Then Dan nearly had a heart attack when, wandering upstairs one night, he uncovered a large, furry body spelunking in his laundry pile. Several things happened at once. An explosive yell and thump sounded from the loft, causing those of us who had been relaxing in the downstairs living room to jump. A fat bundle of gray fur went careering down the stairs, Dan in hot pursuit.

Anna and Brett leapt to their feet. Ali and I leapt onto the couch. The pack rat streaked past us into the kitchen. Dan raced after it, bellowing like a wounded bull.

"That's it! I am killing that little bastard."

Dan was in the kitchen on his hands and knees, one hand clutching his folding knife, the other positioning a large bucket about an inch from the hole in the baseboards through which I assumed the packrat had disappeared. An hour later, Dan was still in the kitchen.

Finally, Dan's battle cry announced the return of The Lurker. There was a clatter and then for the second time that night the pack rat was speeding through the living room with Dan on its tail.

To Dan's credit, it was a close chase. Trying to change directions, the pack rat slid on the hardwood floor, giving Dan the chance to come within striking range. But too late. With a burst of speed it bolted up the stairs and though Dan nearly upset his table lamp trying to nab it, The Lurker slipped through his fingers, diving into the rafters and out into the night. Defeated, the hunter clomped downstairs, sulking.

During the next two nights the cabin became a war zone. The pack rat had climbed on top of the fridge. The pack rat rooted through the garbage. The pack rat was in the loft again. In one particularly intense encounter, Brett and Anna cornered the creature on the kitchen counter and Brett, in a moment of valiant stupidity, lunged forward trying to grab it. The Lurker responded by launching itself into Brett's chest, clawing its way up his body and spring-boarding off his face. After that incident Brett decided to leave the sport of pack rat slaying to the more foolhardy members of the cabin. Not surprisingly, Dan volunteered to take up the mantle.

Dan never did manage to kill The Lurker, though. None of them did. The saga of the pack rat ended much as it had begun, with me sitting alone in the cabin eating Chex Mix at the kitchen table when I heard huffing.

I cast around, searching for the source. There, behind the refrigerator.

Goosebumps ran down my arms. It was the pack rat. After weeks of skillfully eluding the trap, The Lurker had finally given in to temptation and tried to snatch the peanut butter from between the sharp teeth of the trap.

Twenty minutes passed; the gasping cries from behind the fridge gradually slowed, then stopped. Steeling my nerve, I grabbed a flashlight and climbed on the counter, sending a thin beam of light behind the refrigerator. The light fell upon a gray, bushy tail and splayed back feet, both unmoving.

I waited until all four of my cabin mates had trooped through the door before I broke the news.

"The pack rat's dead." My voice came out strange and strained. The others didn't notice; they were too busy whooping and hollering.

Grinning from ear to ear, Brett broke out the cans of Pabst Blue Ribbon and passed them around. When he offered one to me, though, I did not accept.

Somehow, I didn't feel like celebrating.

Lake McDonald has many pleasant activities to offer.
Bob Anderson photo, courtesy Lola Anderson

Onion dicer in paradise
Chris Crump Moench
(Lake McDonald Lodge 1970)

In the summer of 1970 I was an onion dicer in paradise—an onion dicer, mincer, slicer and chopper at Lake McDonald Lodge in Glacier Park.
When I applied to work at Glacier, one of the positions which I indicated my willingness to assume was that of kitchen assistant. I wished to improve my culinary skills.

From Day 1 in the Lake McDonald kitchen my job was secure, though overly specialized. I was one of the only employees able to chop onions without tears.

So that summer the French chef knife was the tool of my trade and it was me and the onions, with occasional green peppers thrown in, until the end of the summer when I had to fill in for the French fries in the snack bar.

This job might have been dreadfully boring except for the camaraderie of other kitchen workers. The other positive element of my job was that it was easy on the mind and allowed for extensive daydreaming and time to plan and anticipate the next day off in the mountains.

From the moment I arrived at Lake McDonald, I was awestruck by the mountains. Having grown up in a suburb of Chicago in an area which was a continuous puzzle of shopping centers, subdivisions, freeways, and towns,

I had had limited exposure to mountains. I was immediately drawn up into the mountains. The purely visual experience was clearly not going to satisfy my soul's craving.

For every six days of onion work, I was awarded one blessed day in the mountains. This one day might be stretched to two by arranging one's shifts the day before and the day after.

I did much of my hiking and climbing with my roommate Pat and her boyfriend. Every hike was more like a spiritual quest. We experienced the thrill of lakes, passes, summits, swimming in mountain lakes, sliding down snow fields, screaming and laughing on summits. The alpine flower fields took my breath away. Such great variety in so fragile a habitat. Such brilliant colors.

The ice cold water of the mountain streams contributed to the spiritual experience. It seemed to me holy, even "living" water. We drank freely and our thirsts were quenched.

Finally, sleeping under the stars without tents was a highlight—sleeping under a canopy of stars in the crisp mountain air. In spite of bear stories, I was never afraid and never remember getting wet from rain or bitten by bugs.

My summer in Glacier gave me infinitely more than an opportunity to sharpen my onion chopping skills. It gave me a chance to experience the beauty and grandeur of the mountain landscape in the company of good-humored comrades and to meet God in that place.

Louis W. Hill, head of the Great Northern Railway, stands beside a Red River cart on display on the west side of Glacier Park Hotel in the summer of 1924. The railway's developments in Glacier were a passion for Hill and he took every opportunity he could to promote them. James J. Hill Library collection, Minnesota Historical Society

Chapter 10

People famous and obscure

Early days at Many Glacier
Warren Hanna
(Many Glacier Hotel 1918, 1920)

My work at Many Glacier Hotel brought me into contact with some of the more important and interesting visitors to whom expense was of little concern. One of these was John D. Rockefeller, who visited with members of his family. Others included the Stout family from Menominee, Wisconsin, which would occupy nine adjoining rooms in the Annex.

Another distinguished guest was Louis Hill, chairman of the board of the Great Northern Railway. With his family, he spent some of each summer at Many Glacier, sometimes taking pack trips into the backcountry. He was very democratic, and gave me his U.S. Geological Survey map of the park when he found that my desk did not have one.

In 1918, Mr. Hill had planned a family pack trip into the Belly River country with his own horses, a guide and a packer. He had also engaged, as a cook, a woman who lived on a ranch near East Glacier.

Unexpected illness in his family after they reached Many Glacier forced cancellation of entire trip. This disappointed all concerned, including the cook. She asked Mr. Hill if she could ride one of his horses back to East Glacier. Louis asked her if she had any preference, and she pointed out a blue mare. Thereupon, he made her a present of the horse.

Warren Hanna

He said, "When someone does something for Louis, she gets something from Louis." The good woman was almost overcome by his generosity.

The 1918 visit of the Hills at Many Glacier happened to coincide with that of Treasury Secretary William G. McAdoo. Also present was the Howard Eaton horse party. Several of the Eaton guides had ridden (or attempted to ride) bucking horses. With all the important visitors present, they decided to stage a bucking exhibition at the Many Glacier corral.

Several riders acquitted themselves well at the exhibition. I passed a four-quart hat among the crowd for their benefit.

I was somewhat amused that neither Hill nor McAdoo had any money on them. Mrs. Hill came to her husband's rescue, tossing a five-dollar bill in the hat. Mr. McAdoo also was able to borrow from a friend and contribute. But it was interesting that neither the railroad king nor the treasury secretary were able to produce any ready cash.

Since the bronc riders came from the Eaton party, I did not know their names at the time. I learned one man's identity 60 years later. In 1978, while on a visit to Glacier Park, I became acquainted with Angus Monroe, a grandson of the "white Blackfoot," Hugh Monroe. We stopped for lunch at St. Mary, and had a chance to reminisce about the park. In describing the Eaton party's 1918 visit to Many Glacier, I told about the bucking exhibition—undoubtedly the only such event staged there. Angus looked at me with a twinkle in his eye, and asked me if I knew who had starred in the bucking exhibition.

When I said, "No," he responded, "You're looking at him."

He then told me that he had served as head guide for the Eaton party every time the party visited the park.

That conversation reminded me of my own contacts with Howard Eaton at Many Glacier. Genial Howard and his brothers were the operators of a dude ranch near Wolf, Wyoming. Each summer, Howard would recruit those of his ranch visitors who wished to participate in a horseback trip through Glacier National Park. Most wanted to go.

In 1915 one of these travelers was the well-known author Mary Roberts Rinehart, who wrote *Through Glacier Park with Howard Eaton*, a book which has since been republished.

The Eaton party rode with guides furnished by the Glacier Park Saddle Horse Company. They would start at East Glacier and ride to St. Mary over the Inside Trail. They then rode over Piegan Pass to Many.

They carried their own tents and travel gear with them, rather than lodging at the hotels or chalets. They took advantage of their sojourn at Many to take some trail trips, before crossing Swiftcurrent Pass to the park's west side.

I well remember the doughty Howard Eaton, a rather large man in western garb. He was outgoing, and when he visited Many, it was my pleasure to meet him. Near my counter in the hotel lobby he unexpectedly encountered one of his former party members. When she inquired about his health, he responded that he was healthy – "disgustingly so, in fact."

He added, "Come and see us, and I'll cook you a meal in five minutes that you can't eat in two weeks."

Howard always was the life of the Eaton party and excelled as a raconteur at the campfire. I enjoyed the return of his party in 1920. However, these annual safaris ended after 1922, the year that Howard died in his 60s. There was no one who could replace him.

Art Burch with his son Scott, who later would help manage the concession his father and grandfather operated since 1938.   Courtesy, Billy Ann Burch

Arthur M. Burch and the boats of Glacier
John Hagen
(Many Glacier Hotel 1970-80)

I first met Art Burch on a stormy day in the spring of 1970. I was a new employee at Many Glacier Hotel. Art and his boat crew were preparing for the new season.

An emergency arose when the *Morning Eagle*, the big motor launch on Lake Josephine, broke loose from its moorings and got broadside to the wind in shallow water. Art hustled over to the hotel, rounded up about 20 off-duty employees, loaded us onto the *Chief Two Guns* and we sped across Swiftcurrent Lake. We raced over the path to Lake Josephine, waded into the lake and lined up along the beam of the *Morning Eagle* in icy water up to our waists. We arduously pushed the boat back to the dock against the force of the wind and waves. Art expertly directed the maneuvers amid driving rain, then took us back to the hotel and bought us all hot drinks.

This episode captured Art's fine qualities of leadership and resourcefulness. He displayed these skills through decades of maintaining and operating the boats in Glacier's wild weather.

Art's father, Arthur J. Burch, bought the east-side boat concession in 1938 from the Capt. William (Billy) Swanson. Swanson built many park launches—the *De Smet, International, Little Chief, Sinopah* and *St. Mary*. Art was 10 years old when his father bought the concession, so he grew up learning the operation.

In 1953 Art married Billy Ann, his wife for 55 years. Soon afterward Art bought the west-side boat concession with the *De Smet* on Lake McDonald. In 1967 he acquired the east-side boat concession on Two Medicine, St. Mary, Swiftcurrent and Josephine Lakes from his father. He owned and operated the *International* from 1976 to 1986.

Art and Billy Ann raised four children (Art Jr., Scott, Kathy, and Susan), spending winters in Kalispell and summers in the boat crew quarters at Lake McDonald, and then at Swiftcurrent Lake. In the winters Art built boats at his shop in Evergreen, Montana. He built the *Chief Two Guns* for Swiftcurrent Lake, several versions of the *Curly Bear* for St. Mary Lake and the *Wanda Mae, Roddy Paul*, and *Connie Marlene* for Stan Kretz at Waterton, large boats for Yellowstone Park and Jackson Hole, and rowboats for Glacier's rental fleet. He also trucked the Glacier Park motor launches down to the shop for periodic maintenance.

The biggest challenge of Art's career was the wreck of the *Chief Two Guns* in 1975. At that time, the *Two Guns* had been transferred to Lake Josephine and shut up in the boat house for the winter. (The *Morning Eagle* had been floated to Swiftcurrent Lake and transported back to Evergreen for refitting.)

Late in the winter of 1975 a huge cornice of snow collapsed on Grinnell Point. An avalanche swept down on a curving path and obliterated the boathouse. The *Two Guns* was carried some 80 yards out across the ice that covered Lake Josephine.

The Park Service gave the Burches permission to take snowmobiles to Lake Josephine to inspect the damage. The *Two Guns* was on its side, with its superstructure torn off and with chunks of the boathouse driven through its hull. The Burches salvaged life-preservers and other items, then roped the hull to trees on the distant shore and waited for the ice to melt.

Spring left the shallow water at the site "an undulating mass of debris" (trees, chunks of the building, and other flotsam) as remembered by Scott Burch. The leaking *Two Guns* floated amid the mess, with about two feet of freeboard. The hull was black with spilled engine oil. Art and his sons towed the *Two Guns* to the outlet of Lake Josephine with a motorboat. In Stump Lake (between Lake Josephine and Swiftcurrent Lake), the hull repeatedly was grounded, and had to be raised with jacks and winched with come-alongs. Finally, the *Two Guns* reached Swiftcurrent Lake, where the Burches beached it near the boathouse, cleaned off the oil and patched the hull.

The next challenge was to move the *Morning Eagle* upstream to its customary place on Lake Josephine. The passage took five days of jacking and winching. (Ordinarily, the boats could have been hauled overland from lake to lake on an old logging road, but a flood in the June of 1975 left the road impassable, so the water route across Stump Lake had to be used.)

The Burches brought the *Little Chief* from Two Medicine to Swiftcurrent Lake to fill the *Two Guns'* place. The *Two Guns* went to Rising Sun, where for the rest of the summer it ran (on sunny days) with no superstructure and tourists riding on open benches. Eventually it was refitted and returned to its former place on Swiftcurrent Lake.

Scott Burch recalls another colorful tale about his father. The *Motor Vessel International*, on Upper Waterton Lake, was sold by Glacier Park, Inc. to the Burches in 1976. That fall Cy Stevenson, GPI's legendary chief engineer, showed the Burches the antiquated arrangements at the boathouse at the south end of the lake. He helped them to raise the 56-ton boat up rails

The motor launch *Chief Two Guns* on Swiftcurrent Lake.   Ray Djuff photo

into the boathouse with a cable attached to a Model T engine (which had to be started with a hand crank, and which powered a leather drive belt).

The following spring the Burches returned to the boathouse, cranked the engine and started to lower the boat down the rails. The cable paid out very slowly, and the *International* inched toward the water at a snail's pace.

Scott recalls, "Art wasn't real patient. He took the motor out of gear and let the boat slide by its own weight. It took off like a freight train. There were crowns in the rails, and the hull flexed when it hit them. Seams split apart and windows shattered. Art's eyes got big as the boat splashed into the lake—we were lucky that it didn't derail."

He said, "I guess we won't do that again."

Art sold the boat concession a few years later to his sons and his nephew, Mark Van Artsdale. He promptly started another business, building docks, and ran it well into his 70s. Hard work and energy were his trademarks.

In 1996 the Park Service released initial proposals for a new General Management Plan for Glacier Park. Some of these proposals were very ill-considered—e.g., razing Swiftcurrent Motor Inn and shutting down numerous auto campgrounds. The public overwhelmingly opposed the plan.

Art gave energetic leadership to the resistance. He organized a group called Friends of Glacier, conducted a public opinion poll, wrote letters to the editor and spoke out at public meetings. Through his efforts and those of the Glacier Park Foundation and many citizens, the final management plan called for maintaining the traditional visitor facilities.

Art died in May 2008 at the age of 79. He played a great role in the history of Glacier, mentoring hundreds of employees and transporting hundreds of thousands of visitors. His many friends will remember him fondly whenever they see a white motor launch cutting a graceful wake in the waters of the park.

Musicians and the Glacier Park hotels
Tessie Bundick
(Many Glacier Hotel 1972-73, 1976-80)

The hiring of park musicians usually entailed a live audition at the Great Northern building in St. Paul. Many small bands returned for several summers. A point of particular note, however, is the number of players who tried very hard to be hired, but were rejected.

Applicants for employment for musical positions were not all typical orchestras. In 1926, the Wade Family Bell Ringers sent an unusual letter to the company. They were traveling on a publicity campaign for Montana and offered to place the emblems of Glacier Park and the Great Northern on their car.

The Wade Family Bell Ringers generally appeared in Chautauqua and

Donn O'Connor's Minnesotans perform in The Grill, in the basement of Glacier Park Hotel, in 1928.
Alice Porter photo, Ray Djuff collection

vaudeville acts, and styled themselves "America's Only Family of Carilloneurs." The family's brochure extolled a "fine collection of musical instruments, the dainty dancing, the beautiful stage settings, the smoke and ray pictures, elaborate costumes."

Howard Noble, general manager of the hotel company, refused.

In 1926, a 12-year-old saxophonist from St. Paul, Minnesota, Ruth Reynolds, wrote to the company wanting to know if there might be a place for her. She had played at banquets and theaters, and in her words, was "fairly successful."

"I play saxophone and also dance," she stated. She was not hired.

The Billings Ladies Ensemble, a group that could provide quartets, quintets, or octets, as desired, offered its services in 1929. Melville Moss, the group's representative, wrote to A.J. Binder of the Great Northern, "The personnel of the orchestra would be fine young ladies." However, as usual, the offer was declined as too expensive.

The orchestra that should have won a blue ribbon for its efforts to be hired was the Murray Family Orchestra of Iowa. This group (consisting of five women and a boy) played the very latest dance and orchestra music for functions in four states—Iowa, Nebraska, and the Dakotas.

Roy Murray, the proud father and manager of the troupe, sent a letter in

August, 1925, proclaiming: "Each player an artist on his own instrument, we carry Iowa's best whistler, soloist, satisfaction guaranteed."

In another letter, he boasted that the orchestra played leading hotels such as the Montrose Hotel, Cedar Rapids, Iowa; the Fort Des Moines Hotel in Des Moines; and the Hotel Lincoln in Lincoln, Nebraska; as well as lyceums, theaters, state fair circuits, and the Iowa governor's inaugural and ball.

He pointed out that an advantage of hiring this family of musicians was that they required less room and could assist with clerical work when not performing. In a letter in February 1926, Roy Murray stated, "We know what is wanted and can deliver the goods."

Noble refused, saying that the Murray Family Orchestra was larger than required, and that only young men had been employed in past seasons, on account of housing conditions.

Roy Murray did not give up, however. In August 1926 he sent the Great Northern a gushing proclamation by the Missouri State Fair Board. It certified the Murray Family Orchestra as the Missouri State Fair Orchestra of the 26th state fair. The proclamation made no impression on Noble.

In December 1926, Murray sent another letter, stating: "The orchestra will this year make a price to Mr. Noble for Glacier National Park playing that he cannot afford to overlook. They had a wonderful season last year and went over big."

More letters followed. Again in 1926, Roy Murray wrote:

"We will play your dinner's [sic] and dances for the season of 1927, Glacier Park Hotel, for $1,500. We're to furnish our own transportation and board and house ourselves, for we are equipped to do it that way."

Noble refused again, for the same reason.

September 1927 saw a letter to E.C. Sheedy, agricultural division agent for the Great Northern, a friend of Murray's, which asked, "Don't you think this specialty orchestra would make a big hit for The Glacier National Park Hotel in 1928?"

And a letter in February 1928 urged Noble: "We will furnish your dance and orchestra music for Glacier Park Hotel, 1928 summer park season, for $1,200, house and board ourselves, we have our own traveling equipment."

None of these pleas ever worked, however. For all their persistence, the Murray Family Orchestra never spent a summer performing in Glacier.

Clark Gable at Lake McDonald Hotel
Bill Wanser
(Crossley Lake Camp 1924-38)

Clark Gable was a regular visitor at Lake McDonald Hotel in its early years. The employees awaited his visits with great anticipation, and always expended spit and polish in preparing the hotel for his arrival. However, they always were disappointed. Gable's limousine and luggage would arrive at the lodge without him. The actor habitually alighted at the Lake McDonald corral to play stud poker with the cowboys. The poker games went on till long after midnight. Gable, reputedly, always lost.

The hotel employees were disillusioned to learn that after their long preparations, the great man had groped his way into the hotel at 3 o'clock in the morning, smelling of horse blankets, beer, and cheap cigars.

Omar the Terrible
Dick Schwab
(Many Glacier Hotel 1947-52)

It all began by a long chance sometime in the spring of 1947, when I was 19 years old and at the University of Minnesota. Bill Lines, my roommate 50 years ago at the university, came in and said he had just got a job for the summer as a busboy at Glacier. I did not know anything about the park, and I am not sure I had ever consciously heard about it before that.

Since I had no job yet back home in Pelican Rapids for the summer, I thought there would be no harm in trying to get one in Glacier. And thus the most casual decision fundamentally transformed a big part of my life and the lives of many in our family.

I went over to St. Paul, Minnesota, where the Great Northern Railway, which held the hotel concession in Glacier, had its main office. In a room set aside there for interviewing prospective summer employees I saw a small, somewhat rotund man with a pink face, round glasses, and pure white hair. When he stood up, his head and shoulders just showed above the counter.

A rare snapshot of Omar Ellis, in the Many Glacier Hotel dining room where he regularly dined.

Ray Djuff collection

He was Omar Ellis, famous manager of Many Glacier Hotel. Omar had long been a sort of legend. Everybody who went to Many Glacier knew from the moment they stepped into the hotel that Omar, and no one else, was the boss. His voice frequently boomed and resounded through the lobby and elsewhere when he occasionally made an inspection tour. For such a small man, he had exceptional vocal powers. Anecdotes about his volcanic outbursts abounded, and they caused us great amusement.

Omar kept an Olympian distance from all the employees and even the guests. He did not sit with the staff for his meals, but ate in silent isolation at his own little table. Making jests, socializing, or charming the guests were completely foreign to him, and the only words most of us heard him utter were occasional barked orders or criticisms.

Omar's ill temper reached such a peak in 1948, his last year, that one has to think he was no longer in possession of himself. When Tom Westbrook was hauled on a stretcher into the lobby with a broken ankle after a near-fatal fall and a night on a cliff ledge, Omar charged out of his office, stood over him, and roared, "You're fired!"

Although while I worked at the hotel Omar never said a word directly to me, I heard him say five words in response to something he overheard me saying one evening at the end of the 1948 season. Those few of us who had stayed behind to close up the hotel were sitting by the fire in the great lobby fireplace after a hard day's work, and I was telling some of them about Bede Clapp's hilarious ape act.

Bede, who had very long arms, would occasionally do a squatting chimpanzee walk, dragging his knuckles on the ground. Then, in true ape fashion, without using opposable thumbs, he would awkwardly pick up something like a tray between his palm and fingers and transport it from one place to another—all the time with the most amazingly ape-like facial contortions and grunts. This never failed to reduce us to helplessness.

Omar, who was sitting silently before the fire in a high-backed bench that completely hid him from the rest of us, boomed out: "He IS a damned ape!"

One memorable Omar episode proved his humanity to us after all. A load of us, departing in a Red bus at the end of the summer, stopped at the entryway of the hotel to pick up something or someone. The high-spirited crowd of employees spied Omar standing on the porch. This was the first time we had seen him in his shirtsleeves—and he was carrying a hammer.

The entire busload began to shout a rousing, "Goodbye, Omar."

He kept his glance fiercely directed elsewhere, and then just as the bus started to leave he turned, smiled and raised his arm and the hammer.

Mrs. Rhody and Edward R. Murrow
Michael Buck
(Many Glacier Hotel 1960-68, Glacier Park Transport Company 2001-02)

Minnie Rhody, in charge of the Many Glacier Hotel kitchen, was a person of uncompromising quality in service, steadfast dedication to duty and unwavering commitment to her position. No one would dare, ever, to invade her domain, her realm, her "sovereign state," if not working there. If you did and escaped, you did so only once, and never did so again.

She had created for her an elevated, glass-enclosed perch at the end of the kitchen. From there she would position herself behind a desk and oversee the efficient operation of the fiefdom. It was like the bridge, above the flight deck of an aircraft carrier.

I was a part-time dishwasher in the kitchen when not handling responsibilities as a houseman in the hotel. I was never quite sure just who the "officers of the day" were who could approach, let alone climb to Mrs. Rhody's command post. Occasionally she would descend to the "draftee" level and direct her movements to the dining room and confirm that all was in order.

Newsman Edward R. Murrow and Minnie Rhody at Many Glacier Hotel.
Courtesy, Michael Buck

During a meal at the governor's conference, in the summer of 1960, she strolled into the dining room on just such a mission.

One of the journalists covering the dinner, Edward R. Murrow, caught sight of her and did the unthinkable—he trailed her back into the kitchen. There he asked if he could have a picture of them taken together, for remembrance's sake. (He, the celebrity, made the request of her—it was not the other way around.) It seems that Mrs. Rhody had been the cook in Murrow's college fraternity house, and that he had not seen her since.

Recollections of Joy Paulsen
Linda Young Kuhn
(Many Glacier Hotel 1976-78, 1980-82;
Glacier seasonal ranger 1983-86, 1988)

During the six summers I spent at Many Glacier, I had the opportunity to get to know a rare person by the name of Joy Paulsen. Joy was a wonderful, unique, inspiring woman who added wisdom, sparkle, thoughtfulness and charm to my summers in Glacier. There was never a more perfect adopted grandmother and friend.

Joy Paulsen had the good fortune to spend her summers with Art and Billy Ann Burch on the shores of Swiftcurrent Lake, just a 10-minute walk from Many Glacier Hotel. [The Burches ran the boat concession in the park.] Not only was this a good arrangement for Art and Billy Ann, because Joy was such good company and made the best huckleberry cheesecake in the world, but this was a wonderful summer home for Joy, who enjoyed two things most in life: young people and fishing (not necessarily in that order).

Joy was ecstatic when Art and Billy Ann gave her a boat of her own to use for fishing: a sturdy rowboat with a fresh coat of white paint and "Joy" painted neatly on one side. Joy's enthusiasm for fishing was boundless. Every evening she'd row out to the best spots and often the next morning there would be fresh trout for breakfast.

On some evenings Joy had guests out with her in the boat. Employees from the hotel were welcome to fish with her, and she loved the company. But one thing never varied: it was Joy who rowed, no matter how strong or willing the young man or woman who accompanied her.

Joy Paulsen with her boat and fishing gear. Courtesy, Diane Heberling

Joy was also an expert berry-picker. I was amazed at her agility in getting up the steep slopes of Grinnell Point headed for her favorite huckleberry patch. I almost needed to run to keep up.

Proper equipment for an afternoon of berry-picking was a large plastic bucket which could be tied to one's belt; it was very important, Joy told me, to be able to keep both hands free to pick the berries. Proof of the success of her method was the warm huckleberry pie, huckleberry cheesecake, huckleberry pancakes and many, many jars of huckleberry jam which appeared and quickly disappeared in the Burch family's kitchen.

Joy's familiarity with Glacier began in the 1920s, when she came out by train from St. Paul to work for a summer at Many Glacier Hotel. I loved to hear her stories about waitressing in 1924. I could hardly imagine picking wildflowers for the tables, a menu in French, earning 60 cents a day, and no days off all summer.

Joy did tell of one redeeming virtue of the job, however: as a reward for a successfully completed contract, each employee was treated to a two-day packhorse expedition to Granite Park Chalet. In addition, employees who finished the season received free train fare home, while those who left early paid their own way.

It was always a treat to visit her, maybe because she had that rare trait of being more interested in other people than in herself. Joy enriched many people's lives with her generosity, enthusiasm, and optimism. I hope I can be like her some day. I'm thankful we could be friends.

Blackie Dillon: last of a breed
Dick Schwab
(Many Glacier Hotel 1947-52)

Buster (Blackie) Dillon was the classic, old-time dude wrangler who had worked for the Park Saddle Horse Company (the Bar X6 Ranch) in the glory days before the Second World War, and he continued to be a wrangler after the war. He was surely one of the most colorful characters to be seen regularly in the lobby at Many Glacier Hotel.

All of these veteran guides, packers and dude wranglers were men of exceptionally strong character, and many of them had unusual talents for storytelling, composing and reciting poetry, and singing range songs. Some were self-taught artists. They knew their jobs, and they were rugged, self-assured, and impressive.

In the 1940s and 1950s, Blackie served pretty much as the last active reminder of this old breed of Glacier wranglers. He was still quite fine looking, with his dark hair, handsome features and impressive carriage. When he stepped into the lobby, everyone looked in his direction. Of all the cowboys, he dressed in the most elegant way, usually wearing a fancy black outfit that was quite striking, but not garish.

He was straightforward, soft-spoken, polite, and reserved. However preposterous some of the questions were that the dudes directed to him, he replied with unfailing patience and left his audience legitimately satisfied that they had encountered a cowboy who was in all respects the real thing.

People like him often generate myths. He was a sort of western version of a classical hero, with one tragic, destructive flaw. In his case it was Drink.

At regular intervals he went on his legendary binges. Again and again he would be fired by the Park Saddle Horse Company, and then after plunging to the worst depths he would pull out of it and be signed on again. His bosses recognized how valuable he was when he was sober, and they were willing to forgive him. Even the flawed Blackie towered head and shoulders above the other dude wranglers. Certainly that was the opinion of the dudes.

Toward the end of my time at Many Glacier, Blackie was given the job of driving the tally-ho, an antique, horse-drawn surrey. The tally-ho was driven out on part of the old high road that originally brought guests to the hotel from Babb before the lower main road was put in. Some clearing of rocks from the primitive track allowed for a short, quite bumpy western surrey ride through a bit of rugged scenery not far north and east of the hotel.

The circumstances are unclear to me, but after our time, apparently, Blackie, who was usually so dependable, got a bit wild on one of these trips and fairly scared the life out of his passengers. Perhaps he had started on one of his binges. In any case, I think that was the end of the tally-ho rides and Blackie's career in the park.

All of us lost track of Blackie for 20 or so years. Then we discovered him again, this time playing the role of the old gold prospector at Knott's Berry Farm in Orange County, California. He still looked magnificent, now with pure white hair, nut-brown face, and a white beard—just the way a prospector ought to look. I was struck again by his great dignity and gentility.

A Recollection of Mr. T
Mike Leach
(Many Glacier Hotel 1972, 1974-75)

During my last two summers, I was Many Glacier Hotel manager Ian B. Tippet's executive secretary. During one of the summers, Many Glacier hosted the Bureau of Indian Affairs annual convention. Part of my job was to arrange many of the particulars of the celebration.

One day we were hosting many dignitaries from Washington, D.C., and the tribal heads from the various Indian nations in the West. We arranged a grand luncheon in the Ptarmigan Room, complete with the Many Glacier Singers.

Many Glacier Hotel manager Ian Tippet with staff. John Hagen collection

As result, the dining room had to be closed to the public until after the luncheon was completed. This necessitated our having to direct guests to the Swiftcurrent Motor Inn dining room a mile or so away or to the St. Moritz Room below stairs for sandwiches.

I was finished with my welcoming the guests and giving a brief history of the hotel, Mr. Tippet put in an appearance at the dining room and then left for his lunch. While he was gone from the office, a couple came in complaining about not being allowed to eat at their desired time. They were not even guests at the hotel. I nicely informed them of the problem we were having. I suggested the alternatives to dining. They refused in not all-too-appropriate language.

I then told them that I would take their name, save them a table on the first seating and that they might take a leisurely walk around the perimeter of the hotel and enjoy the beautiful Swiftcurrent Lake. They still were not happy and were mad about the @#$%!&* Indians taking over the hotel.

They insisted on talking to the "head man."

I informed them that Mr. T was at lunch and would return in about a half hour.

Mr. T arrived back early. I was working at the Telex machine, with my back to the door. He glided past me and inquired if anything noteworthy had transpired.

I quickly informed him about the terrible couple and that I thought they were the worst bitchers we had in the office all summer—only to turn around and find them standing right there. Horrors. Needless to say, I didn't hear a word of their conversation since I typed as fast and as loudly as possible on the Telex. I was certain I would hear a "Down the road, thank you," from Mr. T (his usual manner of releasing someone from employment).

When they left, having not been satisfied by the Englishman, I turned to apologize to Mr. T. for my characterization of them. He immediately put me at ease and said, "Oh, but Mr. Leach, that is pre-cise-ly what they are."

What a man!

Margaret Black—a century of success
Jan Didra Stubbs
(Seasonal visitor 1936-)

Margaret Mary James came into the world displaying many of the characteristics that sustained her for more than 100 years. Strong, spirited, and smart-as-a whip, determined, feisty and beautiful: these admirable attributes are recognized by all who knew her. They are also the same characteristics she used 30 years later in the development of St. Mary at the east entrance to Glacier.

St. Paul, Minnesota, was her birthplace and home for the first quarter of her life. Her father had been a conductor for the Great Northern Railway. After an accident, he was forced to become a brakeman because the railroad thought the sight of someone who was physically impaired was displeasing to the passengers. In already stressful economic times, this meant a reduction in income.

Margaret was named after her mother, the backbone of the family. More serious and practical, Mrs. James was busy with Margaret and the six children who followed. It was not an easy time and money was scarce. Her strong Catholic faith and deep moral convictions were passed on to Margaret. Even as a child, Margaret was given and accepted responsibility for the younger children. This sense of responsibility, combined with a strong work ethic, would be important in the years to come.

Margaret earned a one-year scholarship to St. Joseph's High School.

Going to college was virtually out of the question for a woman. Being practical, she decided to attend secretarial school. In this way she could also help support the family. Her first job was with an insurance company. Margaret continued to live at home, as was the custom for an unmarried woman. Her vivaciousness, quick wit and true beauty made her very popular, but she was extremely particular about whom she dated.

She later secured a good job with a bank. This gave her a solid grounding in sound financial management. A clerk at a rental store told her about an opening at the Great Northern Railway. She applied and was accepted to work in Montana for the general manager of railway's Glacier Park Hotel Company for the summer. In 1928 Margaret James set out on the adventure of her life.

When she arrived at East Glacier, it was rough with nothing more than a couple of dusty buildings and a group of Blackfeet Indians in full regalia that greeted the train. But the mountains, spectacular in the first light of day, made an impact on her that she never forgot.

There were many other young people out there. The economy flourished, and trips West were the height of adventure. At night the employees gathered at a location called Mike's Place in East Glacier to sing and dance and exchange stories. Everyone worked their daily jobs, but on days off they hiked or rode horses.

One day Margaret, on her favorite horse Midget and accompanied by three friends, rode over Mount Henry. On the trail is where she met a park ranger named Hugh Black from Michigan. An instant rapport developed between Margaret and the ranger. Like her father, Hugh was endowed with ideas, drive and an acerbic wit. He visited her in St. Paul, and she returned to Glacier the following summer.

Then the Depression hit, driving a wedge in their burgeoning relationship, but love has a way of prevailing. Margaret and Hugh were married in 1932. Combining what little savings they had, they convinced a local bank to loan them enough money to buy 300 acres of land, the very place where St. Mary Lodge sits today.

Hugh immediately started having cabins built, and St. Mary gradually grew. The Going-to-the-Sun Road was completed and received a great deal of media publicity.

Sometimes tourists would stop by, asking for a cabin. Hugh would reply, "We'll have one ready for you this evening." Then a two-person crew would erect an entire cabin in a day. A table, double bed, one window, wood stove, electricity ... and a communal outhouse. He painted a big sign that said "Hugh Black Cabins."

One day a woman came in and asked, "Where are the cabins you advertise? All I see are those little white cabins."

"What do you mean?" responded Hugh.

"Well I want one of those huge, black cabins."

Both Margaret and Hugh's brothers and sisters worked at St. Mary, but as it grew they needed more and more employees. The Blacks went back to Minnesota to hire students, and quickly learned a few things implicit in successfully staffing their resort. They had to be careful not to hire too many Catholics because the resort had to be fully staffed while the priest came to say mass each Sunday.

They also had to watch the girls very closely. Families back in St. Paul considered the Blacks as chaperones, thus accountable for their children. The girls had curfews, and there was bed check, only for the women, every night. Nonetheless, Margaret admitted to being responsible for many romances and marriages.

Margaret was responsible for the hiring, the books and day-to-day operation of the facility. Hugh was frequently gone, doing whatever he could to make money. He ranged cattle, cut and hauled ice.

Hugh and Margaret Black.
Courtesy, Steve Berg

In 1952 they built the first lodge at St. Mary. Subsequently gas stations, restaurants, gift shop, grocery store, sporting goods store, houses, cottages and a second lodge were added.

Hugh Black died in 1983, leaving Margaret to call on her reserves of fortitude and faith. Margaret Mary James Black died at the age of 105. Life tied to Glacier and St. Mary was her adventure, her dream and her reality.

A tribute to Ray Kinley
Rolf Larson
(Many Glacier Hotel 1975, 1977-80)

During the 1970s, when I was fortunate enough to be a part of the Many Glacier community, that valley and especially that hotel were a very special place.

Hotel manager Ian B. Tippet was certainly the soul and mind of that community, but for many of us, an old, wizened character who was the groundskeeper at that time and master of the men's dormitory was the heart of the place.

Ray Kinley, second from left, with bellmen John Hagen, from left, Tim Vadheim and Ted Mate in 1975.

John Hagen collection

This, of course, was Ray Kinley.

Ray had a way about him. He understood the place. He had real insight into people and a sense of humor that left every one of us at peril. To this day people are probably still discovering little jokes that Ray slipped past them at one time or another.

I gained an insight into the sensitivity of Ray's perceptions of the environment early in my first summer. One bright, cloudless morning I greeted him with hopes for a marvelous day off spent on the trail. Ray set his nose to catch a scent of the air, wrinkled his brow and told me that it would rain by afternoon. I chose to ignore his advice. It rained, and I got wet.

Later, I asked him how he knew that the rain was coming. He said that he could smell rain, but then told me that the morning breeze was from the east, an almost certain sign that a storm was moving into the valley.

I was fortunate enough to be assigned as Ray's assistant during the hotel closing for the 1977 season, his last summer working in the park. My season had ended and I was about to leave, with no destination in mind. When I heard that Ray was seeking transport to East Glacier early the next week, I grabbed at the opportunity to hang around "heaven" for a few extra days.

Those days were rather special. They were filled with stories and a grand tour of all his cubby holes—I got first pick of all that season's fleeing employees had left behind. On all counts, I made a killing. There was Ray's collection of fishing gear and his famous hat collection. Both of these were found in the lake level rooms of the main hotel. In the Annex was another cache. There were also special storage areas in each of the men's dormitories. If anyone needed anything—spats, for example—he'd have it somewhere. It wasn't always without a strange odor, however, and certainly didn't always fit the style of the times, but you could be sure that he would have it.

When the summer ended, there were only Ray, Paul Hoff and me in the dormitory, on a cold, stormy evening at the end of September. It was truly the season's end.

The next day I drove Ray down to East Glacier, where he caught a van connection to Great Falls. It was a gray day, snowing in the high country. As I helped him to the van, I asked the inevitable question: "Be back next year?"

The other five or six times I had asked, Ray essentially had said no. This time, looking toward the peaks, boiling in cloud, he started to answer and then paused. He said, "Oh, probably."

He didn't return the next summer. An era spanning 55 years had come to an end.

Hopalong Cassidy at Many Glacier
Dick Schwab
(Many Glacier Hotel 1948-52)

Mrs. [Maude] Oastler was the last vestige of the wealthy guests who spent a good part of their summer vacations in the park in the earliest days, before and during the First World War and throughout the 1920s and '30s. After the Second World War when all the old wealthy eastern families had forsaken Glacier for Europe or elsewhere, she still faithfully returned every summer to take up residence in the quiet of the Annex for most of the season.

She was the widow of a distinguished New York City surgeon, Dr. Frank Oastler. The two of them had started exploring the Glacier area in 1912, and they returned to the hotel regularly until his death in 1936. She continued to come back to Many Glacier until at least 1956, which is the last I heard of her.

Many Glacier Hotel was Mrs. Oastler's summer duchy, and every year she journeyed in state out from her Park Avenue apartment, stepping onto the entryway to the lobby from a shining limousine. Her arrival was a big event that meant the season had truly begun. She was greeted with great deference by the managerial and clerical staff. By this stage of her life her main activity was to preside as a dignified presence in the lobby when she was not in her room or at her special table in the dining room.

Mrs. Oastler had the appearance of a slightly frail Edwardian lady of means. Always tastefully and somewhat formally dressed, on occasion she wore gloves. She had aristocratic features and carriage, a fine complexion, and hair worn in the conservative style of wealthy eastern matrons of perhaps a generation earlier. Her oval glasses added to the distinction of her appearance. An aura of respectability, gentility, and decorum surrounded her. Normally she stayed quite strictly to herself and could be seen reading alone in a lobby chair; but apparently she observed closely everything that was going on.

When the word passed through the lobby that none other than Hopalong Cassidy and his wife, Tripalong (William and Grace Boyd), were going to come for a stay at the hotel, Mrs. Oastler was indignant. In her view these Hollywood types were not proper guests for Many Glacier.

The flamboyant Hoppy arrived in all sorts of glitter, driving an amazing Hollywood cowboy convertible. Its upholstery was all brown and white spotted cowhide, the door handles were six-shooters, and silver pistols were integrated as spokes in the construction of the splendid steering wheel. Silver dollars were embedded all over the dashboard, and I believe there was a shining set of Texas longhorns at the front of the hood.

Hopalong stepped out of this wonderful vehicle and into the lobby all resplendent in his black, white, and silver Hollywood cowboy getup, set off effectively by his famous pure white hair. He was followed by his petite, charming wife, who was turned out in a magnificent cowgirl's outfit. With her flawless pink complexion and white-blond, slightly pastel hair she looked a bit like Marilyn Monroe in a fancy western costume.

Hopalong and Tripalong were immediately a smash hit at the hotel. They were gregarious, courteous, and totally down to earth, and they showed a genuine old-time western friendliness to everyone. Hopalong sat on the bellhop's bench to chat with us, and both he and Tripalong easily struck up neighborly conversations with the guests at every opportunity. They were obviously truly first-rate people.

They would venture out from the hotel for rides in their magnificent convertible, stopping frequently at viewing places. Often they would be surrounded by people, particularly children, who had been weaned on Hopalong's television reruns, and for whom he was a great hero. Hoppy never tired of talking with them and giving them souvenirs he always carried with him—pins in the shape of boots or stirrups. Someone asked him whether this did not become tiresome for him, and he said, "Absolutely not. I owe everything to those kids." And of course he did.

Mrs. Oastler kept her aristocratic distance from the Hollywood couple for a short time; but Hoppy, pretty well figuring it all out, effortlessly launched a campaign that completely won her over. In no time she became entranced with him and Tripalong. Every evening after that the three of them were seen sitting closely together in the lobby, engrossed in animated conversation.

My shift happened to be on duty when Hopalong and Tripalong departed from the hotel, and I witnessed the whole amusing scene. First Hopalong distributed silver spur pendants to the women employees in the lobby and cuff links to the men, and gave a genial, personal word of thanks to everyone.

Mrs. Oastler was standing at the edge of the crowd, and just before he left, Hopalong went over and gave her a spectacular kiss. It was not some peck on a cheek for an aged aunt. It was a Hollywood kiss in which the lady is swept into the leading man's arms and bent slightly backwards.

Mrs. Oastler, feeling a loss of balance, flayed her arms a bit and then limply gave in to it all. Afterward she walked around the lobby for a while in a dazed state. I was laughing so hard I think I had to go into the bellhop room so as not to make a spectacle of myself.

The Cy Stevenson era
Ian B. Tippet
(Glacier Hotel Company; Glacier Park Inc. 1955-)

Thinking back over all the memories from my dozens of years at the Glacier Park hotels, the safety aspect for our guests and employees is among the top of the list.

Our chief engineer, for most of his life, was Cy Stevenson. Cy was always hot on security. The night guards at all locations patrolled their premises with Detex watchman clocks, punching in at about 20 stations, 12 times a shift. They put in about five miles of walking each night. Each punch put a hole in a paper dial, which was inserted into the clock before each shift and taken out afterward. The punches were proof that a guard visited each station at regular intervals. The dials were sent to Cy directly, and woe betide the guard who missed a station.

Cy formed fire crews at all locations—hose teams, ladder teams, emergency runners, first aid teams. He held unannounced fire drills where it was mandatory for all employees to participate. The location teams became very competitive, wanting to prove that they were the most efficient and more speedy, and effective than their opponents.

Cy personally controlled all engineering aspects at all the locations.

Cy Stevenson

When Don Hummel took over from the Great Northern Railway in 1961, he told Cy: "I want Tippet to have grand master keys"—and Cy just about passed out. Master keys had never been assigned before to anyone but Cy.

He muttered to me how aggravated he was about it, and demanded a $100 deposit on each key. I still have the same master keys and they are working fine. God rest Cy's soul.

The "secret hike"
Harvey Barkowsky
(Many Glacier Hotel 1972-73, 1975)

Well, Glacier National Park—I had received a job there. Ian B. Tippet had chosen me as one of the Many Glacier employees. My assignment was that of a houseman.

We had the best boss in the world. Her name was Mrs. Wilson and she was the head housekeeper in the Annex. I will never forget her piercing voice, her demand for excellence and the absolute love and dedication she bestowed on her staff. Never did we upset her or she us, she simply worked from the philosophy that all problems could be worked through. And she laughed and had as much fun as her staff.

There were some days when the housekeeping staff in the Annex finished early and Mrs. Wilson would let us go early. She warned us not to let Mr. Tippet find out. She told us of a "secret hike" back to the dorms. There were many days when Mr. Tippet would show up and greet us. I swear that man knew everything that was going on in the hotel and he had some special power to know about events before they happened.

One day, I finished my duties early and Mrs. Wilson gave me permission to take the "secret hike" back to the dorm. As I began my ascent to the dorm, I found the most radiant, beautiful woman seated on a boulder. She was knock-down gorgeous.

As I passed her, I stopped and said hello and she started talking to me about the park. I knew a few tidbits about some of the short hikes and some of the interesting facts about the park. We kept talking and we kept talking. I was amazed that this beautiful lady would actually talk to a West Texas boy with a funny accent. She did make a comment about my accent and we had a good laugh over it.

We sat on that rock and talked for about an hour. Then she excused herself and I went on my way back to the dorm. Wow, what a day, I simply could not get the lady out of my mind. I kept thinking how nice she had been, how down-to-earth she was, and how she loved the rugged beauty and the antiquated conditions at the hotel.

Harvey Barkowsky

That evening, several of us were to meet in the lounge by the dining room. Then, out of the dining room came the beautiful lady. She made a little wave to me and I couldn't move. Who was this incredible woman?

A few seconds later, Cliff Reykdal, the dining room manager, came rushing into the lounge and said, "That was Candice Bergen who just walked out of the dining room."

I went into an absolute state of shock. I know my mouth had fallen to my chest and all of my friends looked at me as I was probably turning pale. I was speechless, my legs would not move, my mouth (for once) wouldn't work and I sat there frozen with a drink in my hand.

Finally, some of my friends noticed my condition and started poking me and saying my name and I came back to reality. Everyone seemed a bit worried as I set my glass down and finally muttered— "I talked to Candice Bergen on a rock for about an hour today."

Everyone was silent. It took a second to sink in and then all heck broke loose. Questions started flying at me about what, when, and where. I tried to answer them but was off in la-la stardom land. Most of my friends were impressed, although I know several thought I had completely lost my mind. Some didn't believe me, but I didn't care.

I slowly arose from the table and left for the dorm. As I fell into bed, I lay there and before I dropped off to sleep I thought that I had actually talked to Candice Bergen.

I took many beautiful hikes that first summer, reveled in the beauty and lost my breath at the rugged majesty of Glacier. But when I look back on all of those hikes, I know that the "secret hike" was my favorite.

Glacier Park . . . A Hill family affair
Eileen B. McCormack
(Former associate curator, Hill Papers, James J. Hill Library, St. Paul, Minnesota)

To Louis W. Hill, Glacier National Park was much more than just a tourist destination that would enhance the reputation and financial ledger of his Great Northern Railway. Accounts of the establishment of the area as a national park, and the railway's subsequent activities to make it an accessible and desirable travel option for early 20th century vacation-goers, always give credit for this initiative to Louis Hill. In many of these accounts, Hill's love of Glacier is front and center. This short narrative will give examples of how he passed this love on to his family . . . in their own words.

Louis and his wife Maud had four children, Louis, Jr. (born 1902), Maudie (1903), Jerome (1905), and Corty (1906), and he was very involved in their lives. Family trips and vacations were frequent, and many of them included Glacier as a destination, or as a stop on frequent travels west. Hill's wife Maud had family members living in Seattle, and after 1914, the Hill family owned a home in Pebble Beach, California.

Since the family was usually together on these travels, there are not a great number of letters home. However, those that do exist show how much they enjoyed the area. Louis Hill, Jr.'s brief accounts of visits to the park are especially informative. In 1913 he kept a diary of a family trip in July:

• July 18th - We arrived in Glacier Park and shortly afterwards we went to the store to select the provisions for the trip. After lunch we went a little way up Mount Henry and after that we went in swimming, the water was 45 degrees.

• July 19th - Dad and I started for Two Medicine to look for a good camping place. After lunch we saw some bucking broncos and then went in swimming.

• July 21st - We started for Trick Falls about 9:30. We got 13 trout and one sucker. That afternoon we climbed Rising Wolf.

• July 22nd - We started for Buttercup Basin. We took turns walking and riding and we ate lunch up there. The walkers beat the horses home. That night we all slept well.

• July 23rd - We were to break camp so we got up early . . . when the wagon came it was not long before we had it loaded and then we went to the chalets for breakfast. After breakfast Maudie, Corty, Dad and the two-wheeler set out for Cut Bank camp. From there we had a beautiful climb to the top of the ridge; when nearly to the top we could see Lower Two Medicine.

The rest of his family returned to the park in September, after Louis, Jr.'s classes had begun. His siblings wrote him of their activities which included more hiking, picnicking, exploring, witnessing Indian dances and singing.

During some visits Louis would come and go on railway business, while his family remained in the park. Everything was arranged for their stay, as seen in this 1916 telegram to Charles B. Griffin: "My family expect to leave tomorrow night for the park and want the same guide, George, I believe his last name is Jennings, to meet them and they will take him up to Many Glacier where the horses are. Will you please arrange? L.W. Hill."

Louis, Jr. joined his father on many hunting and fishing trips to Glacier, and wrote an account of one of these in 1921:

• July 12th - No one but George [Jennings] and I were stirring so we decided to take a trip up Altyn peak. The blue haze was beginning to show and it was fairly warm, but we took it easy and had a very pleasant climb. We came to a big overhang . . . here we ate lunch in a very peculiar position, our feet over hanging a 10-foot drop, with a small stream running parallel to the edge some two feet behind us. We only had to reach behind for a drink, and in front lay a fine view. From our lunch place we went up to Josephine. . . . Dad was up there with Corty and they had very good luck bringing home a nice mess.

• July 20th - Corty and I went over Piegan [Pass], on top of the summit southeast of the pass. It was very windy and we had quite a time coming down from the pass to Morning Eagle Falls. The wind was so strong that at times the water off Dawn Mist [Falls] went up instead of down.

Those who have spent time at Glacier Park often talk of the lasting impression the area made on them. This "Glacier effect" is shown in letters Louis Hill, Jr. sent his mother years after his childhood visits. In 1929, he worked for the Great Northern Railway and often stopped in the park, for a day here and there:

• August 17th - Apikuni in the morning. I had the most glorious walk in the warm morning sunshine. Up past the falls, into the basin by a short cut. I swiped huckleberries from God and the bears and came home. It was the most beautiful day – just turning from summer to autumn – hot and dry with a wind that raised dust far below in the valley.

And in 1952 when Louis, Jr. brought his own family for a Glacier Park vacation:

• August 10th - Yesterday we went to Morning Eagle Falls. It was a

The children of Great Northern Railway chairman Louis Hill at Glacier Park Hotel in 1920. From the left are Jerome, Corty, Maudie and Louis Jr.

Maud Hill Schroll collection, Minnesota Historical Society

beautiful day, lots of clouds, sunlight, and the "Feather Plume Falls" that comes right out of the sky over the cliff was disappearing again into the air. They call it Horse Tail Falls now, but I like the old name. Morning Eagle is always beautiful. Just before lunch I took a walk way up near the top of Piegan Pass, to the place you and Dad and I went and watched Mr. Stevenson climb up the rock chimney—as he was looking for the correct way over the Piegan Pass. I remember, as you sat watching him, you started counting flowers and you got over a dozen different varieties as you sat there.

Mark Hufstetler pauses to admire Glacier's beauty. Courtesy, Mark Hufstetler

Chapter 11

Afoot in the backcountry

A grisly episode at Poia Lake
Mark Hufstetler
(Lake McDonald Lodge 1978-83, National Park Service 1987-88)

The lessons of bear awareness are certainly vital ones for Glacier workers to learn, but occasionally all of the reminders and warnings can combine with an employee's active imagination to produce a pretty traumatic experience. Such an incident caused an uneasy night for three Lake McDonald employees during the summer of 1980.

Todd, Betsy and Mark set off one afternoon to backpack the Redgap-Ptarmigan Loop trail, with an overnight stop at the Poia Lake campground. It was early evening before the hikers hit the trail, and the long climb over Swiftcurrent Ridge was made in a cloudy, windy dusk. The clouds soon opened into rain, and the trip became an unpleasant, muddy march toward the comparative warmth and comfort of camp.

The trail was deserted, but an abundance of bear signs made it clear that something, at least, had shared the hikers' route. The lengthening shadows and the howling wind made it seem like a grizzly was lurking behind every bush, and the trio's pace quickened.

The campground was reached just as darkness fell, but any feelings of relief and security were short-lived: the camp was deserted, and the moonlight revealed a torn and bloodstained sleeping bag lying beside the trail. It seemed obvious that something terrible had just happened, and that Poia Lake campground was not the place to be.

The hikers had little choice, though, and nervously pitched their tent as far from the awful sleeping bag as possible. Backpacks were quickly stashed in the outhouse, presumably the best place to obscure any food smell. The group retired for a long and sleepless night.

A tremendous sense of relief came with the dawn, as the campers awoke to find themselves intact and breathing. The ruined sleeping bag was cautiously examined, and the fears dissolved into nervous laughter. The "bloodstains" were nothing more than smoke stains; the bear attack was nothing more than an out-of-hand campfire.

The trio hit the trail with restored spirits, but still with the urge to look cautiously over their shoulders every once in a while. You never know what's hiding in the woods.

The fine art of scree running
Rolf Larson
(Many Glacier Hotel 1975, 1977-80)

Glacier's peaks are carved from soft, sedimentary rock. Their rugged faces belie their gentle backsides, with slopes and ledges that can be walked up by less-than-expert mountaineers. But weathering has left behind an abundance of loose rock—chunky talus and finer scree that blankets the backsides of mountains and accumulates at the base of cliffs. Climbing up such slopes is time consuming and arduous. For every step up, one tends to slide back.

But there is another dimension: descending Glacier's scree slopes. A tradition has been passed along among those who have spent time above the timberline and far from the trails—the fine art of scree running. By following a few common-sense rules, this sport is both fun and safe.

First of all, you must know where you are going and what types of terrain lies below you. Unless you know for a fact that there are no cliffs or staircase ledges below you, be very careful. Cliffs are often hard to pick out where rock shading is similar for several thousand feet below you. Look for fine lines where rock texture or color varies, or where there is a break in the dimensions of rocks and foliage. Also, never run scree above snow fields. Once on snow, it is very difficult to stop until you reach the rocks at the bottom—or cliffs.

When scree running a slope, keep your legs wide apart and knees bent, shifting your weight from side to side. Bending the knees absorbs much of the jolt, saving your joints and helps you adjust to rocks that move too much or too little. By shifting your weight from leg to leg, you break downhill momentum, making it easier to stop or regain your balance. Always lean backwards so that if you fall, you will land on your seat rather than your face.

If you want to go fast, point your toes downward so your feet are parallel to the slope. This enhances sliding. Very rapid scree runners actually leap in the air as they run, allowing gravity to accelerate them. This, however, sacrifices control. To slow down, keep your feet planted in the scree, digging your heels in, so your feet are more or less perpendicular to the slope.

When picking your way down a slope, be on the lookout for local hazards. Choose your route to follow the finest gravel, avoiding larger rocks and outcroppings. The secret to safety is to be aware of both the long view and the short view.

I have spent many memorable moments floating down Glacier's scree slopes, joking about stopping at the "Scree Chalet," and getting in line for the "scree lift." The sensation is without a doubt one of the most pleasing aspects of mountain climbing, but one must always remember to respect the demands of the terrain. Avoid cutting switchbacks, and remember to balance your cavorting with caution.

Hang on tight!
Dave Shoup
(Swiftcurrent Motor Inn 1973-1975, Many Glacier Hotel 1976)

Using simple math, I only had about 48 days off to hit the trails and peaks during my four memorable years of Glacier. I was one of the fortunate few who almost always had beautiful weather on my one day off per week. My long-time hiking and climbing buddies and I used to laugh that we rarely got rain on our day off. Deep down inside, however, I always despised wasting my day off.

Here's one of the memories that I put in my "Longest Day" category: a climb up Little Chief Mountain in 1976 with two of my regular hiking companions, Dan Vandell (Swiftcurrent waiter 1970-71, 1974-75) and Mike Scarano (Swiftcurrent waiter 1974-76).

Generally, most think that the pinnacle of the day would be to reach the summit. Not on this day. The real excitement began after we returned to Going-to-the-Sun Road.

The day did not start well. The early morning skies appeared "iffy." Were the clouds going to open up or burn off? On this particular day, I was the optimist (this was not always the case). It took me almost an hour to convince Dan and Mike that we should "go for it" and at the very least get our ride to the St. Mary Falls trail junction, and then make our final decision.

At the trailhead, nothing had changed: the weather still was hauntingly unpredictable. Another big hurdle was the clock. We knew that Gordon Edwards had specifically warned in the J. Gordon Edwards' *Climber's Guide* that Little Chief was a deceptively long climb and that hikers should start at the crack of dawn to ensure returning before nightfall. I had always respected Edwards' advice, but this time we stubbornly "went for it," trucking down the trail about 9 a.m.

Little Chief is climbed by leaving the trail near Virginia Falls, bushwhacking up the north and northwest slopes, and then following a steep gully that takes one up close to the very big notch on the northern face. Then, (the time consuming portion of the climb) one skirts around the massive vertical cliffs on the west side all the way around to the southwestern slope, where a series of Class 3 and few Class 4 cliffs ascend fairly easily to the summit.

We reached the steep gully by late morning. Then the rain began. We huddled under some overhanging rocks and decided to wait it out. We waited for over an hour. Fortunately, the mountain gods blessed us, as the rain stopped and the skies cleared.

I don't remember what made us continue the climb, since the clock, not the mountain, had become our biggest nemesis. I guess we stubbornly felt that we had just gone too far to turn back ... and, besides, it was our only day off.

We ended up "enjoying" a sinking sun a little past 7 p.m. on the summit of Little Chief. We obviously had ignored the basic safety rule of always ensuring a safe retreat.

Dan, Mike and I "ran" down Little Chief. The adrenalin was flowing freely as we steadily witnessed darkness fall.

The lower third of Little Chief is a descent through thick alders, intermingled with five- to eight-foot cliffs. That was an adventure in itself. In near-total darkness (Where's the moon when you really need it?), we painstakingly inched our way down these Class 3 cliffs. We hung onto alder branches and lowered ourselves over cliffs. Several times we had to jump a foot or two to rocks or ground beneath cliffs that we could not see. It felt like jumping into an abyss. That was scary and something I'll never do again.

As we descended lower and lower, the silhouette of St. Mary Lake below grew larger and larger. Eventually, we were bound to reach the trail that was our ticket back to Going-to-the-Sun Road. Our total focus was on locating the trail in the darkness. I'll never forget hearing Dan, about 20 feet behind me, say, "What's this? Look at this. Is this the trail? I'm not sure."

Our flashlights revealed that it was indeed the trail. Mike and I had bushwhacked right across it. If Dan had not found the trail, we surely would have ended up wandering through the alders all night long. Never, ever did a trail (at about 1:30 in the morning) feel so good beneath my feet.

At this point I had had enough "adventure" for one day . . . but that was not to be. We arrived at Going-to-the-Sun Road exhausted about 2:30 a.m.

We had no access to transportation home but our right thumbs. We had to get back to Swiftcurrent by daybreak to work the morning shift.

As most *Inside Trail* readers know, there's not much traffic on Going-to-the-Sun Road in the middle of the night. Eventually, a couple of cars passed us by. We (rather forcefully) waved down the next car. It was driven by a young lady, 25 to 30 years of age, who was willing to offer us a ride. Unfortunately, the small vehicle was jammed full of luggage and other belongings. There was only room for one person in the passenger seat. At the driver's invitation, Dan and I climbed on top of the car and lay down, gripping the small luggage rack, with our feet dangling on the rear window.

At first, the ride seemed tenuous, but fun. Lying on the car's roof with the cool air rushing over us felt good. The young lady started out at a moderate

Little Chief Mountain as seen from Going-to-the-Sun Road. Chris Morrison photo

rate of speed. My biggest fear was whenever we saw the headlights of an approaching vehicle. At that time of night, the probability seemed very, very high that it would be driven by an unsympathetic ranger.

Then it happened. Our driver, for some unknown reason, developed a lead foot. Was she on drugs or something? I'll never know, but off she sped, with Dan and I hanging on for dear life as she swung around the twists and curves of Going-the-Sun Road. I can attest to the fact that to keep from sliding off the roof of a car, one must hold on very tight. We banged on the car roof and yelled for her to slow down, to no avail. Maybe she thought it was funny, but we did not—although in retrospect the vision of us draped on top of a small car speeding to St. Mary is sort of comical.

We made it back to Swiftcurrent shortly before our morning shifts. This was thanks to Ann Martinson (a Swiftcurrent cook), whom we dragged out of bed with a telephone call and convinced to drive to St. Mary to rescue us. I don't clearly recall heading off to work that morning, but I'm sure that Dan, Mike and I were not very productive employees that day.

The moving handrail
Dick Schwab
(Many Glacier Hotel 1947-52)

My brother Phil and I particularly liked the hotel manager in 1952, Lloyd Seilset, and his charming wife, Gjerda, and the feeling was mutual. They were an outstanding management team, by far the best we ever experienced.

Without sacrificing the respect they merited from the employees, the Seilsets occasionally joined them to enjoy some of the adventures of the park. They were game hikers and excellent company on the trail. I remember especially one expedition with them because it was the occasion of our discovery of what we called "the moving handrail."

This was a hike over the splendid Carthew-Alderson trail from Cameron Lake in Waterton Lakes National Park down to the townsite. As we got up toward the summit, it became evident that Mrs. Seilset was suffering seriously from fear of heights on the narrow track across a very steep scree slope.

Phil suddenly got the brilliant idea of using a five- or six-foot pine pole lying along the trail to give her a sense of security. He got on one end, grasped the pole with his right hand, and I got on the other end, doing the same thing. Mrs. Seilset walked in between us, resting her hand on the pole, and lo, she had a moving handrail as the three of us marched smoothly across the scary part of the trail. Just the existence of the pole between her and the steep slope did the trick.

It was quite an amusing sight for other hikers passing us. We were all delighted by the success of this system. Phil and I used it later to help others who suffered from vertigo and it always worked well.

Where angels dare not tread
Einar Hanson
(Many Glacier Hotel 1976-77, 1979)

"How'd you like to climb Wilbur this afternoon?"

The question was innocent enough. Waiting for an answer, Dave Beneman stood beside me along the steam table line, next to the stoves. With his curly black hair and olive brown eyes, Dave looked like a youngish weightlifter, a son of the mountain king.

I'd heard Dave ask Keith Barbeau, the first cook, the same question earlier, before the lunch rush, before the hundreds of plates of corned beef on rye, fruit plates or grilled trout were fed to tired travelers from Iowa, or Nebraska, or Ohio, who were doing Glacier park for a day, as our guests at Many Glacier Hotel. Guess Keith had turned him down.

"Sure."

"Great. Steve took off this morning to do it before his afternoon shift, and I want to do it, too."

I had caught glimpses of the mountain-climbing rivalry between Dave and my other roommate, Steve Winnett, during the previous three weeks. I knew Dave had taught climbing in the Appalachians, out east near his home, and he and Steve had met last summer working at the park. A blond farm boy from the Midwest, I had never even seen mountains before. Having one summer under his belt, I considered Dave a veteran, even though he was only 18 and I was 19. Besides, he'd climbed Wilbur before.

I knew which mountain was Wilbur. When I'd hiked up Mount Altyn the previous week, my first (and only) climb, Rolf Larson had pointed Wilbur out to me. It was spectacular, rising like a hand of peace above the valley.

My Red Wing work boots, which my novice mind thought could double as hiking boots for the summer, had their crepe soles ground to dust by the red scree of Altyn on our descent. Facing the prospect of shoeless climbing, I had hitchhiked the 120 miles to Kalispell after work yesterday to buy my first hiking boots, a beautiful set of Raichles. What more could I need to climb Wilbur?

Two hours later, with our shift over, we set off. The mid-afternoon sun shone through the June haze, casting shadows across the face of Wilbur's sheer east face. There must be an easy way up, I thought. Dave surely must know that I don't know how to climb anything hard.

We stepped off the trail near Red Rock Falls, picking our way through the scrub and brush on the mountain's lower flanks. For two hours we bushwhacked, pushing through willows, then scree, then boulders, until we finally rested below the towering face. It was five o'clock.

"How much farther is the top?"

"Oh, we're about halfway there."

"That far?"

"The hard part's just beginning."

The next three hours introduced me to fear as I had never known it.

Wilbur's face is an unbroken cliff, wrinkled and furrowed with the erosion of time. These wrinkles, actually deep chimneys in the rock, offer the "easy way up," through "opposition climbing," a technique Dave taught me from above, talking me up over overhangs and through crossovers.

A great vault of midsummer's air hung behind us, under us, over us. An eagle lazily circled far down the valley below. If only I can make it back down, I thought. The hotel, miles away, shone in the late afternoon sun. My thoughts wandered to Connie, the pretty, dark-haired waitress I was nuts about. I wonder if I'll see her again, I mused. Reason enough to make it back down this rock.

"Move one, hold three," urged Dave. My thoughts snapped back, and I was back on the cliffs again, carefully gripping a new handhold, then a foothold, then another handhold, then a foothold. Oops! Not that one.

Mount Wilbur as seen from Many Glacier Hotel. Frank Horsfall photo, courtesy John Horsfall

A chunk of loose rock broke off in my hand. I dropped it and heard it skip away below.

Dave was quiet and sure in his climbing. "Practice not kicking out loose rock," he said. "Other climbers below might get hurt."

Above me, Dave hoisted himself through "Thin Man's Pleasure." This landmark of the climb was a narrow shaft behind a huge chock-rock caught in the chimney we were climbing. The face of the chimney leaned out just before the passageway, creating an overhang. Negotiating this area meant stretching back across the thin air of the chimney, away from the comforting face of the mountain, to inch past the wall swelling toward you.

"Here," Dave called from the ledge above, tossing down the end of a slender purple rope. "Loop this around your wrist. It can provide another handhold if you can't find one."

I looped the rope around my right wrist.

"Yell 'Belay on' when you wish to use the rope for support. That's climber's lingo for me to brace the rope across my hips to take your weight, if necessary."

Gradually, I inched upward, stretching my feet back to footholds on the chimney's side walls.

"I can't find another handhold, Dave."

"Then say, Belay on."

"Belay on."

My heart was pounding heavy and slow. I drew myself up on the "handhold" made of rope, as I sought a new foothold. . . . Suddenly, the rock crumbled beneath my other foot, my left handhold pulled free, and I was dangling in space, suspended from the rope around my wrist.

"Hold on!" cried Dave. Hand over hand, he pulled me up like a bucket from a well, until I regained my footing and scrambled onto the ledge where he stood.

I drank in air. Oh, that was close. For the first time I thanked God that Dave was built like a fireplug. We continued upward. The remainder of the climb was just a scramble to the top. From this perch, above the Continental Divide, the mountains of Glacier Park and beyond marched rank upon rank to the setting sun. It was glorious.

I'll never get down, I thought with calm certainty. I'll die up here.

We ate our lunches, signed the climber's register in the summit cairn and took pictures.

"We must be the first people to climb Wilbur after work," exulted Dave. My answering cheer was a little hollow. How were we ever going to get off this stupid rock, I thought.

It was 8 p.m. when we started down. Getting off the cliffs before dark was going to be a race against time, a race made easier by fear being replaced by the utter numbness of having no choice. Only flashes emerge from the blur: jumping 10 feet down from one ledge to another to save time; Dave guiding me from below where to put my feet as I descended a particularly hairy section.

Then, we were off the cliffs, scree-sliding down the upper slopes. It was 10 p.m. The sun was setting at this northern latitude, two days after the summer solstice. We were still more than a mile up the mountain.

Quickly we were off the scree slopes and into the willows and alder underbrush. It was dark, a moon rising behind the mountains. I found myself in front, as we fought through the tangled growth. Branches whipped our faces.

I heard the sound of falling water grow louder from somewhere ahead. Suddenly, the ground disappeared under my feet. I fell forward, grabbing the branches. I caught myself, suspended by alder branches above the waterfall.

I pulled myself back up onto the ground again. The adrenalin I thought had long ago been burned dry now caught my breath short and pounded my heart. I was exhausted. My body ached all over.

We detoured around the water and on down the slope. Finally, we reached the hiking trail, back where we had started. It was 11:30. A full moon shone down between Mount Grinnell and Mount Allen.

After all that struggle, after fighting with myself not to turn back, and swearing to myself that I would make it, I could keep quiet no longer.

"Dave, that was terrible. Is that considered a hard mountain to climb?"

"Oh, yes. It's probably the second-hardest mountain to climb in Glacier in terms of sheer climbing."

I was silent. I couldn't believe Dave had taken me up a mountain that hard without even telling me what I was getting into; I couldn't believe I had been mule-headed enough to keep going.

"If we hurry, we can still get a beer at the hotel."

"Great!"

We started to jog down the moonlit trail, Dave in the lead. Keeping a steady pace, we made good progress, sometimes stumbling on unseen tree roots.

Soon, we reached the footbridge across Swiftcurrent Creek. Dave stopped short. I bumped into him. Someone was splashing in the stream below.

"Who's swimming?" I yelled.

"Shut-up," hissed Dave. "It's a bear."

Sure enough. Silhouetted in the moon-lit stream, a bear fished for a midnight snack. It turned its head towards us . . . we stared . . . then we bolted down the trail. Forgetting all the park ranger warnings not to run from bears, we tore down the trail like sprinters. Almost there . . . "Oof."

Almost in unison, Dave and I had run full-tilt into a heavy chain, strung across the trail to stop errant motorcycles and ATVs, like two runners hitting the tape. We straightened up, sucking back our wind. This was the Swiftcurrent Motel parking lot. We were back.

Fifteen minutes later, after jogging the last mile to the Many Glacier Hotel bar, we were each gulping down a Coors.

"Did Steve make it up Wilbur?" Dave asked a passing fellow cook. "No, he turned back. Figured it was too hard to get up and back before dark."

I finished my beer then left the bar. I walked towards the laundry-employee lounge, looking for the tall, dark-haired waitress who I hoped would be off work. Connie was. I swung her up, and flopped down on an old green sofa. A few other waitresses and waiters were hanging out, as well, including Scott, of whose dark, wavy good looks and Amherst breeding I was somewhat envious.

"Where were you?" asked Connie. "I heard you went mountain climbing with Dave."

"We climbed Mount Wilbur," I replied.

"You must mean Mount Henkel," interjected Scott.

"No, it was Mount Wilbur," said I, for by that time I was no longer confused about what it was.

Moose fishing at Kootenai Lakes
Chet Bowers
(Glacier Park Transport Company 1941, 1946)

Dick Fossum, the Glacier Park Hotel Company's auditor and general cashier, and I were in Waterton about 1950 when we heard of the sizable brook trout to be found in Kootenai Lakes, about one mile south of the head of Upper Waterton Lake. We rented an inboard 12-foot dinghy from Slim [Udal], who operated the Waterton boat rentals, and took off at 6 the following morning equipped with fishing gear, beverages, and insect repellent. After a couple of hours putting down the western shore we realized that, at three to four knots per hour, it was going to be a long day.

We beached the dinghy about 11 a.m. and packed our gear in to Kootenai Lakes, which are really a group of meandering sloughs. We had caught a couple of nice brookies and were wading along a bank thickly covered

Chet Bowers at Crypt Lake in 1941.

Courtesy, Chet Bowers

by four to five foot brush when a loud crashing sound followed by the appearance of a young bull moose got our immediate attention.

It was close to rutting season and I could count the veins in his fiery red eyeballs. Foss and I tried to walk on water, but were soon up to our chins as we bounced our way to the opposite bank. Swimming was not an option as our boots were full of water.

We arrived back at the Waterton docks about dusk. Slim was glad to get his boat back, and we had again proven that adage, "Any day is a good day at Waterton."

Seventy-five miles on the trail
John Hagen
(Many Glacier Hotel 1970-80)

In 1973 two friends and I attempted a non-stop hike from Glacier Park Lodge to Waterton. My stalwart companions on that adventure were Dave Paulus and Ron Zahn.

We had a breezy nonchalance as we set about this expedition. None of us carried so much as a knapsack. We stuck some candy bars in our pockets, and carried a few odds and ends (beef jerky, athletic tape, and salt to counteract dehydration) in a leather shaving kit. No one carried a water bottle—giardia was unheard of in those days, and we drank from any fast-flowing stream. We each had a windbreaker, a flashlight, and a bear bell or two. None of us thought to bring a hat to ward off the hot summer sun. Yet, despite our attitudes, we all were seasoned hikers.

Our plan was to start at Glacier Park Lodge at midnight on July 13. We would walk north along the Inside Trail—the famous old trail which in Glacier's early years had conveyed horse parties from the lodge to Two Medicine Chalets, Cut Bank Chalets, Red Eagle Tent Camp, and finally St. Mary Chalets. Near St. Mary, we planned to turn west on the trail along the south shore of St. Mary Lake. Then we planned to climb Going-to-the-Sun Road to Logan Pass, walk up the Highline Trail to Goat Haunt, and push on to Waterton—95 miles in all.

The only navigational problem we anticipated was at the start of the hike. None of us ever had taken the first leg of the Inside Trail from East Glacier over Scenic Point to Two Medicine. We were told that the trail was somewhat hard to follow from its starting point along the East Glacier golf course through the first mile of brushy forest. Since we were planning to start in darkness, we made inquiries for a guide.

Tom Doering, a gearjammer, kindly agreed to guide us over the first miles of trail. He expertly led us through the confusing aspen groves at the start of the hike, and then up into rugged foothills. Tom was a genial companion and an excellent astronomer. He pointed out constellations and planets. We set a brisk pace, forging uphill at nearly 4 m.p.h. We came to Scenic Point, a fine vantage point overlooking the high plains with Browning and Cut Bank in the distance. We followed the trail along the stony open shoulders of Mount Henry under the vivid, starry sky. Then we descended to Two Medicine, arriving before 3 a.m. The chalet, the launch *Sinopah*, and the campground all were dark and profoundly still. We gave our earnest thanks to Tom, who set off down the road for East Glacier.

Now Ron, Dave, and I strode off on familiar ground—the long forested trail up the Dry Fork. We yelled and waved our flashlights and jingled our bear bells to warn off wandering bruins. In two hours, we arrived at Old Man Lake and started up the long steep switchbacks leading to Pitamakan Pass. Dawn was spreading over Glacier's mountaintops as we arrived on the pass. Below us, the Cut Bank Valley, Pitamakan Lake and the Lake of the Seven Winds still lay enveloped in inky shadow. We loped down the trail into the valley, having covered about 18 miles in about five hours.

Unexpectedly, trouble arose. As we descended the rough, rocky trail, Dave developed a cramped foot. He gamely tried to shake off the pain and to loosen the muscle, to no avail. After plodding for six more miles down the valley, he felt compelled to abandon the hike. Dave left Ron and me at the trail junction to Cut Bank campground, walked to the campground and hitchhiked back to Many Glacier.

Ron and I turned westward up the steep climb to Triple Divide Pass. We would have appreciated a drink of that water on the arid

John Hagen at Triple Divide Pass. John Hagen collection

pass. At midmorning, the day was already hot and from now on we would be exposed almost constantly to the blazing sun. We descended long, rocky slopes and then long, wooded switchbacks to Red Eagle Lake. We then continued northeastward along Red Eagle Creek, as the heat grew more oppressive. At length we came to the fork in the trail between St. Mary townsite and St. Mary Lake. Here Ron decided to end his hike. He walked out to the townsite and hitchhiked home, having covered about 47 miles.

I took the long trail leading westward along the south shore of St. Mary Lake. The noonday sun was now intense, and the streams were few and far between. I began to see the folly of taking such a trip without a water bottle or a hat. I passed under the spires of Red Eagle, Mahtotopa, Little Chief, and Citadel Mountains, in their stately file along the shoreline of St. Mary Lake. At the lake's west end, I passed the great waterfalls, Virginia and St. Mary, and made my way along spur trails to the pavement of Going-to-the-Sun Road.

In front of me was the most daunting physical challenge that I ever have faced in my life. The temperature was in the high 90s—an extremely hot day for Glacier—and as I walked up the roadside I was completely exposed to the withering sun. I was weary and parched, and there were only a couple of water sources (Siyeh Creek and Lunch Creek) along the last few miles to Logan Pass. The road ran relentlessly uphill. My quadriceps and hamstrings ached, and I was breathing in panting gasps.

I knew that I was too spent to complete the hike to Canada. The question now was whether I had the willpower to push on to Logan Pass. The steep pitch in the road above Siyeh Bend seemed almost impossible to climb. I was near the point of giving up and hitchhiking back down the road. Then a deadheading Red bus taking a group of off-duty Many Glacier employees homeward suddenly passed by. The employees, standing up in the open bus, gave me a cheer, which steeled my will. I pushed up the steep slope and painfully plodded the last two miles to Logan Pass. The visitor center there, nestled below snowy Mount Clements seemed like a vision of paradise—gradually, gradually drawing closer, through enormous effort and pain.

At Logan Pass I threw myself on the ground and rested for a while. The panting gradually subsided and my heartbeat gradually slowed. I drank and drank from the water fountain, took salt to electrolyze the fluid, and managed to eat a little food. Meanwhile, I pondered what to do next. Completing the full hike was out of the question, but if I had strength enough, I thought I should hike on to Granite Park Chalet. We had arranged to rendezvous there with David Manzer, another Many Glacier employee. The plan had been for David, with a cache of food, to join us at 3 p.m. for the last 33 miles to Waterton, but it was now nearly 6 p.m. I thought that David probably would have given up on us and returned to Many Glacier before I could reach the chalet, but I thought that I should try.

I started out along the Highline. I was sore and tired, but I found that I could walk at a normal hiker's pace of about three m.p.h. The heat had subsided and the evening was very beautiful as the sun sank toward the peaks of the Livingston Range. Around sundown I reached Granite Park Chalet. The employees there told me that David had faithfully waited for us until early evening. He finally had left to return to Many only about an hour before. I drank a pitcher of Granite Park Kool-Aid, bought a slice of apple pie and then started uphill toward Swiftcurrent Pass as twilight fell across the park.

I remember the golden lights of the Swiftcurrent fire lookout shining out above me against a sky of deep blue in which stars were just beginning to show. It was a benevolent, peaceful image and it gave me a profound sense of the providence of God. I started down the switchbacks of Swiftcurrent

Pass, unexpectedly renewed in strength. I smiled to find a trail of orange peels along the side of the path left by Manzer.

I reached the floor of the Swiftcurrent Valley about 9 p.m., as full darkness was falling. I switched my flashlight on, and shouted periodically for bears, but I continued to feel a sense of benevolent providence surrounding me, and hiked on unafraid.

I reached the lobby of Many Glacier Hotel at the stroke of 11 p.m. I had completed a hike of 75 miles in 23 hours. Ian Tippet, the manager, was in the lobby. He graciously led me to the cafeteria and I gorged on milk and cake. Then I shuffled off to the dormitory, showered and tumbled into bed. My notebook shows the next day I had written "sore in the ankles," but rose to work my shift as a bellman and was reasonably sound.

I learned from the lessons of this hike. In planning another length-of-the-park attempt the next summer, I made sure that everyone had a hat and that we took a number of water bottles along. We took the hike from north to south, so that the exposed midday walk on the Logan Pass road would be going downhill instead of uphill. And we carried knapsacks containing more food, space blankets, and other emergency gear.

The 1974 adventure brought its own challenges, and the satisfaction of finally completing a non-stop hike across Glacier. But I never will forget the earlier trek, and the exhausting climb up Logan Pass in the withering midsummer heat.

Hiking the Inside Trail
Ginny Leach Mouw
(Glacier Park Hotel 1940-42, 1946-50)

East Glacier to Two Medicine is the easy one. It was the hike that I took every summer that I worked there, sometimes more than once. It was a trail that one almost always took in that direction for two reasons—first, the trail up along Mount Henry was an easy, but long grade, while from Two Med back was a steep, switch-backing climb, more difficult and far less interesting, scenically speaking. Second, you could start early without having to waste time hitchhiking. The hike was about 11 miles, by far the shortest of the Inside Trail.

The first time I hiked it was in 1940. You had to cut across the golf course, climb the stile, and seek out the path. Early on that day we ran across a Basque sheepherder with his flock. I was fascinated. Who knew there were Basque sheepherders here?

I learned that there were a number of them in Montana, and I wanted to find out when he had come, why he left his home terrain, how he had come to Montana, and what life here was like for him. But, alas, he couldn't speak my language, nor I his. I never saw him again.

My most embarrassing episode while hiking occurred on this trail. Lorraine Hartman and I were headed toward Two Med. It was an awfully hot day and we finally shed our shirts. The trail was perfectly open, and we knew that if we saw anyone coming, we could quickly cover up again. Fine reasoning, as far as it went.

Sheep grazing just outside Glacier Park.

Ray Djuff collection

As we came around the shoulder of Mount Henry to view Two Medicine, suddenly here were two fellows coming around the bend. Embarrassment and laughter, but after recovering our clothing, the four of us sat around and chatted a while before going our separate ways.

One year the Glacier Park office employees were treated to a moonlight boat trip on Two Medicine Lake. It was one of those perfect summer nights for a marvelous outing. We got back to the dock about midnight and as we headed for the bus, Karl Klein and I looked at each other and said simultaneously, "Let's hike back."

Everyone else boarded the bus, no doubt thinking what complete idiots we were. It was a long haul up the mountain and much darker through the trees than we had expected. The full moon didn't penetrate as we had thought it would, and we were both afraid we'd run into a bear, although neither of us confessed that until later.

As we rounded Mount Henry, the plains stretched out endlessly before us, bathed in moonlight, with a few lights scattered here and there. It was breathtaking, and one of my loveliest memories. Oh, the joy of being young and crazy.

Dawson Pass is not really on the Inside Trail, but it played its part. The pass is a steep, difficult six miles from Two Medicine, but when you reach the pass, it is, to my mind, the most wild and wonderful view in the park. It explains, in a way, my fascination with hiking in Glacier. Every time you cross a pass, you have an immediate, spectacular, new view, and you are rejuvenated by the beauty and the sense of accomplishment. I often felt like the bear that went over the mountain to see what he could see.

While we were at Dawson, I could see a game trail that stretched out to the right at the same level as the pass. On returning, I sought out Rum Cashman, hiker par excellence, and asked her about it. She said you could follow it, stay at that level, and you would come out at Cut Bank Pass. I had to wait a year before I could try it, and then Rum told me that when they hiked it, they took canned goods along for lunch and what they didn't eat, they buried about halfway between Dawson and Cut Bank passes, and erected a cairn to mark the spot. So Clare Williams and I tossed a can opener and a couple of spoons into our lunch sacks and headed out.

Again, that gorgeous view at Dawson Pass, and then off on the game trail. Sure enough, we found the cairn, dug up the cans, and sat there eating baked beans and peaches. Then we headed on to Cut Bank and Pitamakan Passes and down into the valley to Cut Bank Chalet.

Cut Bank Chalet and campground presented a real problem to hikers, as you couldn't depend on hitchhiking in or out. There simply wasn't enough traffic, so you had to arrange for someone to pick you up.

The only employees who were allowed to have cars were the office force, people who worked year around for the Great Northern. They spent winters in St. Paul and summers in the park, and they were good sports about picking us up in isolated places. We kept our requests to a minimum, but they enabled us to go places we never could have managed otherwise. This leg of the trail was about 18 miles, although going via Dawson was farther.

Rum Cashman
Ray Djuff collection

The last leg of the Inside Trail, from Cut Bank to St. Mary, turned out to be St. Mary back to Cut Bank campground. The year was 1950 and I was keeping the Red bus records for the Transport Company that summer. I talked gearjammers Hal Henkel, from White Bear Lake, Minnesota, and Vaughn Merrill, from Arizona, into accompanying me. We had a ride to St. Mary, and the driver was kind enough to take us as far as he could on the primitive road, thus saving us a mile or two, a big help on what would have been a 23-mile hike.

We made it to Red Eagle Lake, where we ate lunch. From there we hiked along a stream which eventually had washed out the trail completely.

We sloshed back and forth across that stream trying to find our way, and I remember thinking that we had come all this way and might be forced to give up the hike. Eventually, miraculously, the trail reappeared, and we headed up to Triple Divide Pass, where we stopped to rest.

It was then I discovered I had thrown away the remains of my lunch and had hauled a bag of trash all that distance. Still, I was happy to be sitting there, thinking about the water that drained off to the Gulf of Mexico, the Pacific Ocean, and Hudson Bay. When would I ever be in such a spot again?

All I remember about the rest of the trip was being extremely tired and dragging in to the Cut Bank campground after dark. Nothing was left but to collapse in the car while someone else took us home.

Thus ends my saga of the Inside Trail. I'm disappointed, for apparently I didn't complete it, having missed the direct trail from Two Medicine to Cut Bank Pass. Hey, I'm 88, and I won't be hiking there again, but if I were, I'd head straight for Dawson Pass and its incomparable view.

Eighty years of hiking in Glacier
Glenn Mueller
(Glacier visitor since 1920s)

My first hike in Glacier was to either Iceberg Lake or Grinnell Glacier. While I can't be sure which trail it was, it certainly was one of those two "kid-friendly" trails. Both became favorites for my family.

I first hiked those trails with my parents, Oscar and Josephine Mueller, and my younger brother George. There weren't many other hikers on the trails and by the time of the Heavens Peak fire in 1936, I had hiked both those trails more than once. I don't recall the fire itself, but I definitely recall how changed and barren the area was after the fire.

Nineteen thirty-six was also the year I turned 18, and our family trip to the park just after the fire was my last one for several years. That fall, I enrolled in the University of Montana to study forestry and went on to work out of state, serve in the military during the war and then I took a job with the Soil Conservation Service in Malta, Montana.

With friends from Malta, I began what was for 10 years an annual Fourth of July trip backpacking and fishing in Glacier. Our favorite trip in those years was to drive up past Chief Mountain on Highway 17 to the Canadian border. We would spend the night at the trailhead, then hike to the Belly River, past thundering Dawn Mist Falls and set up camp at Lake Elizabeth. Then we would explore Lake Helen, Cosley and Glenns Lakes and Redgap Pass. Other years we would hike from Swiftcurrent camp through the Ptarmigan Tunnel to Elizabeth camp. I have never tired of the breathtaking view of the Belly River drainage from the tunnel.

Freeze-dried, lightweight food was not available in the late 1940s. Camping gear was also heavier. Our canvas packs contained potatoes, cans of Vienna sausage, bacon, eggs, bread, pancake flour and dried and fresh fruit. Our canvas tents were war surplus two-man tents. Some of us had army surplus sleeping bags, but on my first backpacking trips I slept in a bedroll of folded blankets. We cooked on an open fire with coffee cans which had two holes poked through the sides of the can near the top with a wire strung through for a handle. Different sized cans would be nested inside each other in our packs. For frying, we brought along a skillet. Our packs were heavy.

It was in Malta that I met Helen Weinmeister, who was the home econom-

Glenn Mueller, seen here with a family member, has hiked the trails of Glacier Park since the 1920s, first with his parents, then children and grandchildren.

Courtesy, Glenn Mueller

ics teacher at the high school and has now been my wife for over 55 years. Before we married I asked her if she had objections to our Fourth of July trips. She had none, so I continued them after I married. For those 10 years of hikes we seldom ran into other hikers or backpackers, generally having the place to ourselves, except for the wildlife.

During the years I lived in Malta, I was assistant scoutmaster for Boy Scout Troop 29. The troop made several trips to Camp Napi on Lower St. Mary Lake. From there we would often take day hikes, some of them the same ones I had taken as a boy.

By 1956 I was the father of two young girls and took a job with the Forest Service in White Sulphur Springs, later working as district ranger at Meyers Creek in the Beartooh Mountains and then in Libby. By 1961 with a third daughter our annual trips to Glacier became a family affair. When the girls were young, we took day hikes to Grinnell Glacier and Iceberg Lake and then to Sperry Chalets and Granite Park Chalets, which were both full-service at that time. This allowed us to overnight in the mountains without the demands of backpacking.

As the girls got older we took more challenging hikes. On our first trip to Siyeh Pass, it appeared that we were approaching the pass only to find a very steep mountain slope yet to climb. My middle daughter was about

10 years old and she became angry with the National Park Service for "misrepresenting" where the pass was. She took off straight up the mountain, ignoring the trail, with tears streaming down her face. The beautiful alpine flowers and gorgeous view at the pass calmed her. Lunch didn't hurt, either.

When we began to take backpack trips, often their friends would join us. These trips took us all over the park: Two Medicine Lake, Snyder Lake, Gunsight Pass and Bowman Lake among other places.

I recall camping at the Granite Park backpacking camp sometime in the 1970s. A park ranger stopped by to check our camp and was surprised to see us cooking out of coffee cans. I never have upgraded my cooking gear as coffee cans continue to work well.

Gradually, my daughters got married and had children and I have had the opportunity to hike in the park with all of my 10 grandchildren. Helen and I hiked in to Grinnell Lake with all three daughters and many of the grandchildren about five years ago, when we were both in our 80s.

Of all the wonderful trails in Glacier, the Highline Trail remains my favorite. When I was 82 I had the opportunity to again hike to the Granite Park Chalet and was happy to be able to hike out over Swiftcurrent Pass while part of our group went back to Logan Pass for the car. I can truthfully say that I never grow tired of hiking in Glacier. The expansive views, the fields of flowers and the animal life remain beautiful. Glacier is a wonderful place and, God willing, I will be there next summer, hiking with some of my children, grandchildren and, perhaps, great-grandchildren.

Camp Cooking with Aki
Mary Ann Kozel
(Glacier visitor)

To protect the delicate alpine environment and to decrease bear-human encounters, overnight camping in Glacier's backcountry is highly regulated. Food is suspended from bear-proof poles, tents are pitched on designated sites and meals are cooked and consumed in a central area. I have eaten dinner alongside hikers from around the world and delighted in many fascinating conversations. One meeting stands out as particularly memorable.

My husband, Ray, and I approached the last night of our week-long backpacking trip. Hiking through some of the most beautiful scenery in the world, we traversed 6,000-foot Stoney Indian Pass, basked under Feather Plume Falls and waltzed through fields of delicately scented wild flowers. Good weather had blessed our trip, but now rain was driving as we arrived at Flattop campsite and hastily erected our tent. Ray, the designated beast of burden, relished a well-deserved nap as I saw to dinner preparations.

After filling a large pot in icy Flattop Creek, I headed toward the cooking area. Advancing acrobatically, I pirouetted my way over the slippery rocks, concentrating intently to keep from spilling my brim-full pan. Suddenly, shooting flames broke my trance.

The inferno's source was an out-of-control backpacking stove. The chef was Aki, an 18-year-old Japanese student. His English was poor but we managed a parley of primary phrases and gestures. Noticing his stove was the same brand as mine, I pointed to his bonfire and slowly asked if he would like my help. He cautiously nodded. I turned off his stove, reassembled it, and gave him some basic instructions on lighting it and regulating the flame size. Aki responded with the first of many "tank you, tank yous" accompanied by frequent bows.

Aki cooked his Ramen noodles with a nicely controlled flame and I prepared instant cheesecake with cherry topping (most remarkable because we had packed our favorite dessert for the last night of the trip). I carefully carried it to the stream where it jelled in the frigid water. The smell of herb and butter instant pasta cooked al dente enticed Ray to dinner. By that time I had learned that Aki was traveling alone and wanted to see the United States. As Ray and I continued to communicate with him in our combination of sign language and simple English, we learned this was his first time to the U.S., to Glacier Park and backpacking. He was traveling alone into grizzly country and readily admitted he was scared to death.

Later, I pulled our dessert out of the creek; Aki seemed truly amazed by this culinary feat. Dreading the thought of dealing with leftover cheesecake, we gratefully shared our American delicacy. He eagerly scarfed down several pieces, interlacing bites with frequent bows and "tanks." Our interchange continued late into the night until the persistent rain and fatigue drove us to our tents.

By morning the rain had stopped, but the mist hung thick to saturated underbrush as we departed in different directions. Wishing each other good luck, we waved our goodbyes knowing this was an encounter we would all remember fondly whenever we ate instant cheesecake.

Brothers Phil, left, and Dick Schwab at Many Glacier in 1948. Courtesy, Dick Schwab

Chapter 12

Why we keep coming back

Young brothers in Glacier
Dick Schwab
(Many Glacier Hotel 1947-52)

It has now been more than 60 years since my brother Phil and I first discovered the wonders of Glacier in the 1940s, and no part of our lives has been brighter or more packed with rewarding memories than the golden days we have spent there. I stumbled upon the park quite by accident in 1947 when I took a job as houseboy at Many Glacier, with no inkling whatever of the huge and happy impact it would have on everyone in our families for the rest of our lives.

Realizing almost immediately how magnificent the place was, I wanted to get Phil out there as soon as possible, and that happened the next summer when he got a job at the hotel, too. The result was that our young spirits soon became so deeply drawn to everything about the park that I believe we must be ranked among the greatest Glacier enthusiasts of our era.

Only a stroke of good fortune at the outset prevented the year 1948 from being Phil's only one at Glacier. He was originally hired as a busboy, a job whose unreasonable demands at that time wore out and drove away more than one busboy every year in the Glacier Park dining halls.

Phil was very slight of stature then. Week after week of endlessly running back and forth morning, noon, and night with huge trays of dishes cleared from the tables in the great dining room began to pare down his weight pound by pound. Fairly soon it became evident that however game Phil was, he would be reduced to a shadow if he continued. Since there was a rule against switching jobs, he reluctantly decided he would have to leave.

Nobody wanted to see him go. On the eve of his departure we had a goodbye party over at the Swiftcurrent Lake picnic grounds. For the occasion I made a huge investment in an excellent 12-inch model of a teepee made of deer hide sold at the gift shop, and friends at the picnic autographed it for Phil as a farewell gift. The next morning I watched with dismay as he trudged with his bags like Charlie Chaplin's little tramp down the road from the dormitory past the chalet to the intersection with the road to Babb, where he was going to start the long hitchhike back to Minnesota.

Then the great miracle, deus ex machina, occurred. When Leah de Zouche, the gentle head of housekeeping, heard the story a few minutes later in the linen room, she exclaimed, "Stop him. Stop him."

She rushed down to reason with the despotic little manager, Omar Ellis (Omar the Terrible), the original author of that ironclad rule that employees were never permitted to switch jobs. The brave Miss Leah demanded that he hire Phil at once to replace a worthless houseboy she was planning to sack.

Brothers Phil, left, and Dick Schwab at Schwab Falls in 2002. Courtesy, Dick Schwab

To everyone's astonishment, Ellis gave in. Phil had not yet found a ride when we tore down the road to get him. We brought him back victoriously to the housekeeping department where Miss Leah gave him one of the frayed white uniform jackets we all wore. That made it possible for him to have a great, carefree Glacier summer after all.

Years later Phil told me how he shivered every once in awhile at the thought that he might have got a hitchhike ride before we stopped him. That would have changed our lives altogether. Most important of all for Phil, the notable year of 1952 was the year he met Joanne Hanson, who was a waitress in the dining hall at Many Glacier. They were married in 1953 and eventually produced three of the most faithful of all Glacier devotees: Eric, Sara, and Annie, who themselves have produced several other little enthusiasts for the park.

The same thing happened in my family with Mark, Paul, and Heidi. Jo turned out to be the best of us all at keeping in touch with our old Glacier friends, some of whom we might otherwise have lost contact with. Brad Jeffries, who was the head bellhop in our time, noted this in a toast to her as "the glue who held us all together" at a dinner during one of our reunions at Many Glacier. It must be one of the few times when being called "glue" could be considered the highest compliment.

An alpine honeymoon
Don Loeffler
(Glacier Park Hotel, Sun Camp, Many Glacier Hotel 1940-42, 1946-48)

While working at Many Glacier Hotel in June of 1947, I met a beautiful blond from Minneapolis, a fellow employee, named Barbara Burrets. It was love at first sight when I spotted her in the chow line in the cafeteria.

That was the beginning of a beautiful friendship that lasted all summer. It included such interludes as hiking up to Granite Park Chalets for breakfast, a trip over to Lake McDonald and a hitchhiked return with a couple of powder monkeys from the Hungry Horse Dam who were hell-bent on getting to bars on the east side before they closed and other less exciting trips to Grinnell Glacier, Iceberg Lake, Cracker Lake and more.

That winter, back in the Twin Cities, I proposed and she accepted. She had a good job at Dayton's (parent company of Target stores) and I was attending the University of Minnesota majoring in civil engineering. Now we came to the honeymoon. I asked my bride-to-be if she wanted a week's stay at the Ambassador East in Chicago or several weeks scrambling around Glacier Park. After giving it considerable thought, Barbara offered, "How about both?"

Unfortunately, 'both' was not possible, so she selected Glacier. We were married on June 10, 1948, and planned to arrive in the park on the 15th via the west-bound Empire Builder for Whitefish, Montana. Since that train didn't stop at the West Glacier station, we backtracked to West Glacier on the mail train.

The park did not officially open until the next day, so we had to find a place to stay that night. After leaving our heavier gear with the station agent, we crossed the tracks toward town. There was a six-unit motel. We checked in with the nice older lady who owned the place, carrying just our gear sufficient for an overnight stay.

She insisted that we come up to her place for a toddy to celebrate our honeymoon. She seated us in the tiny living room and proceeded to the kitchen to break out the Jack Daniels. What she didn't know was that we could see what she was doing reflected in her dining room mirror.

She poured a shot for the bride, poured and consumed a shot for herself, poured a shot for me, poured and consumed another shot for herself. Then she placed everything on a tray and returned to the living room. We were glad that she didn't need to drive home.

The next morning, back at the West Glacier station, we boarded the first jammer run of the season. When we tried to purchase two one-way tickets to Siyeh Bend, the jammer said with a smile, "No charge to former employees on the first official run of the season." Bless his heart.

We checked our extra gear through to Many Glacier Hotel.

After the required stop at Logan Pass, we proceeded down to Siyeh Bend for an unscheduled stop to drop us off for our hike to Many via Piegan Pass. It had snowed a couple of inches during the night and it looked like white rice.

They bid us adieu from the bus as if we were Columbus leaving for the New World. What the bus dudes didn't know was that I was very familiar with the area, having worked and climbed from Going-to-the-Sun Chalets before the Second World War.

The trail had not been used that season, so we were on our own. Lucky for us the several feet of snow was firm, so we made good progress in the direction of Mount Siyeh. Breaking out of the woods I could see that we were a little too far east of where I wanted us to be, so we traversed in a westerly direction along Siyeh's southern slopes. We could see and hear an occasional avalanche on Going-to-the-Sun Mountain nearby.

Now the sun had set behind Mount Piegan and we hustled to make a shelter for the night. I found a nice, big, east-facing drift in which to excavate a cave. Prevailing winds were from the west. After 30 minutes of scooping snow, we had ourselves a nice igloo where we installed our sleeping bags—USAF survival equipment good for 30 degrees below zero. After a dinner of pemmican, biscuits, hot broth, and Hershey bars, Barbara inquired, "Now comes the Drambuie and petit fours, right?"

Don and Barbara Loeffler on their honeymoon in Glacier in 1948. Courtesy, Don Loeffler

The next morning, after a nice hot breakfast on our trusty Coleman stove, we broke camp. Daily high winds had kept Piegan Pass itself clear of any snow. The marmots in the entire area were holding their spring convention there. These overly friendly guys would overwhelm you if given half a chance. We kept them at bay with our ice axes, putting our packs on the stone pedestal that once held the locomotive bell, now long since gone.

We feasted on gorp while admiring that incredible view south to Citadel, Jackson et al. and north to Piegan, the Garden Wall, Mount Allen, and Siyeh. No wind, bright sun and a dusting of the white stuff. It was Paradise Manifest.

By 5 p.m. we entered the front doors of Many Glacier Hotel. The manager, Omar Ellis, immediately made a classy inquiry as to what Barbara Burrets (a.k.a. "B.B.") was doing with me. He was soon overpowered by a contingent of bellmen, porters and maids who knew both of us and had been informed that we were coming by the jammer who had dropped us off at Siyeh Bend.

Omar disappeared back into his office to get away from all the fuss over which he had lost all control. By this time, every dude in the place came over to the fireplace to join in the festivities. Even Ray Kinley and Sid Couch came over to check out the ruckus. (Nothing fazed Ray or Sid normally.) Frankly, I was embarrassed, but I was beginning to like the attention. I really didn't think what we had done was that spectacular—even though trail crews wouldn't open the trail to Piegan Pass for another two weeks.

We stayed at the Swiftcurrent cabins for the next several weeks, spent a few days renewing friendships from previous years and took many hikes. Our last trip was across the Highline to Granite Park Chalets, where Ma Perkins made sure we had the best stove-warmed rock available to tuck in under vintage railway blankets.

Barbara, my Viking goddess, never complained—not once—on our alpine honeymoon. She told me many years later that I never pushed her past her limit. Besides, she had a sharp ice axe and she knew how to use it.

Our progeny are turning out to be pretty good alpinists themselves. In the summer of 2005, they set a record when our oldest son Bradford led his family of four daughters and a son in a one-day, round-trip assault on Mount Whitney. It's in the genes.

A second career in Glacier
Mark Stokstad
(Many Glacier Hotel 1967, 2007-08)

Spending the summer of 1967 as a bellman at the Many Glacier Hotel was a high point in my young life. Forty years later, Mary, my wife, and I found ourselves asking, "Can you go back?" We now know the answer: Absolutely!

In December 2006, having recently retired, we found ourselves completing the on-line job application. We requested assignment at Many Glacier and hoped to be staying in the crow's nest as couples did in the '60s. We were tickled to have a phone interview in February and be offered positions. Mary was to work in the gift shop and I in Heidi's convenience store downstairs.

We arrived in the park with every toy we owned—camper, kayaks, bikes, backpacks, etc. Since so many couples now work at Many G, part of the Upper Dorm had been converted to couples housing. We were assigned a room there.

Our first challenge was to figure out how to store all of those toys. The room was 12 feet square, with a small dresser, desk and tiny hanging space. Did we really need all that stuff? Fortunately, the folks at Johnson's campground had allowed us to store the camper there for a reasonable fee.

I was delighted to see how little has changed at Many Glacier in 40 years. The shared baths were about the same, though a brand new one had been added for the ladies. The employee dining room looked exactly the same. And just like 1967, there were 200 talented, bright, energetic and hard working kids of all ages to get to know.

At some point I noticed I was living in the same dorm, eating the same food, sitting on the same porch and singing the same music as in 1967. There was not a whit of progress in 40 years.

The work was really quite demanding, a full 40 hours and most of it on your feet. With the flood the previous fall, there was plenty of cleaning needed as well as light repairs to get the stores open. The hotel filled almost immediately and stayed full through September.

Work days started early or ran late. At times we'd wonder why we were doing this for Montana minimum wage. Then we'd look at the view across Swiftcurrent Lake to Grinnell Point and Mount Wilbur. Or we'd join the kids on the steps of the dorm for a cigar and toddy. The question was easily answered. One nice change has been made since 1967. We had two days off each week. So in four months we were able to do a great many of the day hikes, a bit of backpacking and a couple of easy climbs.

Downsides? Sure. After a lifetime of fine home cooking, we found the institutional food to be tiresome. No criticism of the cooks, they were great. The material they had to work with was just OK. And one does get a bit tired of having to get dressed to go potty. Would we do it again? In a heartbeat.

Can you go back? We're delighted that we did.

[Editors note: Mark and Mary returned to Many Glacier Hotel in 2008. They subsequently moved on to seasonal positions with the National Park Service and were last seen in flat hats at the east entrance to Yellowstone. Their dream is to return to Glacier.]

Many memories
Warren Hanna
(Many Glacier Hotel 1918, 1920)

For two summers shortly after the completion of Many Glacier Hotel, I had the great pleasure of serving on the hotel staff. During the summer seasons of 1918 and 1920, I was the transportation agent there, in charge of arrangements for bus trips and horseback rides.

It all began while I was a junior at the law school of the University of

Minnesota in Minneapolis. During the month of May 1918, I began to think about summer employment as a means of ensuring being able to return to school in the autumn. By chance, a friend who had worked in Glacier the preceding summer suggested that I might consider working there. Although I had never previously heard of the park, the idea of working there had instant appeal.

Following his further suggestion that I should apply for park employment at the Great Northern Railway offices in St. Paul, I was signed up for a job as transportation agent at a place called Many Glacier, located in the heart of the park.

After my arrival and lunch in the employees' cafeteria, I hastened over to the hotel's front entrance where I found that my office was to be the first space to the right (occupied today by the bellmen). In those days I was to have sole possession of it, and to be in charge of information as well as transportation. I thought it the best and most attractive location in the lobby.

I was introduced to a tall, bronzed man who had been filling in the arranging of horseback trips pending my arrival. Never having seen a mountain before, let alone a cowboy, I was totally unprepared for this colorful westerner, who gave me a firm handshake and said his name was Cal Peck.

Since it was the beginning of the tourist season, as well as wartime, travel was very light and I was able to avail myself of the opportunity to get to know the area better. Within a week I accompanied horseback parties to Iceberg Lake, Piegan Pass, Granite Park, Cracker Lake and Grinnell Glacier. In the meantime, I settled into my job comfortably.

Warren Hanna with his wife Claire, whom he met at Many Glacier Hotel.
Courtesy, Marilyn Johnson

As I look back, I realize the important role that Glacier Park and Many Glacier have played throughout my life. To begin with, my earnings in the park helped put me through law school. While at Many I was practically given the unused part of a railroad ticket on which I traveled the length of the Pacific Coast (where I made up my mind to eventually settle), and all the way across Canada to New York City, where I spent two delightful years.

It was at Many Glacier that I met the girl who became my wife and the mother of my only child, and it was at Swiftcurrent, across the lake, that we enjoyed a second honeymoon, the first having been spent at Niagara Falls in the traditional way. My first two non-legal books were about the park. All this has culminated in my receiving in 1984 the National Park Service's formal recognition of my contributions to Glacier Park.

The appreciation is, of course, mutual.

Working the mangle at Many Glacier
Diane Selvala Sheldon
(Many Glacier Hotel 1942-61)

I am a rather unusual Glacier park alum. I started my sojourns there when I was just six years old. My parents, Arthur and Ann Selvala, were the long-time managers of the laundry at Many Glacier Hotel. In 1942 they told the manager, Omar Ellis, that they would be unable to return because they couldn't find a babysitter for my brother and me. Mr. Ellis's answer was, "Bring the kids with you."

Needless to say, my first memories of the hotel are hazy. I do recall vividly the smell of Stagger Alley, because that is where we stayed—Rooms 36 and 38 (now 56 and 58).

I loved going to Many Glacier early in the season to help open the hotel. There was a skeleton crew at first, and all the rooms had to be set up. I would help the maids clean up the rooms. The walls had to be washed—splinter time. I also remember the first day off (usually on Sunday) and going for a hike. The trails were still clogged with snow, but that never stopped us from accomplishing the walk around Swiftcurrent and Josephine Lakes.

During the season I had to keep busy. When I was six I washed glasses occasionally in The Grill (now the St. Moritz Room). What a great thrill I would have when I was tipped by a guest. I would run right away to the laundry to show my mom.

By the time I was 14, I was officially on the payroll. Wow! I received $65 a month plus room and board. I worked for my dad, running the mangle (a machine which pressed sheets and other items with heated rollers). I came to know the machine very well because I helped out on it for years.

My memories of working in the laundry are very pleasant. It was warm, friendly, and musical. I always associate singing with the laundry. The girls on the mangle would sing almost all day long.

There were two negatives to working in the laundry. One was the dirty towels from the kitchen—whoa, did they stink. The other was the paucity of tips. A blanket tip from a convention might mean 50 cents apiece to the laundry workers.

When I first started waitressing in 1954, we wore maroon cotton dresses. They had a starched white collar and a starched white apron. We also

Many Glacier Hotel dining room staff take a beark in 1947. Courtesy, Betty Borman

had to wear hair nets, black shoes, stockings, and a lovely crown-shaped, starched, white headpiece. The uniforms were our responsibility to keep clean—thank God my parents ran the laundry.

Once the hustle and bustle of the dinner hour was over the wait staff had duties to perform to set the dining room and kitchen in order for the next meal. Someone was assigned to cleaning the trays. That was an ugly job. Those aluminum trays would be really dirty by the end of a meal. The best part of waitressing was walking home to the dorm—except on those nights when you had to detour the garbage cans because of the bear that had come down to feast.

These are some of my memories of Many and of Glacier. It is truly one of my favorite places on earth. I not only grew up there, but I also had fun there. For years after I quit going to Many I would get very homesick in June for the smell of pine needles, Stagger Alley, and smelly old kitchen towels needing to be washed.

A Siyeh retrospective
Mark Hufstetler
(Lake McDonald Lodge 1978-83, National Park Service 1987-88)

Back when I was a kid, my Dad would take a week off work each summer and the family would head out on vacation. In 1966, when I was eight years old, we were living in central Idaho and Glacier was the chosen summer destination. I was always excited about those annual vacations, but something happened almost the instant we arrived in Glacier: I fell in love with the place.

I only remember a few specifics about that trip, but I know that we camped in my grandparents' trailer and that I convinced my Dad to take me on a ranger-led hike to Avalanche Lake, and at Two Medicine I bought a red felt pennant with a drawing of Mount Sinopah on it.

And I very much remember the little, black-and-white Glacier brochure that the Park Service issued back then. The booklet included a photo of a horseback party working up the spectacular trail along the cliffs just north of Ptarmigan Tunnel, and the image transfixed me. I wanted to go there so very badly, but there was no way an eight-year-old kid with two out-of-shape parents would ever make it. I took the brochure home, though, and kept it in my desk, and looked at that photograph often.

With that sort of memory, it was really no surprise that when it came time to look for a summer job 12 years later, my first thought was Glacier. It was a real thrill in the spring of 1978 when I returned to my college dorm one afternoon to find a fat envelope from Glacier Park Inc. in my mailbox. It contained a slightly quirky employment letter typed on an all-caps typewriter and bearing Ian B. Tippet's signature.

For hundreds of young men and women each year, getting a letter like that marked the beginning of a Montana summer that frequently progressed into a lifelong fondness for Glacier; it was the same for me, too, but was also a rekindling of a dormant infatuation that had been with me since I was a kid.

The summer at Lake McDonald Lodge was great, of course: I had countless adventures, made some amazing new friends, and I even thought I fell in love. I was pretty distraught when it all ended, but I left with a trove of wonderful memories and the certainty that I would return and the knowledge that Glacier would remain a part of my life forever.

Those memories drew me back to Lake McDonald summer jobs the next year, and the next—a total of six seasons in all. After my last summer I moved to Montana full time, and later got to spend two more seasons as a National Park Service employee in Glacier. Eight memorable summers in the park, some better than others, but each one treasured.

At the end of each of those years I wondered if my physical connection to the park would somehow end, but it never did. Even after I finally stopped working at Glacier I kept returning as a visitor, often two or three times a summer.

At first the visits were pure nostalgia, akin to looking at photographs, and they just left me with a sadness for times past. Eventually, though, my continued trips to Glacier started generating fond memories of their own, and I began valuing my continued relationship with the park almost as much as those early encounters of my youth.

Each trip—with old friends, new ones or alone—added another layer of experience and intimacy to my long-standing relationship with the park.

Today, it seems that almost every spot in Glacier is associated with a memory for me and often a succession of memories, built up over the years. It's a remarkable thing, and something that makes me more eager than ever to keep returning to Glacier and keep being involved in the park.

I was thinking about all this as my friend Joel and I were starting a trip over Siyeh Pass, among my favorite of Glacier's shorter trails. I first did Siyeh back in August 1978 with a couple of friends named Danny and Bill. Befitting my then-20-year-old physique, our day included side trips to Sexton Glacier as well as the top of Piegan Pass, probably accomplished with an effortlessness that would appall me today. I had that cheap red daypack that I'd bought at the lodge's camp store, and an employee sack lunch that was probably smashed flat by the time I was ready to eat it. And I'm sure we had to hitchhike all the way back to the hotel after it was all done.

Oh, and there was the Siyeh trip in 1981 with Joe, my intrepid fellow bellman. He took a photo of me atop the pass that is still one of my favorites today. I remember some shorter trips, too—visits to Preston Park to see the wildflowers; a trudge along the terminally dull connector trail from Preston to Jackson Glacier overlook, just so I could ink it in on my trail map; and a failed attempt to climb Mount Siyeh, abandoned at a pitifully low elevation probably in favor of a million-calorie lunch at Johnson's Cafe.

The experiences of recent years have added still more depth to my memories of Siyeh. I hiked the trail early in the summer of 2002 with another friend named Dan; we were among the first over the pass that year, and nearly the entire descent from Siyeh to Baring Basin was covered in a steep and pristine snowfield. We skied down the thing on our hiking boots, with a feeling of euphoria that would be hard to match anywhere.

No matter who I'm with, the next time I do Siyeh, all of these memories—and more—will come back to me, and similar recollections will surface as I revisit other hikes and drives and favorite places. It's reason enough for me to keep returning to Glacier again and again, and it's a continual reminder of how special the place is, and how it's become such a part of my life.

Index

Accardo, Mike 41
Adams, Bob 135
Adams, Edie 36
Amtrak 146
Anderson, Louie 66
Apgar Mountain fire
 lookout 80
Astor, Lord and Lady 46
Babb Bar 149
Baker Family 89-90
Baker, Christine 133
Bar X6 Ranch 171
Barbeau, Keith 190
Barkowsky, Harvey 118, 179
Batson, Douglas 29
Bazan, Mark 102
Bell, John 147
Belsaas, Ino 12, 66, 69
Belton Chalet 149, 150
Beneman, Dave 190
Bentley, Carl 74
Berg, Steve 37, 98
Bergen, Candice 180-181
Billings Ladies Ensemble 165
Binder, A.J. 165
Black, Cary 109
Black, Hugh and Margaret 12, 37-38, 98, 173-175
Blackfeet Highway 141
Bohnert, Karen (Koller) 113
Bormann, Clark 112
Bowers, Chet 195
Boyd, William and Grace 177-178
Bridegroom, Dick 132
Brown, Bonnie 28, 110
Buck, Michael 168

Bundick, Tessie 13, 15, 101, 164
Burch, Arthur M. 12, 161
Burch, Billy Ann 169-170
Burch family 12, 161-164, 169-170
Burke, Chris 134
Burton, Larry 84, 86
Burrows, Colin 138
Campbell, Malcolm R. 127
Cashman, Rum 200
Cassidy, Hopalong and Tripalong 177-178
Chadwick, Mrs. 45-46
Chamberlain, Jack G. 58
Chewing Blackbones Campground 141
Chief Mountain International Highway 33, 57
Christmas 53, 98, 118-119, 150-152
Clapp, Bede 168
Clark, Tom C. 50
Clarke, John L. 50
Cleland, Bob 145
Coddington, Liz Gehring 18, 82
Cornish, Janet Eisner 150
Cosley, Joe 9
Cotham, John 19
Couch, Sid 12, 58-59, 65, 76, 211
Cross, Bonham 144
Dahle, Carol Repulski 13, 118
Dam Town Tavern 150
Daubney, John E. 38
Davis, Clint 138
De Zouche, Leah 208
Deer Lick 150

DeGarmo, Ned 71-72
Dew Drop Inn 149, 150
Diamond, Dick 87
Dillon, Buster (Blackie) 171-172
Dobbertin, John 47
Doering, Tom 196
Doherty, Rosellen (Finley) 52
Dusty's Tavern 46, 51, 52, 55, 98
Eaton, Howard 17, 159-160
Edwards, Gordon 187
Ek, Kay Schwenk 51
Ellis, Omar 83, 112, 130, 167-168, 208, 211, 214
Empire Builder (train) 54, 146-147, 209
Erickson, Ralph 45
Ewald, Tom 69
Finley, Charles 52
Fleming, Orville 111
Fossum, Dick 195
Francis, Tom 122
Frase, Mama 12, 143-144
Frieda's Bar 149
Friends of Glacier 164, 223
Fuller, Lance 52
Gable, Clark 166-167
Galvin, Mary Grace Severson 136
Gamble, O. A. (Pappy) 69-70
Geshell, Sylvia 83, 84
Giles, Al 69
Glacier Park Station 24, 146
Granite Park Chalets 12, 92-95, 134, 170, 198, 203, 204, 209, 211
Great Northern Railway 14, 16, 17, 18, 23, 24, 33, 45-48, 50, 52, 96, 127, 146, 149, 158, 159, 164-167, 173-174, 179, 181-183, 201, 213
Griffin, Charles B. 182,
Grill, The 47, 82, 83, 111, 112, 214
Griskey, Lou 71
Haase, Bob 66
Hagen, John 9, 11, 23, 28, 35, 36, 43, 73, 79, 103, 115, 118, 121, 161, 196

Hallock, Ken 91
Hanna, Warren 159, 212
Hanson, "Dusty" 52
Hanson, Einar 40, 190
Hanson, Joanne 208
Hanson, Marit 152
Harris, John 20
Hart, Neil 147
Hartman, Lorraine 200
Harwood Bar 98
Hatch, "Tib" Gloria 109, 110
Hawley, Harold 132
Hays, Howard H. 57, 64
Hays, William 57
Heidi's Ice Cream Parlor 125
Helgeson, Julie 70
Henkel, Hal 201
Hicks, Dick 67
Hileman, Tomer J. 22
Hill, Louis Jr. 181, 182
Hill, Louis W. 158, 181
Hinrichs, Cheri 36
Hoff, Paul 176
Holm, Mick 136
Holmen, Rey 22
Horodyski, Bob 79
Huckleberry fire lookout 133
Hudak, Karen 119
Hufstetler, Mark 146, 149, 185, 215
Hummel, Don 47-50, 92, 150, 179
Hussey, Keith 22
Jacobson, Bob 66
Jeffries, Brad 208
Jenkins, Rachel 135
Jenner, Brian 80-81
Jennings, George 182
Johnson's Café 217
Jones, Lydia "Casey" 36, 37
Kelly's Camp 136, 137
Kinley, Ray 11, 16, 24, 30, 31, 36, 115, 127, 128, 129, 175-177, 211
Kinsella, Pat 20
Klein, Karl 200

Koons, Michele 70
Kozel, Mary Ann 204
Kozel, Ray 20
Kracaleea, Gene 59
Kretz, Stan 162
Kuhn, Brian 80
Kuhn, Linda Young 169
Kurr, Mark and Linda 136
Larson, Rolf 13, 83, 175, 186, 191
Laurie, Piper 52
Leach, Mike 172-173
Lees, Jim 30
Lindsay, Carol 143
Link, Carl 46
Lloyd, Bill 75
Loeffler, Barbara Burrets 209-211
Loeffler, Don 80, 83, 96, 111, 141, 209-211
Logan, Charlie 136
Lutz, Buzz 55
MacRae, Don 38
Mann, Ray 120
Manzer, David 198-199
Martick, Tom (Baby Huey) 147
Martinson, Ann 189
Mathews, Dave 111
Matney, Claude 34
Mature, Victor 52
McAdoo, William G. 159-160
McCormack, Eileen B. 181
McFarling, Tom I. 60
McMullin, Lyle 54
Merrill, Vaughn 201
Mieras, Susie 119
Mike's Place 174
Moccasin Room 140
Moench, Chris Crump 156
Monroe, Angus 160
Monroe, Hugh 160
Monson, James W. 63, 66
Moose's 150
Moss, Melville 165
Mouw, Ginny Leach 53, 199
Movie: *Dangerous Mission* 52

Movie: *Cattle Queen of Montana* 52, 76
Mueller, George 202
Mueller, Glenn 202
Mueller, Oscar and Josephine 202
Murray Family Orchestra 165, 166
Murray, Roy 165-166
Murrow, Edward R. 168-169
Natta, Dino 67
Nave, Mark 72
Nichols, Jimmy 66
Noble, Fred 57, 63, 64, 76
Noble, Howard 165-166
Noffsinger, George 90
Norby, Eric 34
North Circle Tour 89
O'Connor's Minnesotans 165
O'Connor, Pat 20
Oastler, Maude 177-178
Ognjanov, Cindy 138
Olson, Howard 128
Overturf, Hank 31
Packer's Roost 150
Park Saddle Horse Company 86, 89, 160, 171
Parsons, Harriet 36
Parsons, Louella 36
Pat O'Connor 20
Paul Bunyan's 150
Paulsen, Joy 12, 169-171
Paulus, Dave 196
Pearson, June 83
Peck, Cal 213
Perkins, Ema (Ma) 12, 92-95, 211
Perkins, Millie Jean 92-95
Perry, Don 76
Phillips, Mary Shepherd 53
Piper, Doug 48
Plumer, George 49
Porter, Mr. and Mrs. 58
Price, Van 66
Price, Vincent 52
Prince of Wales Hotel 57, 64, 65, 66

Ptarmigan Room 35, 109, 113-115, 172
Putney, Ruth 147
Randolph, Tom (Motor Mouth) 147
Reagan, Ronald 52, 76
Reiss, Winold 46
Reykdal, Cliff 180
Reynolds, Ruth 165
Rhein, Rob 114
Rhody, Minnie 168-169
Rinehart, Mary Roberts 17, 160
River Bridge Inn 150
Rixon, Bill 69
Rockefeller, John D. 159
Rockne, Ellen 110
Rollie, Bill 114
Ronning, Mary "Sarge" 52
Roosevelt, Franklin D. 67
Sanitation inspectors 40
Sayles, Fred 54
Scarano, Mike 187
Schade, Bill 67
Schade, Fritz 67
Schwab, Dick 92, 167, 171, 177, 190, 207-208
Schwab, Phil 207-208
Scott, Neil 67
Seilset, Lloyd and Gjerda 190
Selleck, Jeff 39
Selvala, Arthur and Ann 214
Settles, Tony 102
Sheedy, E. C. 166
Sheldon, Diane Selvala 214
Shipley, Joan Fritz 45
Shore, Jim 67
Shoup, Dave 187
Singleton, Jim 102
Slater, John 24, 117
Smith, Chip 74
Speltz, Bishop George 53
Springer, Patrick 147
St. Moritz Room 102, 108, 127, 172, 214
Stagger Alley 36, 43, 127, 214, 215

Staley, Jay 54
Stanwick, Barbara 52
Stephens, Roger L. 109
Sterrett, Bill 58
Stevens, Roger 117
Stevenson, Breck 66
Stevenson, Cy 12, 97-98, 111, 120, 128-129, 163, 179
Stimson, Henry L. 67
Stockade Room 147, 149
Stokstad, Mark 211
Stone, Terri (Saunders) 118
Stoner's 150
Stubbs, Jan Didra 173
Swanson, William 115, 116, 162
Swiftcurrent fire lookout 133, 198
Taylor, Rick 102
Thronson, Oscar 17
Timbers, Bryan 69
Tippet, Ian B. 11-13, 15, 19, 24, 27, 31, 34, 35, 101-102, 106, 109, 110, 111, 113, 116-117, 120, 127, 128, 147-148, 172, 175, 179, 180, 199, 216
Tointon, Roger 67
Treacy, Bill 47
Treacy, Steve 47
Trimble, Bill (Deacon) 66
Udal, Slim 195
Van Artsdale, Mark 164
Vandell, Dan 187
Vick, Chris (Wizard) 24, 104
Wade Family Bell Ringers 164
Wades-in-the-Water, Julia 47
Walker, Annette (Haussler) 27
Walsh, Michaela 53
Wanser, Berith 89, 90
Wanser, Bill 86, 89, 95, 166
Waterton Lakes National Park 57, 64, 69, 98, 162, 190, 195, 196, 198
Weaver, Dennis 52
Westbrook, Tom 168
West Glacier, Montana 65, 67, 81, 82, 136, 137, 140, 146, 147, 209

Wiese, Tracey 124
Wilcox, Donna 50
Willemssen, Mac 13, 34, 91, 117
Williams, Clare 201
Williams, Sean 109
Wilson, Mrs. 179-180
Winnett, Steve 191
Wontorski, Pat 41, 116
Woods, Cathy Crossland 18
Yearout, Bill 68
Zahn, Ron 196

Join the

Glacier Park Foundation

All friends of Glacier National Park in Montana are invited to join the Glacier Park Foundation. Membership includes a subscription to *The Inside Trail* and the right to vote for directors. Please download a membership form from our website (www.glacierparkfoundation.org) or send your name, address, phone number and park experience to Glacier Park Foundation, Box 15641, Minneapolis, MN 55415.

An annual membership in the foundation costs $10. A "Friend of the Park" membership costs $25 annually, culminating in a "Lifetime" membership in five installments. A Lifetime membership paid in one installment costs $100. All prices are U.S. dollars.

The Glacier Park Foundation is a § 501(c)(3) non-profit corporation. Contributions are tax deductible to the extent permitted by law.

www.ingramcontent.com/pod-product-compliance
Lightning Source LLC
Chambersburg PA
CBHW072344100426
42738CB00049B/1626